Comparative Constitutional Federalism

Recent Titles in
Contributions in Legal Studies

Comparative Constitutional Federalism

EUROPE AND AMERICA

Edited by
Mark Tushnet

Foreword by
Lord Mackenzie-Stuart

CONTRIBUTIONS IN
LEGAL STUDIES,
NUMBER 61

GREENWOOD PRESS
New York • Westport, Connecticut • London

Library of Congress Cataloging-in-Publication Data

Comparative constitutional federalism : Europe and America / edited by
  Mark Tushnet ; foreword by Lord Mackenzie-Stuart.
      p.   cm.—(Contributions in legal studies, ISSN 0147–1074 ;
  no. 61)
    Includes bibliographical references and index.
    ISBN 0–313–26888–6 (lib. bdg. : alk. paper)
      1. Federal government—United States.   2. Federal government—
  European Economic Community countries.   I. Tushnet. Mark V.
  II. Series.
  K3185.C66   1990
  342.4′042—dc20
  [344.0242]   90–37838

British Library Cataloguing in Publication Data is available.

Library of Congress Catalog Card Number: 90–37838
ISBN: 0–313–26888–6
ISSN: 0147–1074

First published in 1990

Greenwood Press, 88 Post Road West, Westport, CT 06881
An imprint of Greenwood Publishing Group, Inc.

Printed in the United States of America

The paper used in this book complies with the
Permanent Paper Standard issued by the National
Information Standards Organization (Z39.48–1984).

10 9 8 7 6 5 4 3 2 1

Contents

Foreword:
Toward a National Identity in the European Economic Community

This book presupposes the existence of a federal society or association and has as its object the discussion and, one hopes, the elucidation of a number of problems that such a society or association necessarily creates.

The primary question as regards the European Community is whether or not it can be regarded as a federation. The term *federation* gives rise to many difficulties, largely of a semantic nature. In one sense any association of independent states that band together for a common purpose can be called a federation. In normal usage, however, I suggest that a federation of nation-states needs, at least, to adopt the criteria enunciated by Sir Harry Hinsley: "A single Foreign Office, a single military establishment, a single intelligence service,"[1] and to which I would add, "a single currency."

By these standards the European Economic Community is not a federation; it is an association of states and no more. In many respects, certainly, it is a highly integrated association of states, but one that falls short of the requirements just mentioned. To quote Sir Harry Hinsley again

[T]he transition from being the closest possible association of states to being even the loosest of all possible single body-politics, is a leap—a momentous step. It requires the dramatic exercise of political will, and the requisite will is generated only when exceptional pressures of force or fear, internal or external, prevail over obstacles that are normally insuperable.

Sir Harry Hinsley instances the threat of war that impelled the North German States, in the middle of the nineteenth century, to move from the *Zollverein*, a customs union, to a confederation; the conditions in 1776 facing the colonies that became the United States; and the offer of union that Britain made to France in 1940 under even more severe pressures.

In the Europe of forty years ago the external pressures were great—the Iron Curtain, the Berlin air-lift, the Korean War. These pressures were sufficient, in 1951, to bring about the first European Community, in which six countries— Belgium, France, Germany, Italy, Luxembourg, and the Netherlands—joined together to put their coal and steel production under common management, a step that paved the way for Germany's economic revival. The momentum was powerful enough in 1957 to see the birth of the Economic Community. It was still sufficiently strong to ensure the first enlargement in 1973 when Denmark, Ireland, and the United Kingdom acceded. That the ball did not stop rolling is evidenced by the subsequent accession of Greece and later of Spain and Portugal.

The momentum was strong but it was never strong enough to bring about the creation of a body politic, even if some of the founding statesmen might have wished it. Today with an easing of international tension there is no sign of its taking place. Let us, perhaps for that reason, be thankful for it.

I need not labor the other differences between postwar Europe and the United States of 1776 and 1787. The latter had even then a common language, a common currency, and at the risk of offending both North and South, a common intellectual heritage. Yet, as Professor Jack Rakove's contribution to this book shows, even there the construction of a fully unified nation occurred in fits and starts over an extended period.

Today in the European Community the sense of national identity remains very real. The British prime minister, Margaret Thatcher, irritated many who had chosen to work for the Community when, in a speech she gave at Bruges in September 1988, she referred to "identi-kit Europeans." Such an animal, and this should please Mrs. Thatcher, does not exist.

What the European Communities seek to achieve is limited by the terms of the constituent treaties. These seek to create, in the widest sense of the term, a "Common Market." They provide for the free movement of goods and persons, the freedom of establishment, and the free rendering of services, goals that have substantially been realized for many years and that 1992—for all its attendant hype—is but the final step, albeit an important one. Of 1992 one can literally transcribe Alexander Hamilton's words about the Constitution (Federalist No. 43): "[I]t will be found that the change which it proposes consists much less in the addition of NEW POWERS to the Union, than in the invigoration of its ORIGINAL POWERS."

For example, the agricultural sector and coal and steel sector are fully integrated. The fundamental freedoms already operate well. The Common Market, however, is more than that. The treaties provide for a common external commercial policy. For example, the Community speaks with a single voice in the GATT (General Agreements on Tariffs and Trade) negotiations. Any commercial behavior that offends against the principle of fair trading—cartels, concerted practices, dumping—is penalized. Political cooperation, which always existed in fact, has recently been institutionalized. Professor Varat's discussion of the relation between economic and political integration suggests that the connections, which many proponents of further integration believe to be strong, are actually rather weak.

The constitutional structures of the European Community, then, provide a great deal more integration than existed a few decades ago but fall short of the creation of a body politic. Certainly, efforts have been made to create a sense of belonging to a community. These efforts are wholly praiseworthy but have a limited scope. All members of the Community receive the same treatment at airports and on arrival by boat at a Community harbor. The Community passport is in the course of being introduced, but slowly. Cultural manifestations, such as the European Youth Orchestra, are encouraged. Perhaps the most significant contribution to a European identity is to be found in the European Schools set up by a separate treaty in the 1950s. These are intended primarily for the children of Community officials. The curriculum is the same in each school and language training has a special place. The final examination is recognized in all the member states as an entry qualification for their universities. While there is no one more fiercely nationalist than a seven-year-old, it is fascinating to observe how national barriers dissolve under the impact of daily face-to-face contact. These schools, however, concern a minority. They may be qualitatively important but they are statistically unimportant.

The constitutional structure of the European Treaties still retains an important role for the member states. One of the most common legislative devices employed by the Council of Ministers is the "Directive," an order addressed to the member states setting out a series of goals and objects, often in considerable detail, but, as the Treaties provide, leaving it to each member state to choose its own way to bring about the ends prescribed. Moreover, the daily administration of the Community is, for the most part, handled by national agencies. To give one example, the American exporter to the United Kingdom will find his goods, which are subject to the Community's external tariff, handled by the British Customs and Excise. For and on behalf of the Community, certainly, but the officials are British and wear the uniform of their national service.

In his excellent introduction to *The Federalist Papers*, Professor Isaac Kramnick says, "Along with the flag, the Constitution stands alone as a symbol of national unity. America has no royal family, no heritage of timeless and integrative state institutions or symbols, no national church."[2] In contrast, in the countries comprising the Community, the symbols of statehood abound and will continue to do so. It is true that some of the member states are relatively recent creations. Belgium dates only from 1830, Luxembourg in its present form from 1839. Italy and the Federal Republic of Germany did not emerge in a unified shape until the second half of the nineteenth century. Nonetheless, each member state has its own badges of identity and nothing has occurred to displace them. One cannot elevate the European Treaties to a European constitution in the sense of that of the United States.

In particular, the European Treaties (although perhaps increasingly so) affect only marginally the daily life of most Community citizens. In generalizations of this sort it is difficult to get the balance right, but the human rights element of the United States Constitution, the social dimension if you will, lies for the most part outside the European Treaties and remains entrenched at the national level.[3] Professor Howard demonstrates the complexities of structuring the protection of human rights, which one might think universal, in a federal system in which one of the primary characteristics is the toleration of diversity.

Paradoxically, while there has been little progress in Europe toward a nation, or rather, toward a Community identity, Professor Majone shows that there has been a resurgence of regional identity, some of it with unpleasant consequences. One might cite the Basque separatist movement that straddles the Pyrenees. The Irish problem might be placed in the same category, but here there is a long, sad history and, in truth, it escapes classification. On a more tranquil level, Catalonia, the Italian regions, Dutch-speaking Belgium, and the Netherlands all have regional affinities that are becoming more marked. To assert a direct connection between such movements and the creation of the European Community would be going too far, but it seems to me, a connection is there. As the existing frontiers of the old Europe begin to disappear, a series of new (or very old) entities are arising with which the European citizen can identity. This trend results from the toleration of diversity, discussed as well by Professor Minow, which simultaneously provides opportunities for growth and retrogression.

The federal system of the United States has been in place for over two hundred years, developing in ways that its framers might not have fully anticipated. The incipient federal system of Europe has just begun on its path of development. Reflection on the problems encountered by constitutional federalism in the United States may illuminate what Europeans may find themselves living with in the next century.

NOTES

1. World Today, Chatham House, London, January 1989, p. 1.
2. *The Federalist Papers* (Penguin Classics ed. 1987), p. 12.
3. That is not to say that the Court of Justice of the European Communities ignores all questions involving human rights. Far from it, but that is another chapter.

Lord Mackenzie-Stuart

Preface

The near conjunction of the bicentennial of the United States Constitution in 1989 and the completion of the European Common Market in 1992 provides the occasion for comparative consideration of the constitutional aspects of federal systems. The United States presents a mature federal system, while 1992 symbolizes federalism in its early or incipient stage—or, if that presumes without justification that 1992 will mark the beginning of an extended process of further federalization of the European Community, a "small" form of federalism.

The Delegation of the Commission of the European Communities believed that it would be useful to sponsor a conference on comparative constitutional federalism to generate interest among legal academics in the United States regarding the development of federalism in the Community. The Delegation therefore provided a generous grant to the Georgetown University Law Center to sponsor the conference that resulted in the preparation of the papers published in this volume.

Law schools in the United States, alert to the impact of 1992 on trade between the United States and Europe, have increasingly supported courses and research on Community law. The focus of those courses, though, has tended to be on issues of trade law, and they are frequently taught by instructors outside the core of the law schools' faculties. The Delegation believed that it would be helpful to have the more general aspects of federalism in the Community examined by United States legal scholars whose primary interests lay outside trade and Community law. At the same time, it was clear that some comparisons between the Community and the United States would be provocative, yet precisely because the Delegation sought to interest scholars who had not yet studied the Community in detail, the United States scholars were not in a position to provide that comparative focus themselves. Instead, legal scholars from the Community were invited to address themes common to the systems in Europe and the United States in the hope that comparisons would emerge from the juxtaposition of studies focused on each system separately. Those who attended the conference believe that this strategy succeeded; readers of this volume are in a position to make their own judgment.

As the coordinator of the conference and editor of this volume, I would like to thank the Delegation of the Commission of the European Communities for the financial and logistical support it provided to the Georgetown University Law Center. Giancarlo Chevallard, Auke Haagsma, and especially, Cesira Klayman provided essential help. At the Law Center June Jones gave more than I should reasonably have asked in dealing with the details of arrangements for the conference. The Technical Support Services staff of the Law Center assisted in the preparation of the manuscript of this volume.

Comparative Constitutional Federalism

The First Phases of American Federalism

JACK N. RAKOVE

One would be hard pressed to imagine a subject more open-ended than nation-building, or a concept less amenable to neat definition or resolution than federalism. Nation-building embraces virtually all of the social and political processes that make up the collective life of a people, from aspects of popular culture or language or religious belief, to the economic linkages of labor and capital markets, to the coalescence of ruling elites or voter coalitions, to the formal organization of governing structures. When the great American historian Henry Adams tried to describe something he would never have entitled "The Process of Nation-building during the Administrations of Jefferson and Madison," he found himself driven to talk about the elusive concept of "national intelligence." So, too, the concept of federalism can hardly be considered at all without exploring the complicated interplay of national, provincial, and local institutions of governance. As the most celebrated European observer of American society noted a century and a half ago, the American "federal system . . . rests upon a theory which is complicated at the best, and which demands the daily exercise of a considerable share of discretion on the part of those it governs"—and also, Alexis de Tocqueville might have added, on the part of those who, like himself, attempt to study its character and evolution.[1]

To discuss problems of nation-building in a federal system, then, is not a task one takes on lightly, even when one has been safely confined to a well-defined historical period. This chapter provides a brief interpretive overview of perhaps the best-known conjunction of nation-building and federalism in modern history: the founding era of the American republic. The central purpose here will be to trace the emergence and evolution of early American ideas of federalism and to identify the major factors that shaped the somewhat uneven process of nation-building during the first decades of American independence.

Federalism is by nature an inherently messy topic. The concept itself demands repeated definition, and its practical operation in the extended republic of the United States, with its crazy-quilt pattern of overlapping jurisdictions, defies ready description. Our understanding of the role that federalism plays in the contemporary American constitutional order, or has played at various points in the past, has to some extent been limited by the preference that historians, political scientists, and legal scholars often show for studying national events and developments as opposed to politics and governance at the state and local levels of the federal system. Whether federalism is still an animate part of the constitutional order has itself become something of a question. Was it "killed" by the creation of the modern regulatory state, the "nationalization" of the Bill of Rights, and the modern interpretation of the commerce clause? If so, could federalism be revived by a return to a "jurisprudence of original intention," whose logical consequence would be to enlarge the autonomous realm of state and local authority at the expense of federal judicial oversight? Or does federalism simply inhere in the multiple levels of governance that make up the entire public sector, from sanitary districts, school committees, and state legislatures, to the formidable concentrations of national power inside the Beltway girdling Washington?

Our understanding of American federalism has also been distorted by the prominence given to the classic chicken-and-egg question of which came first, the union or the states? This "continuing if fruitless debate . . . over the priority of the union or the states"[2] has gone on since at least the Federal Convention of 1787,[3] shedding more heat than light, with serious scholarly exchanges on the subject appearing even in the bicentennial year itself.[4] It is a debate whose staying power far outweighs its substance, because it illustrates our tendency to substitute formulaic simplicity for the inherent complexity—or messiness—of both the American federal system and the circumstances that led to its creation. While historians have done more than their share to keep this debate alive, the question of the relative priority of the union and states is fundamentally ahistorical. The legal fiction of priority cannot begin to describe the revolutionary situation of 1774–1776, when all authority was extralegal and legitimacy flowed reciprocally and simultaneously up and down the ladder of resistance.[5]

Rather than freeze the original meaning of federalism at some pristine moment of clairvoyant understanding, it makes more sense to identify the major phases in the development of American ideas on this subject.

THE COLONIAL LEGACY

From the start, a federal solution to the problem of union was implicit in the history of the thirteen colonies that became the independent states of 1776. Each of the colonies had substantial prior experience of self-government, while the authority of the empire never penetrated very deeply into the American countryside—especially to the level of town meetings and country courts that regulated the ordinary affairs of a predominantly agricultural society. The occasional acts that Parliament adopted to regulate American commerce or restrict the growth of particular industries were also enforced with great difficulty. The British navigation system worked, not because it was well designed or well administered, but because producers, consumers, and merchants on both sides of the Atlantic kept the channels of commerce flowing largely as mercantilist theory suggested they should.

Historians have never found it easy to explain why the British Empire had evolved in this way. What does bear emphasis is the extent to which the high degree of autonomy that the colonies had attained by 1750 was sanctioned by English tradition as well as their own cumulative experience since settlement. As a number of legal scholars have recently argued, the claims of an indivisible parliamentary sovereignty that were used after 1765 to justify the British Parliament's efforts to legislate for America were not as well grounded or widely accepted as was once asssumed. The alternative idea that each colony possessed a customary constitution that could not be unilaterally superseded by Parliament (or the Crown) was not a contrivance whipped up as a pretense for resisting parliamentary taxation.[6] It was indeed deeply rooted in the political history of each of the colonies, going back to the seventeenth-century efforts of the provincial assemblies to secure substantial legislative rights at a time when the outcome of the struggle between the Stuart Crown and Parliament was far from settled.[7]

Thus American leaders came to the controversies of the prerevolutionary decade (1765–1775) well prepared to argue that their individual assemblies were fully competent and fully entitled to exercise complete legislative authority over their own "internal police," and that Parliament accordingly had no inherent right to legislate for individual colonies. Yet neither did they enter the imperial debate willing to pretend that the colonies—either individually or collectively— were competent to conduct the great affairs of state. Until 1775, most colonists conceded that, in the interest of reconciliation, Parliament could continue to regulate American trade (though on grounds of convenience rather than as a matter of right). Nor did they challenge the Crown's authority over war and foreign affairs, although a number of American leaders, including Benjamin Franklin and Thomas Jefferson, began to deny that the disposition of western lands should remain part of the royal prerogative. But the course of the imperial debate did not favor the distinctions the colonists sought to draw. They repeatedly sought to reconcile the preservation of substantial provincial autonomy with membership in a larger polity possessing transcendent needs and concerns of its own. Only after British spokesmen refused to draw the line between what Parliament could and could not do did the colonists advance the more radical position that the empire could remain united only through a common allegiance to the Crown and a recognition that Parliament and the colonial assemblies were endowed with identical and mutually exclusive rights.[8]

The Articles of Confederation

In their efforts to define the extent of Parliament's authority over America, colonial spokesmen had, in effect, been groping to develop their own theory of federalism, and with it to challenge the hoary notion of unitary sovereignty. Arguably, the imperial debate should have left its American participants more sensitive to the difficulties that would await them when they replaced the failed union of the first British Empire with a better model of their own. They should have been led, that is, to consider the nature of the union they were forming with something of the same theoretical intensity they displayed both in the dispute with Parliament and the writing of the first state constitutions. Instead, what is remarkable about the drafting of the Articles of Confederation by the Continental Congress in 1776 and 1777 was how little concern or attention the theoretical dimensions of federalism commanded.[9] In fact, neither sovereignty nor the problem of enforcing national policy became a serious topic of debate during the framing of the Articles of Confederation.[10]

Although one can identify individual delegates who held expansive views on either national power or state sovereignty, Congress as a whole approached the subject of confederation in a pragmatic cast of mind that reflected wartime urgency. Under the proposed Articles, Congress would control everything relating to external affairs—decisions as to war and peace, the direction of the armed forces, and foreign relations. The states would retain full legislative power over their internal police, including the elusive power to levy taxes, subject only to a handful of ambiguous restrictions. In many ways, Congress simply supplanted the Crown in the overall scheme of governance, perhaps in part because the Americans felt a need to replace the monarchical element now missing from their regime.[11]

To implement the decisions and policies of Congress, the framers of the Articles of Confederation relied on the states to act as administrative auxiliaries by recruiting armed forces, levying taxes, collecting supplies, and aiding in the general mobilization for war. In this sense, the Articles recognized what the colonists had previously argued: that plenary legislative power resided in the provincial governments. As is well known, the Articles gave Congress neither the power to coerce delinquent states nor to legislate directly for individuals. But that was less because the delegates actively feared the abuse of congressional power than because, as James Madison correctly observed a decade later, they shared

a mistaken confidence that the justice, the good faith, the honor, the sound policy of the several legislative assemblies would render superfluous any appeal to the ordinary motives by which the laws secure the obedience of individuals; a confidence which does honor to the enthusiastic virtue of the compilers, as much as the inexperience of the crisis apologizes for their errors.[12]

In the patriotic atmosphere of the mid–1770s, it was still plausible to assume that Congress, a body commonly hailed in its first years as "the collected wisdom of America," would continue to command the implicit support of the population.

Moreover, even had the framers of the Confederation been less confident that the states would act in "good faith," it is difficult to imagine what alternative course they could have taken. Pragmatic considerations were again paramount. It made much more sense to think that the states, with their knowledge of local situations, would prove effective at mobilizing their respective populations for war than to imagine how one could possibly create a national administrative apparatus out of whole cloth in the midst of the struggle. In the real world of eighteenth-century government, the initial decision to rely on the states *was* the pragmatic choice.

Vices of the Political System

From the dual political experiments of the mid–1770s—the Articles of Confederation and the first state constitutions—American leaders pursued two separate vectors toward the rethinking of federalism and republicanism that would take place in the late 1780s.

The first and more prosaic of these involved the manifest weakness of Congress. It took, of course, the experience of the war and the "imbecility" of Congress during the early years of peace to point out the lessons that had eluded the framers of 1776/77. By the time the Articles were finally ratified in 1781, a number of national leaders thought that Congress needed independent sources of revenue as well as some authority to "coerce" the states to carry out their federal duties. These concerns carried over into peacetime, when two additional problems came to the fore. When state noncompliance with the treaty of peace of 1783 gave Britain a pretext to retain its forts along the northern frontier— and thus to threaten American expansion into the Northwest Territory[13]—Congress had no means to force the states to repeal their offending acts. Its ability to conduct foreign relations was further hampered by its lack of authority over foreign trade, which was the crucial issue of the mid–1780s, given the dumping of British goods in the United States and Britain's exclusion of American ships from West Indian markets.[14]

To deal with these problems, Congress proposed a series of discrete amendments that would have modestly increased its power without altering the essential character of the confederation or even enlarging its basic duties. When none of these amendments surmounted the barrier of unanimous state ratification, the supporters of an effective federal government finally adopted the risky strategy of calling a general convention to revise the Articles of Confederation. Somewhat to their surprise, the original call issued by the Annapolis Convention of September 1786 brought delegates from twelve states to Philadelphia to attend the Federal Convention of 1787.

The most telling summary of the defects of the American system of federalism was made by James Madison in his famous preparations for the Convention and largely accepted by most of the delegates at Philadelphia. They drew two lessons from the refusal or simple failure of the states to act with the good faith the framers of the Articles had anticipated. First, the union had to be allowed to govern the American people directly through ordinary acts of legislation and taxation, circumventing the need to work through the states. Second, the national government would need further authority to restrain the states from interfering with or frustrating its acts. These decisions in turn raised two crucial and closely connected questions about the new notion of federalism. The first asked how two lawmaking bodies—the reconstructed Congress and the state assemblies— could legislate for one people. The second presumed that they would not always do so harmoniously and sought to ask how the ensuing conflicts could be resolved without requiring either party to resort to force. Much of the theoretical ingenuity of 1787 was devoted to resolving these problems.

The concerns of the framers of the Constitution, however, were not confined to the failings of the Articles of Confederation alone. Equally important, in the thinking of Madison and many of his colleagues, was the character of republican government *within* the states, that is, at the level of internal police. In Madison's formulation, the most alarming of all the "vices of the political system of the U.States" was the tendency of popular majorities in the states and their elected representatives in the omnipotent state legislatures to violate just claims of individual and minority rights. From his analysis of the causes of this behavior, Madison made a radical leap to the image of a national government that could act as a "disinterested & dispassionate umpire in disputes between different passions & interests" within the individual states, preventing "the aggressions of interested majorities on the rights of minorities and of individuals." Madisonian federalism in its original form would thus enable the national government to intervene in the states through the exercise of a proposed congressional veto on all state laws, a power that its author frankly equated with the identical prerogative held by the Crown prior to the Revolution.[15]

DEBILITIES OF STATEHOOD

Before examining how the Federal Convention sought to remedy the "imbecility" of the Articles of Confederation and the "vices" of the states, it would be useful to consider the nature of the political communities that would reunite under the Constitution from a different perspective.

In the revolutionary interregnum of 1774–76, the existing thirteen colonies that formed the new American union were transformed into independent (if not fully sovereign) states, and the new map of America looked essentially the same as it had before, save for the emergence of Vermont as an independent republic. Statehood, in a sense, was a given; preexisting laws remained in force; and the idea that the colonies needed to reemerge from the literal state of nature into which they felt they had been forced by the withdrawal of royal protection in 1775 meant only that lawful government had to be reconstituted, not that the entire social order required re-creation.

In the decade after 1776, however, the idea of statehood was exposed to two fundamental challenges. One roughly paralleled the problems of Congress. The demands of a protracted war placed unprecedented strains on all levels of government. Much of what Madison denounced in 1787 as the "multiplicity," "mutability," and "injustice" of state lawmaking could be more charitably explained as the consequence of the desperate expedients that the war had forced each state to adopt. By the 1780s, disillusionment with the state legislatures was shared, not only by such nationally oriented leaders as Madison, Hamilton, and Washington, but by masses of a resentful citizenry. In some states, such as Connecticut, opposition to particular acts or policies provoked a populist response, which held that even locally elected legislatures could not legitimately claim to represent the people.[16] By the mid–1780s, all of the states—small and large alike—appeared not as homogeneous communities but as fractious polities.

The second challenge to notions of statehood grew out of jurisdictional controversies both between and within the states. Some of these reflected the vagueness and extravagance of the seventeenth-century colonial charters and the closely related demand that the so-called "landed" states (those with substantial western claims) cede territory for the creation of a national domain whose eventual sale would help pay off the staggering national debt. Others involved separatist movements within individual states, which affected both landed and landless states alike. As the historian Peter S. Onuf has argued in his recent compelling analysis of these jurisdictional controversies, the difficulties that the states encountered either in resolving territorial disputes or in commanding the allegiance of dissident settlers made the acceptance of federalism the most satisfactory alternative to the debilities of statehood. Polities that were too weak to secure the minimal territorial criterion of statehood could best remedy their own jurisdictional defects through a process of mutual recognition based on common membership in a federal union. Far from enhancing the authority of the states, the collapse of the union might make it more difficult for individual states to maintain their own cohesion. For whatever affection and loyalty the states might command from residents of long-settled seaboard communities or descendants of the early "adventurers" of the seventeenth century, they could not count upon the unquestioned allegiance of migrants moving west or of the new immigrants whose entry into American society had been only temporarily disrupted by the Revolution.[17]

With the creation of a national domain in the Northwest Territory, the allegiance of the mass of settlers who had surged westward even during the war became a federal as well as a state problem. It was indeed the preeminent challenge of domestic policy facing the new American nation after 1783—far more important than such other issues as paper money or barriers to interstate trade. A union that could not muster the force to suppress native American resistance to white expansion or to persuade Spain to permit the United States access to the Gulf of Mexico through New Orleans would risk losing control of the liberal territorial settlement that Britain had granted in the treaty of peace. No one pretended that individual states would be able to succeed where Congress seemed destined to fail.

THE 1787 CONVENTION

Madison's proposed national veto on all state laws was the most radical assault on state autonomy that the Federal Convention seriously entertained. The protracted debate over representation, though, exposed the potential debilities of statehood most clearly. In seeking to apportion representation in *both* houses of the new Congress on principles of proportionality, the large-state delegates had to argue that states, as states, did not deserve representation. They did this, not only by denying that the states were the sovereign constituencies of which the union was originally and immutably composed, but by insisting as well that the only just scheme of republican representation was one tied to individuals and the interests they possessed (that is, forms of property). States possessed interests but were not interests themselves.[18]

In advancing this argument, the large-state delegates also offered a new understanding of the potential flexibility of political attachment within a federal system. Whatever prior advantages the states might enjoy over the union by virtue of history and custom might not survive the establishment of an effective national government. "A private citizen of a State is indifferent whether power be exercised by the Genl. or State Legislatures, provided it be exercised most for his happiness," James Wilson reminded the delegates.[19] As a Scots immigrant, Wilson knew from his own experience just how volitional political attachment could be.[20] Nor was he alone in suspecting that the astonishing geographical mobility of both natives and immigrants might work to weaken provincial attachments, reducing cultural differences among states as it promoted loyalty to the union that would be responsible for opening the frontier. As Madison argued, the fact that "the Govts., the laws, and the manners of all [the states] were nearly the same, and the intercourse between different parts [of the union] perfectly free, population, industry, arts, and the value of labour, would constantly tend to equalize themselves."[21]

These perceptions foresaw a day when a citizen's sense of national identity would count for far more than the accident of residence in a particular state—when, in Wilson's words, "the people would be rather more attached to the national Govt. than to the State Govts. as being more important in itself, and more flattering to their pride."[22] Had the Convention denied the claim of equal state representation in the Senate or approved Madison's unlimited veto on state laws, the proposed Constitution might have gone forth from Philadelphia as a far less ambiguous document than in fact it was. For while the Constitution clearly envisioned a national government far more potent than its predecessor, it left the existing authority of the states largely intact. Avoiding a "zero-sum" solution to the distribution of public power in the federal system, the framers did not so much transfer power from one level of governance to another as find independent sources of energy upon which the national government could thereafter draw.

In part, they were far more concerned with freeing the union from its debilitating dependence on the states than on radically expanding the duties of national government. During the heated debate over representation, it is true, many delegates on both sides had spoken as if the new government would be Leviathan indeed. But after the so-called Great Compromise settled that issue in mid-July, the language of debate grew more moderate. Delegates who had once talked, almost condescendingly, of the residual functions the states might still exercise "within their proper orbits" now conceded, with Rufus King, that "The most numerous objects of legislation belong to the states," while "Those of the Natl. Legislature were but few. The chief of them were commerce & revenue. When these should be once settled, alterations would be rarely necessary & easily made." Some delegates even thought that Congress would not have to meet annually.[23]

The framers' notions of the principal duties of national government had thus evolved little beyond the commonplace ideas of the previous decade. Even Madison's congressional veto on state lawmaking assumed that the states would necessarily retain the dominant role in regulating the daily concerns of society. This presumption in turn exposed the utter impracticality of the proposal itself. "Are all laws whatever to be brought up?" George Mason asked. Was Congress to "sit constantly in order to receive & revise the State Laws?"[24] The Constitution did promise to restrict the legislative power of the states in limited cases, notably through the prohibitions of laws impairing contracts and the emission of paper money; and through the supremacy clause, it allowed the federal judiciary to act to protect individual rights in the same way that Madison had meant the veto to operate. But many of the framers thought that the national government would be hard pressed to defend itself against interference from the states, much less to "secure individuals agst. encroachments on their rights."[25]

One can argue, further, that the Constitution actually enhanced the political capacities of the states far more than it reduced their claims of "sovereignty." The most conspicuous example of this was the decision to allow the state legislatures to elect the national Senate in which the states would moreover be represented as equal corporate units. But other provisions, often overlooked, were just as important. Madison and many of his allies in the Federalist movement had hoped to liberate national politics from the parochialism they associated with state-based politicians.[26] But the Constitution left the composition of all the political branches of the government subject to the influence and control of the state legislatures, which retained legal authority over procedures for electing members of both the Electoral College and the House of Representatives, and as experience from the first federal elections of 1788/89 down to the present has shown, state leaders have always understood how to exploit this power for practical purposes. Article 5 amendment procedures, though more liberal than the corresponding Article 13 of the Confederation, also allowed the states to remain the essential locus of constitutional change. The preservation of the states as the essential electoral jurisdictions of the national government thus guaranteed that national and state politics would always remain closely intertwined.

The Constitution further confirmed the political integrity of the states by ending the danger they faced from separatist movements. No state could be divided without its own consent, and territorial disputes between states would now be resolved by an independent federal judiciary.[27] As Onuf notes, these provisions helped to create a "diminutive notion of state sovereignty." For "if the states were defined by boundaries that were guaranteed by a powerful central government, they would never have to exercise sovereign powers—preeminently those of war and peace—to uphold their 'sovereignty.' "[28] But the states gained far more than they lost by surrendering powers they probably were incompetent to exercise. What army would Pennsylvania have mobilized to advance its desire for beach frontage on the New Jersey shore?

MAKING SENSE OF THE CONSTITUTION

Antifederalists transfixed by the force of the "necessary and proper" and "supremacy" clauses can be forgiven for failing to appreciate how much the Constitution had done to secure the position of the states within the federal system. Their efforts to block ratification of the Constitution emphasized its violation of the sacred axiom of *imperium in imperio* and the enormous danger it posed to the autonomy of the states. For however many specific sovereign powers of government the states retained, the opponents of the Constitution argued, true sovereignty (defined as the ultimate authority to rule) clearly promised to become the exclusive property of the national government.

Antifederalist objections had the virtue of the simplicity that results from an appeal to axiom. The Federalist defenders of the Constitution, by contrast, faced the daunting task of explaining how the new federalism, in all its complexity, would work. They, too, sought to simplify the issue wherever possible. Thus the most notable line of their analysis sought to rebut the familiar argument against the illogic of divided sovereignty with the ingenious "fiction" of popular sovereignty. Unitary sovereignty was an attribute of neither the states nor the union but of a sovereign republican people whose consent alone bestowed legitimacy on government, and who could freely choose to parcel out particular aspects (powers) of sovereignty to the different levels of the federal system.[29]

Yet the theoretically ingenious discovery of popular sovereignty could hardly describe how American federalism would operate in practice. No one better appreciated the difficulty of this task than Madison, precisely because he left Philadelphia fearful that the new Constitution had *not* overcome the danger of *imperium in imperio*. In his view, the supremacy clause offered too weak a solution to the centrifugal forces of state and regional loyalty. Part of the problem was that its enforcement would rest with the weakest branch of government, the judiciary, whose members would be reluctant, Madison thought, to impose their judgment over and against popularly elected representatives (even in the states).[30]

The potential weakness of the judiciary might have alarmed Madison less had he thought that the line between federal and state jurisdictions would be plain for all to see. But Madison instead remained convinced of "the impossibility of dividing powers of legislation, in such a manner, as to be free from different constructions by different interests, or even from ambiguity in the judgment of the impartial." Madison had in fact come to the same opinion that such defenders of British rule as Thomas Hutchinson had reached before the Revolution: line-drawing was unsatisfactory in theory and futile in practice. Conflict between state and national levels of government was inevitable, given the overlapping character of the legislative powers a sovereign people would now delegate to each and the unlikelihood of framing national laws and policies that would find equal favor in every state. Madison's veto would not have removed these potential sources of conflict, but it would have avoided "the evil of imperia in imperio."[31]

Madison realized that the Convention's other decisions had further muddied the waters. The Convention had repeatedly been "compelled to sacrifice theoretical propriety to the force of extraneous considerations," thereby producing "deviations from that artificial structure and regular symmetry, which an abstract view of the subject might lead an ingenious theorist to bestow on a constitution planned in his closet or his imagination."[32] A misplaced emphasis on the issue of sovereignty would not prove very useful in describing the new federalism in its complex details. Thus, in *Federalist* 39, Madison emphasized the novel and hybrid features of the federal system, substituting a detailed balancing of its national and federal aspects for the axiomatic view that detected no middle ground between state sovereignty and national consolidation. After applying a five-pronged test for assaying the respective federal and national features of the proposed Constitution, he concluded that it was "in strictness, neither a national nor a federal constitution; but a composition of both."[33] And, with a similar respect for the untidiness of the Constitution, his co-author Alexander Hamilton devoted several of his contributions to *The Federalist* to explaining how both Congress and the states could concurrently maintain independent sources of revenue without forcing each other into insolvency.[34]

Ideally, Madison and Hamilton would both have preferred to describe a federal system constructed along more elegant lines, that is, one giving the national government more effective means of asserting its authority and supremacy. In one sense at least, there was nothing insincere about the emphasis they placed in *The Federalist* on the substantial residual powers of the states. What they had no need to confess in their public defense of the Constitution were their private doubts about the adequacy of the powers of the national government.

THE AFTERMATH

In the best of all possible eighteenth-century worlds, the American "political nation" would have read the exegesis of federalism in *The Federalist* with the greatest care, grasped the nuances of Madison's five-pronged analysis, and come away from the unprecedented ratification debate of 1787/88 possessed of a mature understanding of the inherent complexities of federalism. Some contemporary commentators on the Constitution seem to presume that something like this is indeed what happened during the "miracle" of "the founding." What else can sustain a "jurisprudence of original intention" than the belief that the Constitution had some fixed original meaning that was correctly perceived by an informed citizenry who gave the Constitution the force of supreme law through their first exercise of popular sovereignty?

Historians, among others, prefer a more skeptical view of the founding. The meaning of the Constitution was controversial almost from the moment it went into operation. In the quarter-century after ratification, both Federalists and Republicans[35] sought to use national power vigorously in pursuit of their foreign policy objectives, which were in turn closely linked to their differing notions of the optimal development of a national economy. From the start, these disputes over foreign policies and domestic programs took constitutional form. As early as 1791, in the debate over the chartering of a national bank, Madison and Jefferson challenged Hamilton's broad reading of the "necessary and proper" clause as an illegitimate effort to extend the lawmaking authority of Congress far beyond anything anticipated a few years earlier. Republicans responded by stressing the limited nature of the legislative powers the Constitution had granted to Congress. From this notion of the limited sway of national government it was but a short step to a view of the Constitution as a traditional compact among sovereign states, and from there to a revival of the hackneyed issue of *imperium in imperio*, which gained new currency during the nineteenth-century debate over states' rights.

Yet disagreements over the meaning of the Constitution did nothing to impeach its authority. Even though the early divisions in national politics were far more serious and bitter than any the country had known under the Articles of Confederation, no one thought to suggest that the Constitution itself was somehow part of the problem. The opposite was more nearly the case. As the historian John Murrin has wryly noted, "The Constitution became a substitute for any deeper kind of national identity. . . . People knew that without the Constitution there would be no America."[36] Seen in this way, its great contribution to nation-building was not so much to solve the theoretical problem of *imperium in imperio* but simply to have preserved the union at a time when many observers had good reason to fear that it might soon devolve into two or three regional confederacies.

Constitutional reform had provided a new and improved forum within which national decision-making could take place, and it promised to give the national government greater resources with which to implement its decision once taken. In their most optimistic moments, the framers even hoped that this new forum would attract only men of "enlightened views and virtuous sentiments" who would be capable of recognizing and pursuing a transcendent national interest.[37] But, as they quickly learned, constitutional reform could not by itself magically remove underlying sources of political division. Nor could it prevent external events—most notably the wars of the French Revolution and Napoleon—from exposing the existing divisions within the country.

The framers of the Constitution had understood perfectly well which sources of division seemed most threatening. For all their preoccupation with the struggle between large and small states over representation in the Senate, they knew, as Madison reminded them, that the states were ultimately "divided into different interests not by their difference of size, but by other circumstances; the most material of which resulted partly from climate, but principally from (the effects of) their having or not having slaves."[38] One could, of course, describe this fundamental cleavage in the more decorous terms of differences in regional economies. The northern states were populated largely by subsistence farmers producing modest agricultural surpluses, but they also possessed substantial maritime interests in commerce and fishing; the economies of the southern states, by contrast, were dominated by the production for export of such agricultural commodities as tobacco, rice, and indigo (cotton would come along soon enough).[39] But however one described or explained regional differences, no one at Philadelphia pretended that the future development of the nation would see a convergence of the social orders of the existing states. The differences between northern and southern states were taken as fixed, and unless one could imagine the miraculous disappearance of chattel slavery, they seemed likely to remain so indefinitely.

The acceptance of this brutal fact led the Convention to deal with the reality of sectional differences in the most direct way. To allow Congress to frame the navigation laws that northern merchants and artisans had been clamoring for since 1784, the Convention agreed that laws regulating commerce could be passed by simple majorities, rather than the supermajorities some southern delegates had sought. Treaties of commerce, however, would need two-thirds approval in the Senate, and in the House the southern states would benefit from the three-fifths clause allowing slaves to be counted for purposes of representation. At the same time, the lower South was assured of a grace period of twenty years in which it could continue the legal importation of new African slaves.

In theory this kind of hard bargaining could easily have presaged future accommodations along equally pragmatic lines. The cause of intersectional accommodation would be further advanced if the new states in the West entered the union as a balancing force between the regions. In the 1780s, it was widely believed that the axis of migration would flow southwest toward the Gulf of Mexico rather than northwest toward the Great Lakes, so that many southern leaders expected that the free population of their expanding region would soon come closer to parity with the North. Some New England leaders shared that expectation, and accordingly viewed the development of the West with alarm. Their fears of depopulation and a loss of political influence could not outweigh the attractive force and evident benefits of western development. After six generations of a remarkably fruitful multiplication of its original population, New England needed the West as much as anyone. If New England and the South could agree upon the importance of the West, and if the new territories were settled by migrants from all the Atlantic states, the development of the interior might well provide a powerful impetus for the further coalescence of the union.[40] One crucial measure of the appreciation that the Federal Convention had for the role of the West came when it handily rejected the idea that representation in Congress should be apportioned in a way that would permit the lasting dominance of the Atlantic states.

Over the course of the succeeding decades, the development of the West became the sole significant domestic function of the national government and the one area in which the new regime met the high expectations of the founding. Seen from the vantage point of the next half-century of American history, much of the original debate over the adoption of the Constitution seems splendidly and ironically irrelevant to the subsequent evolution of the federal system. The United States were not much less of a confederation in 1836, when Madison, the last of the framers, passed away, than they had been in 1786, when he and Hamilton and a handful of others had joined at Annapolis to call for general constitutional reform. In the realm of foreign affairs, the hope that the United States would conduct an effective foreign policy based on a mature sense of a "true" or "permanent" national interest soon gave way to the extreme partisanship that led to the organization of the country's first system of political parties. Much of the divisiveness that issues of foreign policy provoked before 1815 can be traced to the unavoidable buffeting that the United States experienced from the principal belligerents in the wars of the French Revolution and Napoleon. Yet party conflict was ultimately rooted in rival conceptions of the national interest that were so sharply divergent and sectionally based as to call into question the idea of national interest itself.

Similarly, while the framers who met at Philadelphia in 1787 "believed that constitutional reform would make the United States a more efficient military power,"[41] the next war the country fought found the nation far less prepared to sustain a conflict with Britain than it had been during the Revolution. One whole region of the country (New England) virtually sat out the War of 1812 and by its close was at least flirting with the idea of secession. Republican efforts to use the government's new power to regulate foreign commerce to bring economic pressure to bear on Britain and France proved unavailing overseas even while they inspired such massive efforts as evasion at home that the militia had to be mobilized to crack down on the extensive smuggling trade with Canada.

The coming of peace in 1815 finally permitted the quieting of foreign policy issues. In their absence, the role of the national government seemed to decline almost from year to year. No observer of the American scene in the 1820s and 1830s—De Tocqueville, for instance—could possibly have concluded that the Constitution had in fact created a vigorous nation-state. The federal government, as John Murrin has observed,

remained minuscule, a midget institution in a giant land. It had almost no internal functions except the postal system and the sale of western lands. Its role scarcely went beyond what would have pleased even most Antifederalists in the 1780s, the use of port duties and the revenue from land sales to meet its own limited expenses.[42]

Much of the lassitude of the federal government after 1800 can be traced squarely to the ideology of the Jeffersonian Republicans—that is to say, to the notions of federalism that they had forged in their opposition to Hamiltonian policies. Though prepared to use national power vigorously in pursuit of their foreign policy objectives, Republican domestic concerns did not extend beyond monetary and fiscal matters, the development of the West, and a modest tariff. After 1815 the crucial public decisions fostering American economic development were taken individually by the states through their promotion of canals, turnpikes, and railroads and their liberal allocation of corporate privileges to banking and manufacturing enterprises. Elements of a national economy were certainly emerging in these years, in the development of infrastructure or the growth of a northern textile manufacture relying on southern cotton, and one can see the nationalist decisions of the Supreme Court under Chief Justice John Marshall as both a recognition and a harbinger of that process. Yet the essential locus of economic activity and public investment and support remained largely local.[43]

Only in the West can one plausibly argue that the federal government played a major role in the process of American nation-building. Even here, there were ominous signs that the hopeful expectations of the 1780s would go unfulfilled. Far from bringing the southern states into rough population parity with the North or of working to moderate prior antagonisms between the Atlantic states, the settlement of the West widened the population gap while it worked to replicate the slave and free societies of the parent regions. The growth of the cotton economy and the opening of the fertile lands of the Southwest dashed whatever faint hopes the founders had nursed for the extinction of slavery. Ownership of slaves remained the dominant ambition of all southern whites—a condition attested to by the fact that while the great majority of slaves lived on the large plantations always associated with the antebellum South, the overwhelming majority of slaveholders possessed only a few slaves.[44] Conversely, a fear that the extension of slavery into western territories would circumscribe the geographical expansion of the mobile agricultural population of the North and thus encourage a proletarianization of northern society was probably the most important factor in the development of political antislavery—as opposed to abolitionism—in the free states.[45]

Although northern public opinion did not begin to swing decisively in this direction until the midpoint of the nineteenth century, the implications of expansion for the future of American federalism became apparent with the Missouri Crisis of 1819–21, which was largely resolved through a compromise that would admit slave and free states to the union in equal numbers, so that the Senate would henceforth serve as the principal institutional defense for the South. This was a formula, not for nation-building, but for the mere preservation of an uneasy status quo. During this same period of hothouse politics, the Marshall Court issued some of its most famous nationalist opinions. From this point on, American ideas of federalism increasingly expressed the hoary logic of *imperium in imperio*, with all its reductionist tendencies. Even with the federal government maintaining its minimalist activities, the lines of conflict between the rival claims of national and state sovereignty were drawn with increasing clarity. So it was that James Madison could leave as his final political testament only a brief plea "that the Union of the States be cherished and perpetuated" and his assent to the posthumous publication of his notes of debates at the 1787 Convention, which he must have hoped would teach its readers that the deepest problems of nation-building were not beyond their powers of reason and politics alike. In this, of course, he would have been disappointed.[46]

NOTES

1. Alexis de Tocqueville, *Democracy in America*, Phillips Bradley, ed. (1945), vol. I, at 166.

2. Gordon S. Wood, *The Creation of the American Republic, 1776–1787* (1969), at 355.

3. See, for example, the June 19 exchange between Luther Martin and James Wilson in *The Records of the Federal Convention of 1787* (Max Farrand ed., 2d rev. ed., 1987), vol. I, at 322.

4. See H. Jefferson Powell, "The Modern Misunderstanding of Original Intent," *University of Chicago Law Review* 54(1987), at 1513–44, reviewing Raoul Berger, *Federalism: The Original Design* (1987), affirming the priority of the states under a theory of original intention.

5. This point is briefly discussed in Jack N. Rakove, *The Beginnings of National Politics: An Interpretive History of the Continental Congress* (1979), pp. 51–52, 65–66.

6. Much of this literature is summarized and elaborated in Jack P. Green, *Peripheries and Center: Constitutional Development in the Extended Polities of the British Empire and the United States, 1607–1788* (1986).

7. Michael G. Kammen, *Deputyes and Libertyes: The Origins of Representative Government in Colonial America* (1969), at 3–68.

8. Bernard Bailyn, *The Ideological Origins of the American Revolution* (1967), pp. 198–229.

9. Wood, supra note 2, at 354–55, and Rakove, supra note 5, at 135–91, trace the drafting of the Articles.

10. In May 1777, it is true, the militantly states'-rightist delegate Thomas Burke of North Carolina secured the adoption of an Article affirming that "Each state retains its sovereignty, freedom, and independence, and every power, jurisdiction, and right, which is not by this confederation expressly delegated to the United States, in Congress, assembled." But this formulaic statement, while stronger than the Tenth Amendment to the 1787 Constitution, did nothing to illuminate where the lines of authority described elsewhere in the Articles would run. See Rakove, supra note 5, at 164–76.

11. On the substitution of Congress for Crown, see Jerrilyn Greene Marston, *King and Congress: The Transfer of Political Legitimacy, 1774–1776* (1987).

12. From Madison's memorandum, "Vices of the Political System of the United States," in *The Papers of James Madison* (Robert Rutland et al. eds. 1962–), vol. IX, at 351.

13. The lands northwest of the Ohio River, which by 1785 had come under federal control through the voluntary cessions of the individual states with claims (however dubious) to the interior. See the extensive analysis in Peter S. Onuf, *The Origins of the Federal Republic: Jurisdictional Controversies in the United States, 1775–1787* (1983).

14. Rakove, supra note 5, at 342–52.

15. On the centrality of the veto to Madison's thinking, see his letters to Washington, April 16, 1787, and Jefferson, October 24, 1787, in Rutland, ed., *Papers of Madison*, vol. IX, at 383–84; vol. X, at 209–14; and the discussion in Charles F. Hobson, "The Negative on State Laws: James Madison, the Constitution, and the Crisis of Republican Government," *William and Mary Quarterly*, 3d ser., 36 (1979), at 215–35, and Jack N. Rakove, "The Madisonian Moment," *University of Chicago Law Review*, 55 (1988), at 473–505.

16. On this point see especially Wood, supra note 2, at 319–43, 363–89.

17. Onuf, supra note 13, passim. The story is carried forward in Peter S. Onuf, *Statehood and Union: A History of the Northwest Ordinance* (1987).

18. For a more extensive discussion, see Jack N. Rakove, "The Great Compromise: Ideas, Interests, and the Politics of Constitution Making," *William and Mary Quarterly*, 3d ser., 44 (1987), at 424–57.

19. Speech of June 20, 1787, Farrand, ed., *Records*, vol. I, at 344; and cf. his earlier speech of June 6, ibid., at 132–33.

20. The idea that political allegiance and citizenship should be volitional was itself deeply reinforced by the events of the Revolutionary era. See James H. Kettner, *The Development of American Citizenship, 1608–1870* (1978).

21. Speech of July 11, 1787, in Farrand, ed., *Records*, vol. I, p. 585; for a general discussion, see Drew McCoy, "James Madison and Visions of American Nationality in the Confederation Period: A Regional Perspective," in *Beyond Confederation: Origins of the Constitution and American National Identity* (Richard Beeman, Stephen Botein, and Edward C. Carter II eds. 1987), at 226–58.

22. Farrand, ed., *Records*, vol. I, at 133.

23. Farrand, ed., *Records*, vol. II, at 197–99; Jack N. Rakove, "The Legacy of the Articles of Confederation," *Publius*, 12 (1982–83), at 62–63.

24. Farrand, ed., *Records*, vol. II, at 390–91.

25. On this point, no one was more skeptical than Madison himself; Madison to Jefferson, October 24, 1787, Rutland, ed., *Papers of Madison*, vol. X, at 209–14.

26. Federalist expectations for creating a "filtration of talent" into the ranks of national government have been a major theme of much recent historiography. See Wood, supra note 2, at 506–18; Robert J. Morgan, "Madison's Theory of Representation in the Tenth Federalist," *Journal of Politics*, 36 (1974), at 852–85; and Jack N. Rakove, "The Structure of Politics at the Accession of George Washington," in *Beyond Confederation*, supra note 21, at 261–94.

27. Article 9 of the Confederation had established an awkward procedure whereby the states immediately concerned could constitute a special court that would meet under the general authority of the union, but its unwieldy procedures were found nearly impracticable.

28. Onuf, supra note 13, at 194.

29. Wood, supra note 2, at 524–36, 543–47; and for a more extended (and skeptical) treatment, Edmund S. Morgan, *Inventing the People: The Rise of Popular Sovereignty in England and America* (1988).

30. His proposed congressional veto, by contrast, would have brought the political clout of an elected national legislature to bear against the wishes of a mere state assembly.

31. Madison to Jefferson, October 24, 1787, Rutland, ed., *Papers of Madison*, vol. X, at 209–11.

32. From the concluding paragraphs of *Federalist* 37, in Rutland, ed., *Papers of Madison*, vol. X, at 363–64.

33. *Federalist* 39, id., at 379–84.

34. Hamilson's extended discussion of taxation can be found in essays 30–36 of *The Federalist*. In the landmark case of *McCulloch v. Maryland* (1819), *Federalist* 32 was prominently invoked in support of Maryland's right to impose a state tax on the Second Bank of the United States.

35. After 1789 the term Federalist no longer denoted the supporters of the Constitution, but rather those loyal to the administrations of Washington and John Adams and especially the programs of Hamilton; Republican denotes the opposition originally grouped around Congressman Madison and Secretary of State Thomas Jefferson.

36. John Murrin, "A Roof without Walls: The Dilemma of American National Identity," in *Beyond Confederation*, supra note 21, at 346–47; and see Lance Banning, "Republican Ideology and the Triumph of the Constitution, 1789 to 1793," *William and Mary Quarterly*, 3d ser., 31 (1978), at 167–88.

37. *Federalist* 10, in Rutland, ed., *Papers of Madison*, vol. X, at 269.

38. Farrand, ed., *Records*, vol. I, at 468–69.

39. This more general perception of regional difference is discussed in McCoy, "Madison and American Nationality," in *Beyond Confederation*, supra note 21, at 230–39.

40. On this point, see especially McCoy, "Madison and American Nationality," in *Beyond Confederation*, supra note 21, at 230–39, 247–50; and Peter S. Onuf, *Statehood and Union: A History of the Northwest Ordinance* (1987), at 1–20.

41. J. C. A. Stagg, *Mr. Madison's War: Politics, Diplomacy and Warfare in the Early American Republic, 1783–1830* (1983), at 120.

42. John Murrin, "The Great Inversion, or Court versus Country: A Comparison of the Revolution Settlements in England (1688–1721) and America (1776–1816)," in *Three British Revolutions: 1641, 1688, 1776* (J. G. A. Pocock ed. 1980), at 425.

43. For a suggestive survey, see Harry N. Scheiber, "Federalism and the American Economic Order, 1789–1910," *Law and Society Review*, 10 (1975–76), at 67–70, 86–92.

44. This theme is repeatedly stressed in James Oakes, *The Ruling Race: A History of American Slaveholders* (1982).

45. Eric Foner, *Free Soil, Free Labor, Free Men: The Ideology of the Republican Party before the Civil War* (1970).

46. *The Writings of James Madison* (Gaillard Hunt ed. 1900–1910), vol. X, at 610–11. His final reflections on the fate of the federal experiment are the subject of Drew McCoy, *The Last of the Fathers: James Madison and the Republican Legacy* (1989).

2

Economic Integration and Interregional Migration in the United States Federal System

JONATHAN D. VARAT

The United States Constitution was designed to help achieve a multiplicity of national objectives.[1] The most important of these were directed at strengthening the ties among the people and governments of the United States. Economic union and freedom of interstate migration were, and remain, primary integrative or centralizing objectives included within the general aims of forming a "more perfect Union," promoting "the general Welfare," and securing the "Blessings of Liberty."[2] But they are not the only two unifying values in the Constitution, and they cannot be understood in isolation. Of greatest significance, the "more perfect Union" the Constitution contemplates is a political union even more fundamental than economic union.

The Constitution's integrative values cannot be fully appreciated without acknowledging that their enforcement is constrained by adherence to the value of preserving decentralized power in the individual states. The Constitution was formulated, and continues to function, on the major premise that the states of the union retain substantial policy autonomy to regulate their internal affairs and to exercise independent taxing and spending powers to serve the needs and wants of their respective inhabitants. The preservation of state policy autonomy is itself a federal constitutional value,[3] one which necessarily exists in considerable tension with the integrative aims of the Constitution.[4]

The nature and degree of U.S. legal commitment to economic integration and interstate mobility are best understood, therefore, by taking full account of the Constitution's simultaneous commitments to both political union and the preservation of meaningful spheres of state authority. In the complex system of United States federalism, each integrative value—economic union, political union, and interstate mobility—potentially must contend with a conflicting constitutional commitment to local autonomy. Moreover, how much weight to give state prerogatives when balanced against any one of these integrative values is at least partially a function of the balance reached with respect to the others. Economic and political integration in particular are often mutually reinforcing. The nature and degree of economic integration and freedom of interregional migration among a group of countries that have decided to join together only to develop an economic common market, at least initially, may well differ considerably from that in a group of states that have joined together to build a politically integrated, individual rights-conscious federal nation, with centralized exclusive power over that nation's external foreign policy and military security concerns, and extensive, virtually plenary power to adopt uniform rules for governing domestic economic and social matters.

In what respects, if at all, the balance between state autonomy and economic integration, and between state autonomy and freedom of interregional migration, may differ as between an entity like the European Economic Community (EEC) and a nation like the United States will undoubtedly depend on a wide range of factors. Perhaps none will be more significant than the reasons why, and the degree to which, member-state autonomy, economic integration, and interstate migratory freedom are valued in the respective systems. Even in a comparison of two systems with the same set of objectives, these balances might be weighed differently. Yet it is that much harder to compare the legal status of these balances as between systems with different overall sets of objectives. Without undertaking such a difficult comparative analysis here, let me suggest that, to the extent that there is any relationship between objectives such as political integration and economic integration, the extent of enforcement of one is likely to be affected by the extent of the enforcement of the other, perhaps in complicated ways. Perhaps, too, the more overlapping objectives a federal system seeks to achieve, the more difficult it will be to ascertain the independent strength of each.

Even without a comparative focus, untangling the extent of American legal attachment to economic integration and interregional migration from its attachment to political unification is a daunting task. More daunting still is to assess for what reasons, to what degree, and in what ways U.S. law simultaneously sought to foster and, when necessary, accommodate those values and the value of state autonomy. After a brief description of the primary rationales for embracing these four national values and some commentary on the relationships among them, this chapter will attempt to ascertain how strongly each is enforced in the United States in the context of issues of economic integration and interstate mobility. The aim is to determine, first, to what extent each may or may not be given priority in discretionary policy decisions, and second, to what extent each is a fundamentally grounded constitutional mandate. This requires some attention to the relationships between Congress and the states, the Supreme Court and the states, and the Supreme Court and Congress. The emphasis is on constitutional *powers* to promote integration as much as, if not more than, on *limits* on constitutional power to impair integration or to promote it, and to therefore focus on the available means of building integration. These are varied, because the Constitution not only seeks multiple objectives, but in widely dispersing power among many levels and branches of government, provides for multiple mechanisms that have been used to foster integration. The constitutional priority of economic integration and interstate mobility in particular contexts is examined by addressing three questions. First, what are the constitutional limits on state power to impair economic integration and free interregional migration? Second, what, if any, elements of economic integration or interstate mobility are so fundamental that even Congress may not impair them? And third, what elements, if any, may the states infringe that Congress is powerless to override?

THE VALUES OF STATE AUTONOMY, POLITICAL UNIFICATION, INTERSTATE MOBILITY, AND ECONOMIC INTEGRATION

Each of these national values has been the subject of extensive analysis, but a few reminders about the central benefits of each, and some of the relationships among them, will facilitate the inquiry.

State policy autonomy within a larger federal system is valued by some because it provides more—and more accessible—opportunities for political participation.[5] Others value its relatively greater responsiveness to diverse local needs, values, and culture.[6] Still others value its effect as a counterweight to concentration of central power that potentially may threaten individual liberty.[7] Yet others appreciate that state policy autonomy has educational and experimental value.[8] It allows comparative evaluation of differing policies in actual operation in different states before deciding whether the national government should adopt uniform rules of governance and, when uniformity seems desirable, what the content of the uniform rule should be.

When individual state regulatory schemes prove successful enough to warrant national adoption, state autonomy has served as an aid to economic integration.[9] State policy diversity is also related to the value of interstate mobility, because taken together, mobility and diversity enlarge the options available for people motivated by distinctive legal climates to live or work or even vacation in particular states.[10] As state policies change, so may opportunities, and policy differences among states constitute one factor among many that may encourage or deter moving among jurisdictions. Given maximum freedom of mobility, people may choose either to migrate permanently or to divide their time among different states to take advantage of the best that each has to offer them. The freedom to live in one state and work in another is frequently exercised in contemporary life, sometimes because of differences in state law.

Political unification is highly valued primarily for the strength it provides to guard against external threats from other nations and for its value as a safeguard against internal strife, that is, for "domestic tranquility."[11] No doubt political union also brings increased capacity to deal more effectively with national economic welfare in dealing with both domestic and international concerns,[12] but this seems distinctly secondary in the formation of "a more perfect Union" as contemplated in the Constitution.[13] Political union is an interest sometimes at odds with state autonomy but intimately related to freedom of interstate mobility and often supportive of, if also superior to, economic integration.

The freedom of interregional migration is valued for its own inherent worth to individuals;[14] for its contribution to freedom of choice generally;[15] and for its contribution to political, social, and economic integration.[16] It has been derived from each of these other values, and its relationship to the diversity that accompanies state autonomy has already been mentioned. It is a serious question whether migratory freedom is derivative of economic or political integration values or is independent of them. Developed U.S. constitutional law suggests, however, that an independent liberty foundation supplements—or perhaps more firmly grounds—the freedom of interregional mobility that derives from a unified nation.[17]

Economic integration may be valued by some for its contribution to aggregate consumer welfare;[18] by others for its contribution to increasing opportunities of owners, workers, and management;[19] by others for its part in reducing economic conflict among states;[20] and by still others to the extent that it may prevent social, political, and even military conflict among states.[21] In the United States, given the degree to which state regulatory, taxing, and spending autonomy is acknowledged, and the degree to which economic integration may be seen as important because of its instrumental relationship to both political unification and interstate mobility, it is a serious question of how much, if any, independent value economic integration has.[22]

DISCRETIONARY POWERS AND METHODS FOR FURTHERING ECONOMIC INTEGRATION AND INTERREGIONAL MIGRATION

The legal status of economic integration and interregional migration in the United States is not just a matter of the relevant constitutional limitations imposed on the states or the federal government. It is, in fact, much more a matter of what affirmative powers to build a system of economic integration and interstate mobility are available and have been used to achieve those ends. This is not the place to undertake a comprehensive examination of the multitude of specific measures adopted to further these goals, but it is appropriate to briefly survey the nature and extent of the powers residing in the federal system that have been used toward these goals. Moreover, in thinking about the value of these constructive methods, it will be worth considering the mutually reinforcing effects of the availability of alternative mechanisms, as well as the potential for antagonistic policies to be pursued through different means.

It is possible that the whole is more than the sum of its parts, that is, that economic integration may occur more swiftly and more certainly given that different institutions may be working simultaneously toward the same end. Thus, if the Supreme Court and Congress or the president simultaneously pursue an integrative agenda that limits the options available to individual states to implement divergent policies or policies that discriminate against interstate relationships, economic integration will be achieved more readily and more durably than if only one branch of government is pushing in this direction. Such is the case also if, in addition, states cooperate with each other to minimize disintegrative tendencies stemming from lack of tax or regulatory uniformity.

It may also be that even if the will is lacking in some of these government institutions to pursue integration aggressively, the existence of alternative mechanisms decreases the likelihood that the goal will be neglected completely. Those devoted to integration may be able to obtain substantive support somewhere and may be able to enlist powerful voices that provoke attention to integrationist needs in other forms. If the courts are unreceptive, legislators may not be. If pleas to state legislatures fall on deaf ears, pleas to Congress may not, or vice versa. If one or another method or institution falls into disfavor for reasons independent of the desire to pursue or not pursue integration, other avenues remain to fill the void. These all remain strong possibilities, but not certainties, because it is also possible that the system's methods can be used in similar ways to accentuate the values of state policy autonomy or that some methods may apply pressure in the direction of integration while others apply centrifugal pressure. All this emphasizes the dynamic quality of policy adjustments between integration and diversity over time and in different spheres that the wide array of mechanisms makes available, but there are at least strong indications of pro-integrative policies at work.

It will also be worth considering the degree to which the wide scope of available power—the capacity of the system as a whole to counter serious dangers to economic integration and interregional migration as they arise—renders particular exercises of state autonomy more tolerable than they would be were the power to curb excesses weaker and so, perhaps ironically, renders the need or desire to exercise these integrative powers less frequent or compelling. The presence of the backstop security of available integrative power may make it easier to give the benefit of the doubt to local measures whose balance of positive effects in serving local needs and adverse effects on integration cannot be accurately gauged in advance. Moreover, to whatever extent economic integration in particular is constitutionally valued as a means of achieving political integration, contentment with the overall status of political integration is bound to affect the perception of whether local measures that depart from the economic integration norm are acceptable.

A final introductory point about the scope of discretionary powers to build economic and migratory union distinguishes the kind of integration that can be furthered as a matter of discretionary policy from the kind that is constitutionally required. The discretionary powers can, and often do, seek integration in the strong sense of uniform regulation that puts aside state policy diversity. A national minimum wage law or federal legislation that establishes uniform requirements governing corporate issuance of securities or control of the terms on which credit is offered to consumers throughout the nation displaces state regulation of these matters, sometimes completely and sometimes only to the extent of barring conflicting regulations and allowing supplemental ones.[23]

By contrast, constitutional limits primarily focus on integration and mobility in a weaker sense, the sense that allows for state policy diversity but generally requires whatever diverse policy a particular state has adopted to be applied equally to in-state and interstate activity and to residents and nonresidents. Thus, each state is generally free to choose the forms and levels of local taxation but must apply its chosen tax policy equally.[24] Absent preemptive federal legislation, regulation of economic activity also may differ from state to state, but such regulations as are adopted generally must be applied equally among intrastate and interstate business[25] and among residents and nonresidents of the state.[26] Insofar as the constitutional restraints on state power extend only to regulations and taxes that facially discriminate against interstate commerce or nonresidents, and do not extend to those that have a disproportionate impact on them,[27] more-over, the discretionary powers can, of course, be used to eliminate the unequal impact. The power to impose uniformity, or even to minimize the dispropor-tionate effects of state laws on nonresidents or interstate commerce, is a much more strongly integrative power than is the constitutional demand of interstate equality, and correspondingly, it exacts a much greater cost in its interference with state autonomy.

National Legislative Power

The most powerful, as well as the most obvious, integrative mechanism in the United States is the scope of the power given to Congress to adopt uniform regulations directly governing the activities of the private sector and, to an astounding degree, the activities of the states themselves. National legislative power is exclusive over foreign affairs, military policy, and external security, as well as the determination of immigration laws.[28] These exclusive powers have significant effects on the internal integration of the country, if for no other reason than that they remove potential sources of conflicting policy among the states and thereby make cooperation among them on all levels more likely than conflict. More directly integrative is Congress' exclusive power to control the currency of the United States, a matter with which the states are forbidden to interfere. A common currency predates the Constitution[29] and is one of the least contro-versial, if also one of the most effective, of the centralizing measures incorporated in that document. Only Congress may coin money and regulate its value and that of foreign coin.[30] The states must accept the common currency of the United States, and they must abide by the value of the dollar (or foreign currencies) as set by the federal government.[31] To what degree this has contributed to economic integration, and to what degree its economic integrative effects were intended independently of the political integrative effects of a common currency, is difficult to say,[32] but surely it has simplified and facilitated interstate trade and has defined a major difference in reality and perception between interstate trade and international trade.[33]

Congress' taxing and spending powers, although not exclusive of similar powers possessed by the states, can and have been used for important integrationist purposes.[34] The most direct example is the funding of interstate transportation improvements that facilitate commerce and personal mobility.[35] Important indirect examples include government procurement policies that standardize commercial behavior among the private sectors of the various states and monetary grants to the states conditioned on compliance with uniform minimum standards, some of which Congress arguably could not legislate directly.[36] In many programs of "cooperative federalism," in fields such as the provision of welfare assistance and the regulation of environmental hazards, Congress has deliberately imposed some uniform federal guidelines and left supplemental regulation to diverse state policy choices.[37]

The powers delegated to Congress to establish uniform bankruptcy laws, copyright and patent laws, and a postal system, although also not completely exclusive of state power, are so plenary and have been exercised so extensively that those areas are virtually within the exclusive domain of federal uniform regulation.[38] All these powers are supplemented, of course, by the grant of the partially exclusive power to "regulate Commerce . . . among the several States," a power that today, despite an earlier period of crabbed Supreme Court interpretation,[39] extends to permit federal uniform regulation of virtually any kind of local activities with arguably aggregate effects on interstate commerce.[40] Not only local commercial activity, but local criminal and social activity is subject to federal regulation.[41] Common standards for the electronic communications industry, one of the most potent of integrative forces, also fall within the power of uniform regulation,[42] although again federal policy to some degree authorizes and supports local participation, as, for example, with local franchising of cable television.[43]

Federal legislative power is clearly more than ample to ensure and facilitate economic integration and interregional mobility, and it has increasingly been used towards this end since the late nineteenth century. What is perhaps surprising is how much diversity of state regulatory policy remains despite the federal capacity for imposing uniformity. Traditional valuing of the benefits of local policy autonomy has much to do with it, but so does the often noted structural means through which that continuing tradition is expressed, namely, the ability of the states to have their interest in policy autonomy respected at the national level through the structural responsiveness of the national government's representative institutions to state political interests.[44] Were the American legislative process to borrow a page from the EEC,[45] and incorporate into the structure of congressional deliberations systematic representation of consumer groups and a requirement that the states carry the burden of notifying Congress of new diverse regulations with significant anti-integrative effects, to the same degree that representation of state autonomy interests is presently integrated into congressional deliberations, the balance between integrationist policy and diverse state policy would perhaps tilt in the direction of more uniformity. The degree to which particular government structures provide systematic representation for certain values cannot help but affect the substantive outcome of deliberations if there is any open-mindedness in the system at all.

Federal Judicial Power

Potent as the national legislative powers are to achieve integration, they do not stand alone. The national judicial power has also played a role in the development of nonconstitutional uniform policy, and its role in promoting integration has sometimes been prominent when the president or Congress have held back, just as it has at other times held back integrationist policies of Congress on constitutional grounds.

The very existence of national courts in each states, available, not only for the independent enforcement of federal law, but to ensure unbiased adjudication of state law as between the citizens of the forum state and citizens from other states who have come to do business or otherwise engage in activity in the forum state, is a powerful integrationist influence—just as it was intended to be.[46] The judicial creation and enforcement of uniform federal common law in admiralty, the definition and enforcement of a national common law governing collective bargaining agreements between labor and management, and the resolution of disputes between states has had a major hand in economic integration.[47] So, too, the flexibility possessed by the Supreme Court to vary the degree to which it finds state authority preempted by federal legislation can be, and has been, used to foster uniformity.[48]

That was also the object during the era of *Swift v. Tyson*,[49] if not before,[50] of the attempt to develop a federal general common law to be applied in federal courts to resolve disputes between merchants of different states where state statutes did not apply.[51] In fact, when it applied, the reach of that federal common law exceeded the scope of the contemporaneously acknowledged federal legislative power.[52] The attempt at uniformity, at a time when Congress had used exceedingly little of its available power to adopt uniform law governing commercial transactions in or affecting interstate commerce,[53] however, had only limited potential. Federal general common law did not bind the state courts in their decisions and did not apply even in federal court diversity of citizenship cases when state statutes governed the issue.[54] Yet Justice Story's attempt at uniformity through federal common law is an important instance of bending federal judicial power in the direction of economic integration.

The timing of the Supreme Court's ultimate rejection of this haphazard notion of federal general common law in *Erie Railroad Co. v. Tompkins*[55] nearly a hundred years later was highly illuminating. The Court's conclusion that the federal courts under the regime of *Swift* had unconstitutionally usurped state lawmaking authority came just as the Court began to back away from its restrictive interpretations of the scope of Congress' power to regulate interstate commerce.[56] Discarding a sporadic, largely ineffective judicial effort at economic integration through uniform law[57] surely had to be easier when comprehensive power to effectively legislate uniform rules was being solidified.

State Efforts at Economic Integration

Not infrequently, the states themselves have voluntarily fostered integration. The Constitution provides a means for formal agreements or "Compacts" among states, which require congressional consent only if they have aggregated their powers in such a way as to threaten federal supremacy.[58] Moreover, the Supreme Court has allowed cooperative efforts, such as the Multistate Tax Commission, in which twenty-one states have joined to develop proposals for uniform tax treatment of multistate businesses, without even requiring congressional consent.[59] In this way, the Court has facilitated voluntary state efforts at economic integration, so long as they do not threaten the existing structure of political integration.[60]

States can, of course, independently decide to adopt similar regulations, and they will often be pushed to do so by interstate enterprises for whom diverse sets of regulations are costly or burdensome. A formal body, the National Conference of Commissioners on Uniform State Laws, begun in the 1880s at the instigation of the then fledgling American Bar Association, has assisted in the integrative effort by drafting proposed uniform laws and model acts for legislative consideration by the states.[61] The most successful is the Uniform Commercial Code, adopted by every state except Louisiana and governing most of the contractual and other commercial relationships among intrastate and interstate businesses.[62] Many of these "uniform laws" have been widely adopted, although not always by all jurisdictions and not always in exactly the same form.[63] State common law, developed by judges, is often prone to integrative influences as a result of the work of drafters of Restatements of the law or of persuasive opinions rendered by judges in other states or even by the influences of legal educators in their writings or teaching.[64]

Many states also have voluntarily adopted reciprocity laws waiving the examination usually required as a condition to practice a profession for those professionals who are admitted to practice and have had a specified amount of experience in another state. For example, some thirty-two states recognize the validity of lawyers' professional licenses plus experience obtained in another state, but twelve do so only on condition of mutual reciprocity, that is, the original state of admission would recognize the validity of professional licenses obtained in the state offering reciprocity.[65] Until recently, almost all jurisdictions granting reciprocity required the professional to establish residence in the state in order to take advantage of this benefit.[66] Even so, voluntary reciprocity laws of this kind have ameliorated impediments to economic integration, particularly interstate migration, which stem from recognizing the validity of differing standards for professional licensing from state to state. Taking into account the recent Supreme Court decisions invalidating residency requirements as conditions to professional practice,[67] "[a]dmission by reciprocity in the absence of residency requirements could create the opportunity for experienced attorneys to establish a multistate or nationwide practice of law.''[68]

Finally, states sometimes even provide favored treatment for nonresident business over resident business, a policy that may increase mobility and interstate commerce. The Supreme Court has held explicitly that such policy decisions are constitutional.[69]

THE CONSTITUTIONAL FUNDAMENTALS OF ECONOMIC INTEGRATION AND INTERREGIONAL MIGRATION

The scope of the discretionary powers within the American federal system to further economic integration and interregional migration, and to vary the balance between state policy autonomy and integrative measures over time and in different spheres of activity at any one time, is not the only matter best understood in the context of the system's political integration and personal liberty goals. The constitutional restraints on state and federal discretion to interfere with the values of economic integration and freedom of personal movement are also judicially defined and enforced, ultimately by the Supreme Court, in the context of constitutional values of political unification and personal liberty, including values of interstate and intrastate equality. These multiple values have often not been readily separable, and some have served to vindicate others without it being clear to what degree each is independently thought fundamental enough to restrain government flexibility. Some attention to their relationships and their individual force in specific problem areas can be enlightening.

Constitutional Limits

Comparing the constitutional limitations on state barriers to interstate movement of goods and services with those restricting state interference with interstate movement of people demonstrates the considerable degree to which personal and commercial integration are overlapping fundamental norms. That comparison also reveals the respects in which personal movement interstate, temporarily for work, study, or pleasure or permanently to make a new home, is a more fundamental freedom than interstate commercial activity. At the most elementary level, apart from doctrine, one would expect a considerable degree of overlapping protection simply because it is people who bring goods, and especially services, across state borders. Interstate movement of people for commercial purposes necessarily involves both interstate commerce and interstate travel of persons.

The protection of commercial interaction would bring with it the protection of personal movement.

One would expect more protection for personal noncommercial travel than for interstate trading activity if political and social integration, rather than, or as well as, economic integration, is sought to be protected. The same should be true if protection for interstate commercial activity derives from a more general set of personal rights to travel interstate. That would be especially true insofar as the right of persons to settle permanently in a new state within the United States is acknowledged to be a broader right, of deeper dimensions, than the right to move goods from state to state. Ultimately, interstate commerce is protected for its instrumental value in benefiting people through building unified communities or providing economic welfare, and perhaps for the wider range of intrinsic economic liberty it provides for those who would engage in it. Personal mobility shares each of those values, but also embraces a more comprehensive, intrinsically valuable range of personal life-defining liberties. In fact, since governments are instituted for the benefit of people, not goods, one of the very values of preserving state autonomy—to preserve diverse communities for the benefit of its people—points, in a unified nation, to the preservation of the right of people to move freely between states as a means of taking advantage of the benefits of state autonomy. That choice is, after all, a national value.

A Doctrinal Comparison of Interstate Personal and Commercial Mobility: The Constitutional Sources of Doctrine

Constitutional doctrine reflects both the overlap and the extended protection afforded interstate personal mobility. Consider first the constitutional provisions that the Supreme Court has used to limit state impairment of commercial integration and personal mobility, respectively. To restrain state authority to interfere with interstate commerce, the Supreme Court has for well over a century interpreted the Constitution's affirmative grant to Congress of the power to regulate interstate commerce as containing a negative implication that at least some preexisting power to interfere with interstate commerce was taken away from the states.[70] At a minimum, the scope of those limits is defined in accordance with the objective of eliminating those local practices likely to provoke destructive interstate trade wars that originally were at least perceived[71] to be a major problem.

The Court also has employed the interstate privileges and immunities clause to protect interstate commercial relationships, although much less frequently. That clause, which provides that the "Citizens of each State shall be entitled to all Privileges and Immunities of Citizens in the several States,"[72] protects the residents of one state from unwarranted discrimination by another into whose jurisdiction they venture. Political integration is the main focus of the clause. As the Supreme Court said in *Toomer v. Witsell*:

The primary purpose of this clause, like the clauses between which it is located—those relating to full faith and credit and to interstate extradition of fugitives from justice—was to help fuse into one Nation a collection of independent, sovereign States. It was designed to insure a citizen of State A who ventures into State B the same privileges which the citizens of State B enjoy. For protection of such equality the citizen of State A was not to be restricted to the uncertain remedies afforded by diplomatic processes and official retaliation.[73]

The protection it affords to interstate business is curiously haphazard, however. Its protection is not extended to corporations, which are not construed to be "citizens" within the meaning of the clause.[74] Second, it most aptly applies only to protect the rights of nonresidents to do business in the state—such as barring taxation of nonresident fishermen at higher rates than resident fishermen to fish in waters within the state[75] or prohibiting the imposition of more onerous requirements on nonresident lawyers to practice law in the state than are imposed on resident attorneys[76]—and not to protect the rights of residents to do business outside the state.[77]

The dormant commerce clause, by contrast, is applicable to corporations and protects interstate business relationships whatever the residence of the parties to the relationship and regardless of whether the activity is carried out primarily in-state or out-of-state.[78] So, for example, under the commerce clause New York may not impose a corporate tax on the transfer of securities traded on the New York Stock Exchange—no matter where the parties to the transfer reside—that taxes sales transactions consummated out-of-state more heavily than those consummated in-state.[79] Nor may a state impose a corporate tax on one group of in-state manufacturers and exempt another group, just because the former sell their goods out-of-state and the latter sell in-state.[80]

It is firmly established, on the other hand, that although nonresidents are only entitled to be treated the same as residents with respect to fundamental activities "basic to the maintenance or well-being of the Union" or "basic to the livelihood of the Nation,"[81] the right to pursue a trade or business is fundamental in that sense.[82] There is every indication that the interstate privileges and immunities clause was first and foremost designed to build political union,[83] but the non-discriminatory ability to pursue a trade or profession outside one's home state, at least in the personal form contemplated by an eighteenth-century Constitution, has been perceived as a vital part of the broader political unification objective.[84] Moreover, a state's Fourteenth Amendment obligation not to deny persons within its jurisdiction the equal protection of the laws, a provision adopted after the Civil War, is theoretically available to prevent local discrimination against out-of-state corporations that may claim neither the protection of the dormant commerce clause nor the interstate privileges and immunities clause.[85]

The Supreme Court has employed even more constitutional sources to protect the right of interstate travel and migration. Indeed, it has yet to settle finally on any one,[86] perhaps because the Constitution did not carry over the express guarantee in Article IV of the Articles of Confederation that "the people of each State shall have free ingress and egress to and from any other State, and shall enjoy therein all the privileges of trade and commerce, subject to the same impositions and restrictions as the inhabitants thereof respectively."[87] The omission of such direct language has never been thought to be a reason for questioning the continuing vitality of the freedom, however. Rather, the Court has sometimes relied on the interstate privileges and immunities clause;[88] sometimes on structural restrictions on state power to interfere with the right of the federal government to call upon its citizens, construed to include a correlative right of its citizens to pass unimpeded throughout the states to respond to or make claims upon the federal government wherever it might be present;[89] sometimes on the dormant commerce clause;[90] sometimes on the Fourteenth Amendment's prohibition on state abridgement of privileges and immunities of national citizenship;[91] sometimes on the protection against state deprivations of liberty without due process;[92] and sometimes on the requirements of intrastate equal protection, which call upon the states to share the benefits of their state autonomy equally among old and new residents.[93]

Despite the fact that protection of interstate commercial activity and protection of interstate personal mobility are occasionally drawn from the same constitutional provisions, the emphasis has been different in ways that suggest strong resistance to ignoring the distinction between commercial and noncommercial movement. In *Edwards v. California*,[94] the Court unanimously held unconstitutional a state law criminalizing the act of bringing a nonresident indigent into the state but divided sharply over the proper basis for the decision. The majority of five held the law "an unconstitutional barrier to interstate commerce,"[95] leaving open the "scope of Congressional power to deal with this problem"[96] of state inability to deal with the consequences of large-scale migration of indigent persons from state to state. The minority of four thought the decison would better rest on the Fourteenth Amendment prohibition against state interference with the privileges and immunities of national citizenship, of which interstate mobility was one.[97] Justice Douglas thought "the right of persons freely to move from State to State occupies a more protected position in our constitutional system than does the movement of cattle, fruit, steel and coal across state lines."[98] Justice Jackson thought that "the migrations of a human being, of whom it is charged that he possesses nothing that can be sold and has no wherewithal to buy, do not fit easily into my notions as to what is commerce" and that "[t]o hold that the measure of his rights is the commerce clause is likely to result eventually either in distorting the commercial law or in denaturing human rights."[99]

More recently, in a series of equal protection cases, the Court sharply restricted state power to withhold from newly arrived residents such benefits as welfare assistance,[100] nonemergency health care,[101] and the right to vote in state elections until they had resided in the state for a lengthy period.[102] The Court emphasized that it has long "recognized that the nature of our Federal Union and our constitutional concepts of personal liberty unite to require that all citizens be free to travel throughout the length and breadth of our land uninhibited by statutes, rules or regulations which unreasonably burden or restrict this movement."[103] Even if durational residence requirements "neither seek to nor actually do deter ... travel,"[104] the "right of interstate travel must be seen as insuring new residents the same right to vital government benefits and privileges in the States to which they migrate as are enjoyed by other residents."[105]

The debate in *Edwards* and the bases of the durational residence decisions should make clear that much more than economic integration is at stake in free interstate migration; that, in fact, political unification and personal liberty are also, and more centrally, at stake. Moreover, there are important systemic connections among the right freely to migrate from state to state, the right of new residents to be treated equally with longer-term residents, and the right of state autonomy. When all are taken together, what is enforced is the right of Americans to freely choose where to settle, knowing that, as bona fide residents, they will enjoy the equal benefits of whatever diverse effects state autonomy has produced.

A Doctrinal Comparison of Interstate Personal and Commercial Mobility: A Comparison of Doctrinal Content

This section turns from comparing the constitutional provisions employed as *sources* of protection for personal and commercial mobility to comparing the rules and doctrines that comprise the *content* of the protection each is afforded. The similarities in the scope of protection may be much more obvious than the differences, but it will help to consider the range of controls on movement of goods and movement of people that states may not impose. First, however, it will be well to recognize that different taxing, spending, or regulatory policies among the states need not be completely sacrificed to uniformity in order to ensure that either commerce or people are undeterred from interstate movement. Neither laissez faire nor any other uniform rule is a constitutional requirement to protect interstate movement. A higher income tax level in one state than another may just as effectively deter or encourage personal as commercial migration. So may stricter professional licensing requirements or financial responsibility laws or any of a myriad of other legal differences that reflect state policy autonomy. But that alone has never been thought to create an unconstitutional barrier or stimulus to either personal or commercial travel.

Export Controls. Some kinds of state barriers appear to be equally unconstitutional whether applied to interstate movement of goods or people, but there are some subtle differences both in result and rationale. Generally, embargoes of goods are no more permissible than refusals to allow people to leave the state.[106] Yet claims that residents are entitled to priority access to local natural resources are taken more seriously than claims that state residents are entitled to keep in the state, or have special access to, fellow residents who may have special talents.[107] Intuitively, the objection to embargoes on goods does seem to go to its potential for damaging economic and thereby political unification with states who are anxious to have access to the goods. Embargoes on people are not objectionable primarily because other states will be angry that they are being deprived of new residents or the potential services of out-of-staters and will likely retaliate. Such emigration controls are mostly objectionable because the basic freedom of those who desire to emigrate is being infringed. Still, the constitutional rule seems firm enough that neither form of exit control is permissible.

Import Controls. Import controls actually reveal some differences between movement of goods and people. Generally, tariffs and quota controls are no more constitutionally permissible for goods than for people.[108] Moreover, the core requirement, both under the dormant commerce clause and the interstate privileges and immunities clause (and occasionally even the equal protection clause), that discrimination against interstate commerce or nonresident business is only very rarely permitted is applicable to both.[109] But the few exceptions in the case of commodities, for inspections and quarantines,[110] are probably not likely to be applicable in the case of people, despite a few early cases acknowledging some state power to exclude persons with contagious diseases.[111]

If one looks to the recent case of *Maine v. Taylor*,[112] the point seems clear enough. There the Court allowed a state import ban on live baitfish on the rarely satisfied ground that this discriminatory law served a legitimate local purpose in a way that could not "be served as well by available nondiscriminatory means."[113] The Court was satisfied that Maine had acted legitimately to protect local fish from parasites more prevalent in out-of-state than in-state baitfish and to prevent accidental introduction of non-native species that might upset the aquatic environment of Maine to an unpredictable extent. The Court also accepted a lower court finding that "less discriminatory means of protecting against these threats were currently unavailable."[114] The Court rejected the lone dissenting argument of Justice Stevens that uncertainty about dangers posed by out-of-state baitfish and ambiguities about alternative means to deal with the potential risks "should actually defeat, rather than sustain, the discriminatory measure."[115]

It is difficult to imagine that the Court would allow a state to restrict entry of people who pose a possible, but uncertain, threat of infection to residents, even if the state could demonstrate that no other feasible method of protection were available. At the very least, a much higher level of risk of harm to other people would likely be required than the level of risk, not directly to people, but to the aquatic environment, that was found sufficient in *Taylor*.

In-State Spending Preferences. It bears repeating that the general ban on discrimination against interstate commerce and nonresidents applicable to state taxing and regulatory measures is not a requirement of interstate uniformity. Rather, it is a requirement, absent special justification, that each state's diverse regulatory or tax policy not subject interstate or nonresident business—or nonresidents generally—to worse treatment than intrastate business or residents are accorded. Even that requirement is lifted, however, when the state is unconditionally choosing how to spend its own money.[116] In the realm of social welfare programs, states may reserve for residents many benefits financed by state funds, such as welfare payments,[117] education,[118] public employment,[119] public housing, or the like. In the commercial realm the Supreme Court has formally recognized state power to favor residents under the "market participant" exemption from otherwise applicable commerce clause restrictions.[120] That exemption allows states, when spending their own money or operating their own businesses, the same freedom to prefer resident suppliers or resident purchasers that private enterprises would have.

The fact that states generally may favor residents in spending programs but not in tax and regulatory measures does not provide obvious insights concerning the comparative protection afforded personal and commercial mobility, however, or even concerning that afforded economic and political integration. Especially since the permissible discriminatory spending authority embraces spending for both commercial and noncommercial purposes, the line between spending and taxation/regulation does not correspond directly to the line between the personal and the commercial or the line between economic and political integration. Nonetheless, indirectly there are interesting connections among these distinctions that are relevant to this inquiry.

It will help in understanding the subtleties to mention briefly the rationales underlying the conclusion that local favoritism in spending is legitimate despite powerful norms of interstate equality that severely limit favoritism in taxation and regulation. Several justifications have been offered in addition to the Supreme Court's rationale equating the freedom of public entities acting as participants in the market with the freedom of private market actors.[121] It has previously been argued that, subject to some important exceptions, spending that prefers residents—for commercial or other purposes—may be justified by a state autonomy interest in using the tax monies primarily raised from residents to serve their community.[122] Others have urged that judicial intervention is unnecessary when the state acts as a commercial enterprise, because the very cost of such programs may render self-limiting the degree to which one state can isolate itself from the others.[123] Some believe that the only crucial restraint on state power under the dormant commerce clause is the prevention of traditional forms of state protectionism that create a danger to political union.[124] For them, discriminatory spending may be acceptable for two related reasons. First, it is not, or at least does not seem, so hostile as the coercive imposition of taxes or regulations that impose burdens out-of-state.[125] Second, it cannot as effectively be used as a retaliatory weapon for the same self-limiting reasons of cost that render it less likely to be abused in the first place.[126]

Whatever the basis for permitting state spending that favors residents, however, the possession of the power has a number of implications. First, the fact that the discriminatory spending power appears to extend to the important case of state business subsidies limited to resident business indicates only that economic integration is being sacrificed for state autonomy in a way that political integration would not likely be.[127] Second, the appeal of permissible parochialism theoretically enhances the likelihood that the state will increase public expenditures in support of the public or private sectors. In practice, however, the parochial impulse is significantly offset—even putting aside ideological objections to a more pervasive state—by the economic reality that public funds normally must come from taxation.[128] Where the state itself successfully engages in profit-making activity, resident preference may satisfy parochial impulses *and* not be costly.[129] Nonetheless, even there the incentive to prefer residents is limited. States generally may not insist that private actors prefer residents.[130] Thus, whenever public enterprises compete with private firms free from having to absorb the added costs of parochial bias, competitive pressures are likely to reduce the costly parochial impulses of state profit-making ventures as well.

Thus far in making these observations about the implications of permissible resident preference in spending programs, it has been suggested that one implication is greater attachment to political union than to economic union. The analysis has not focused yet, however, on the implications arising from a comparison of discriminatory spending for commercial purposes and discriminatory spending for personal or social welfare purposes. That comparison tends to reinforce the view that political integration is more highly valued than economic integration in the United States. It also tends to indicate that personal mobility is more highly regarded than commercial mobility.

Superficially, this might not appear to be true. Although both have been accepted thus far, state power to favor residents in social welfare funding is undoubtedly more secure from constitutional challenge than is state power to limit public subsidies to in-state businesses.[131] This might be thought to suggest that the national interest in personal interstate mobility would be sacrificed to state autonomy more readily than would be the national interest in interstate commercial mobility or, put another way, that personal mobility is less highly valued than economic integration. But any such suggestion would miss important differences between interstate private sector competition and interstate public sector competition that actually suggest the reverse ordering is a more accurate description.

State authority to confine social welfare assistance exclusively to residents enables adoption of such programs and undoubtedly permits states to increase their attractiveness to those contemplating migration.[132] It is important here to distinguish between the nonresident temporary traveller and the permanent migrant. The temporary, if daily, traveller may avail himself or herself fully of the private sector opportunities in another state but generally may not share in the opportunities for which the state paid with taxes raised primarily from its own residents.[133] If people choose to move permanently from one state to another because of differences in the quantity or quality of publicly funded programs available to residents, that is not a distortion of any competitive market for migration. It is rather an implementation of that market, because the states are the ''firms'' offering ''goods'' to people.[134] And the protection of the right of interstate migration through decisions that forbid states from denying such goods to recently arrived but bona fide residents[135] is a protection of the access of people to the interstate market in state-offered, not privately offered, goods or services.

If state subsidies to local business seem more problematic, the reason is not that economic mobility is more valued than personal mobility. State social welfare programs limited to residents do not interfere with temporary interstate mobility but potentially encourage permanent interstate mobility so long as new residents must be treated equally with long-term residents. By contrast, subsidies to resident businesses adversely affect interstate private sector competition at the same time that they may promote interstate public sector competition.

Interstate competition in the private sector is harmed because unsubsidized out-of-state businesses must compete with subsidized resident businesses on an artificial basis that does not reflect inherent productivity advantages. Competition among states for public spending to support local business is promoted to the extent that states adopt subsidy policies in order to induce businesses to stay or relocate within their jurisdictions and so long as interstate migration is unimpeded. That the subsidy-related distortion of interstate private sector market competition thus far has been accepted again suggests a willingness to compromise economic union in ways that personal mobility or political integration would not be compromised. The business subsidy to local firms is more questionable than the welfare subsidy to local residents because economic integration is an important value and, more importantly in the comparative analysis, because personal mobility is not threatened by the welfare subsidy. But precisely because the economic integration value that is impaired is insufficient to make the business subsidy unconstitutional, the current constitutional rules appear to withhold the same level of enforcement from economic integration values that they provide to interstate migration and political integration.

That same impulse probably underlies as well the Supreme Court's seemingly divergent decisions in *White v. Massachusetts Council of Construction Employers*[136] and *United Building & Construction Trades Council v. Mayor of Camden*.[137] Both cases considered the constitutionality of city policies requiring private contractors working on construction projects funded by the city to hire a substantial portion of their employees from local residents. *White* involved a challenge based on the dormant commerce clause, whereas *Camden* involved a challenge based on the interstate privileges and immunities clause. The Court rejected the commerce clause challenge in *White* on the ground that the city was acting as a market participant in buying construction services and that the usual commerce clause restraints were therefore inapplicable. In *Camden*, however, the Court held that the city's scheme was subject to review under the privileges and immunities clause, although it did suggest that on remand of the case the fact that the city was spending its own funds might be "the crucial factor . . . to be considered" in determining whether the clause was violated.[138] Perhaps the Court is having second thoughts about the costs of a total "market participant" exemption from commerce clause analysis,[139] and perhaps its hesitation is reflected in the more cautious approach taken in *Camden*.[140] But it is also quite possible, and quite revealing, that its initial reaction to a commerce clause challenge differed from its initial reaction to a privileges and immunities clause challenge to the same local policy. The commerce clause most obviously puts in question the conflict between state autonomy and economic integration, whereas the privileges and immunities clause raises the potential conflict between state autonomy and political union/migratory freedom. The commercial focus of the commerce clause might ultimately be doing service for the primary value of political union and migratory freedom, and perhaps the clauses will also be interpreted congruently with respect to issues of resident preference in local spending. Yet the Court's decisions may reflect, even if based on erroneous assumptions, the stronger attachment to political union and freedom of interstate migration than to economic integration.

ECONOMIC UNION IN CONTEXT: A DISTINCT CONSTITUTIONAL VALUE BUT SECONDARY TO POLITICAL AND MIGRATORY UNION

It should be clear by now that states are not constitutionally required to comply with norms of economic integration either in the strongest senses of adhering to uniformity, laissez faire, or efficiency, or even always in the weaker but still crucial sense of not distinguishing between in-state and out-of-state business.[141] The comparative analysis goes further. Not only is migratory freedom more highly valued than economic integration, but I quite agree with Donald Regan that the interest in political integration is also a much more important limit on state power.[142] I am not as convinced as he that economic integration norms lack independent force under the dormant commerce clause or that the Court's long tradition of weighing state autonomy interests against the interest in national economic integration is misguided. After all, that tradition, by furthering economic integration, also furthers political union. Nonetheless, it is important to appreciate that the Court's primary concern is political integration.

That view surely is supported, not only by the evidence already examined, but by at least two other examples from current doctrine. First, the dormant commerce clause almost always forbids facial or categorical discrimination against interstate commerce but not state regulation that disproportionately affects interstate commerce or nonresident business.[143] A good example of the latter is *Minnesota v. Clover Leaf Creamery Co.*,[144] which upheld a state law that "evenhandedly" forbids both resident and nonresident businesses from selling milk in plastic bottles, even though it is the out-of-state plastics manufacturers who bear the practical impact of the law and the producers of paperboard milk containers, a major in-state industry, who significantly benefit. To similar effect is *Exxon Corporation v. Governor of Maryland*,[145] which upheld a state law, enacted after the 1973 worldwide oil shortage, barring producers or refiners of petroleum products from operating retail service stations in the state. Despite the fact that every oil producer or refiner is an out-of-state business that the law prevented from engaging in retail operations in competition with independent in-state retailers, the Supreme Court concluded that there was no impermissible discrimination against interstate commerce. All the petroleum products to be sold in Maryland must come from out-of-state, and there was no restriction on interstate independent dealers who compete with local dealers, only a restriction on refiners and producers. The majority held that the commerce clause "protects the interstate market, not particular interstate firms, from prohibitive or burdensome regulation."[146] Laurence Tribe has expressed a view of this decision with which I agree:

> Behind the Court's analysis in *Exxon* stands an important doctrinal theme: the negative implications of the commerce clause derive principally from a *political* theory of union, not from an *economic* theory of free trade. The function of the clause is to ensure national solidarity, not economic efficiency.[147]

It should be added that the line separating impermissible intentional discrimination from permissible disproportionate impact also suggests a greater concern for the political hostility among states that emanates from categorical discrimination than for economic integration.

So, too, does the constitutional prohibition on compelled reciprocity requirements, a problem that arises because states may have different standards with respect to product quality so long as the standards are the same for intrastate and interstate traders. Some state legislators who believe that other states are setting the standards too high, and thereby raising barriers to interstate commerce, have attempted to refuse to permit such goods to be sold in their jurisdiction unless the state with higher standards allows reciprocal rights of entry. As the Court said in a milk-quality case, however, "Mississippi may not use the threat of economic isolation as a weapon to force sister States to enter into even a desirable reciprocity agreement,"[148] especially since the Court itself was available to prevent the sister states from imposing unreasonable burdens on commerce.[149]

The doctrine could be based on the notion that compelled reciprocity requirements are more likely to result in economic disintegration than economic integration, but the Court's more immediate and central concern appears to be the potential for political divisiveness, even if the threat should work to achieve a desirable reciprocity agreement. (Incidentally, the notion of applying quality standards to exclude people, rather than goods, is so alien to our notions of the equal moral worth of persons that it highlights the vast degree of difference between the power to control the movement of goods and the power to control the movement of people, even if the regulation were evenhanded in both cases as between local and interstate movement. There simply are a greater number of legitimate reasons for restricting the movement of goods than for restricting the movement of people.)

It is not within the scope of this chapter to undertake extended discussion of that branch of dormant commerce clause doctrine that goes beyond antidiscrimination rules to prohibit evenhanded local regulation that nonetheless unduly burdens interstate commerce.[150] Both the academic criticism of this branch of the doctrine and the Supreme Court's evident lack of interest in responding to that criticism are worthy of mention, however. The criticism tends to center around three different objections, combining institutional criticisms (economic union is not a *judicially* enforceable constitutional value) and substantive criticisms (economic union is not a constitutional value at all, but a matter best left completely to policy discretion).

The first objection is that the Court should not weigh the benefits of nondiscriminatory local regulation against the burdens imposed on interstate commerce, because fostering economic integration in the stronger sense of moving in the direction of uniformity or not disproportionately affecting interstate commerce is better accomplished, if at all, by other government bodies with superior institutional capacities for this task, such as Congress,[151] by federal administrative agencies to which Congress can delegate the task,[152] or even by the states cooperating with each other.[153] The second objection is that it is not only unnecessary, but inappropriate, for the Court to do more than guard against discrimination, because the balance of state autonomy and economic integration in the stronger senses is quintessentially a legislative policy matter, not a matter of constitutional requirement.[154] The third objection is actually a species of the second, the fear that the Court will incorporate values of laissez-faire economics into the location of the appropriate constitutional demands of economic integration.[155]

There is little evidence of abuse of the latter kind in the Court's rulings, however.[156] The most one can say is that in some areas the Court has sought to ensure against gross burdens on interstate commerce. In particular, in cases focused on the facilities of interstate transportation, the Court has shown hostility to state laws imposing significant risks of cumulative or conflicting burdens that might significantly disadvantage interstate commerce in its competition with intrastate commerce.[157]

That the academic criticism, occasionally echoed by justices in the minority on the Court,[158] has thus far been rejected by a strong majority of the Court certainly does tend to suggest that economic integration is an independent constitutional value.[159] It is true that the cases the Court has cared about could also be described as concerned with political integration, as, in a sense, could all cases in which economic integration is furthered. But the focus of undue burden analysis, unlike discrimination analysis, is much less a focus on hostility among state governments than on state policy having to give way in some few respects to the needs of economic integration.

The other salient point about the academic criticism is that it is mostly focused on the Court's role in weighing the constitutional validity of evenhanded state regulation that unduly burdens interstate commerce and does not extend to abandonment of review of discriminatory state regulation and taxation, although some would shift the focus of analysis from the dormant commerce clause to the interstate privileges and immunities clause.[160] The broad acceptance of the importance of judicial enforcement of interstate equality indicates the greater attachment to political unification and unimpeded interregional travel, not only for permanent change of residence, but temporarily for business, vacation, or other purposes.

The Court appears to share that core concern for interstate equality to an increasing extent. Its recent decisions disallowing states from treating nonresident lawyers differently than resident lawyers with respect to qualifying to practice law[161] indicate that, although the states may have licensing standards that differ from one another, they may not apply them to the disadvantage of nonresidents without good reason. The Court is preserving both state autonomy and interstate equality, as it has done for some time in cases dealing with businesses that do not have professional licensing requirements, and the Court is now moving to protect more forcefully the right of professionals to live in one state and work in another on an equal basis with the state's residents. This salutary development helps strengthen political attachments and personal freedom of interstate travel, as it is intended to do.

Perhaps the Court is only strengthening the constitutional requirements of interstate equality as a response to changing economic and social arrangements, rather than leading the movement to increased integration. At the least, it is facilitating these integrative changes, however, and not allowing the states to impair economic and political union by holding back the people's increasing tendency to function and interact across state borders.

CONSTITUTIONAL LIMITS ON FEDERAL IMPAIRMENT OF ECONOMIC INTEGRATION AND INTERREGIONAL MIGRATION

In the interests of economic and political union many powers are denied the states that are not necessarily denied the federal government, presumably because it is assumed that national policymakers are much less likely than state policymakers to be subject to parochial incentives that create significant risks of national disintegration. Insofar as the political safeguards of federalism[162] operate to provide a strong voice for state autonomy in national political processes, however, national policies may sometimes favor state autonomy over values of integration. In the area of economic integration, in particular, Congress has sometimes even authorized the states to discriminate against interstate commerce, something the states are constitutionally forbidden to do on their own authority.[163] Congressional authorization of discriminatory state taxation of out-of-state insurance companies[164] and discriminatory state restrictions on the acquisition of local banks of out-of-state bank holding companies[165] are prime examples.

In the grant of the commerce power the Supreme Court has found ample congressional authority to value state autonomy over economic integration in these ways. It has also held that the power to regulate commerce includes the power to prohibit it,[166] although it is conceivable that if the power were employed for the purpose of hindering economic integration without the regulation being in aid of the preservation of legitimate state autonomy or other federal policy interests,[167] such an exercise of the power could be invalidated as irrational and arbitrary. Hindrance of interstate commerce for hindrance's sake would seem to be a purely hypothetical situation, however. In addition, the power to regulate commerce has been construed expansively to include the prohibition of interstate movement of persons for criminal or immoral purposes.[168] Thus, there is considerable recognition that congressional power over interregional migration is greater than state power in this area. In short, economic integration, and even some aspects of interstate travel, are not such powerful constitutional values that they may not sometimes be put aside by Congress.

For the sake of accuracy it is important to acknowledge the wide scope of congressional power to interfere with economic integration and the considerably narrower scope of congressional power to interfere with interstate personal mobility. It is equally important to understand the nature and extent of the limits on congressional power to hinder economic integration, political unification, and interregional travel and migration, respectively, in order to isolate those integrative elements that are so fundamental that neither state nor federal legislative power may impair them. In many instances one can give no firm answers based on judicial rulings, simply because Congress has not acted in these disintegrative ways. That may merely demonstrate, however, that the central power to value state autonomy over economic integration is much more acceptable than the central power to value state autonomy over political union or personal mobility.

Economic Union

Although Congress has significant power to sacrifice economic integration, it does not seem to be unlimited. Congress constitutionally could not authorize the states to develop and control separate currencies, for example.[169] Moreover, there is at least one additional set of restraints on federal legislative power that works in favor of economic integration. The primary aim of these restraints is to prevent Congress from discriminating among the states. They serve as protection against the possibility that one group of states might be able to so control the federal government that other states would be at their mercy. Although their primary objective is undoubtedly to prevent interstate and interregional political conflict, they are directly relevant to economic integration of the nation.

Thus, the bankruptcy laws and indirect federal taxation are required to be geographically uniform throughout the country,[170] and the Supreme Court reviews federal legislation to ensure that Congress has not violated the uniformity requirements.[171] Similarly, Congress may not give tax or commercial preferences to the ports of one state over those of another and may not impose duties on the movement of vessels from one state to another.[172] The Supreme Court, in an earlier era, also held that admiralty law must be geographically uniform, a view that may or may not survive today.[173] A requirement of equal federal treatment among the states in these respects serves the goal of common rules of commerce throughout the nation, even if the primary motivation for having the restraints is to prevent political hostility and disintegration among the states and even if Congress is not forbidden from evenhandedly authorizing all the states to act in economically disintegrative fashion.

Political Union and Free Migration

May Congress authorize the states to regulate in ways that would be inimical to political integration or rights of interregional migration to the same degree that it can consent to their adoption of economically isolationist policies? These problems have arisen much less frequently, but the constitutional underpinnings of these values suggest that the answer is no. Article IV of the Constitution on states' relations, speaks to this area, if only by implication.

Three facets of Article IV should be stressed. First, it limits state power to treat other states as foreign jurisdictions. Each state is constitutionally required to give "Full Faith and Credit . . . to the public Acts, Records, and judicial Proceeding of every other State";[174] to treat the citizens of other states who come within its jurisdiction the same as its own citizens with respect to almost all fundamental privileges and immunities;[175] and, on request, to extradite fugitives from justice "to the State having Jurisdiction of the Crime."[176] Second, Article IV grants some circumscribed powers to Congress to effectuate growth and integration of the union. Thus, Congress is granted the power to prescribe the "Manner" in which the states' full faith and credit obligations shall be carried out.[177] Further, Congress has the power to admit new states but not to form one out of an existing state and not to form one by joining different states or parts of them "without the Consent of the Legislatures of the States concerned."[178] Third, Article IV obligates the federal government to guarantee every state "a Republican Form of Government" against invasion or domestic violence.[179]

Nothing in these nation-building provisions suggests any power in Congress to disintegrate political union or to authorize the states so to act. Quite the contrary. It is true that the guarantee clause, at least, has been held to be a "political question" that is not judicially enforceable to protect individuals.[180] But one need not be so Court-centered as to conclude that the Constitution therefore is not binding against congressional acts of political disintegration.[181] More fundamentally, the limited powers conferred on Congress in Article IV are powers to implement, not to defeat, political integration. The limitation of the power to admit and form new states makes this explicit, but the structure carries further. Quite unlike the plenary power in Article I to regulate interstate commerce, the powers in Article IV are far more circumscribed.

Congress has had little incentive to act to break down the union, but if one asks whether Congress, contrary to the implementing measures it in fact took from the earliest formation of the nation,[182] could constitutionally authorize the states to refuse to give full faith and credit to the judgments of the courts of other states, would there be much doubt that such a power is inconsistent with Article IV? I think not.

What, then, of the power of Congress to authorize a state to discriminate against the citizens of other states in a manner that would otherwise violate the interstate privileges and immunities clause of Article IV, §2? Whether construed as a provision protecting political unification for political unification's sake, or as a set of personal rights that are inherent in the recognition of national citizenship that accompanies the value of national union, the fundamental values protected by this clause would not seem open to congressional impairment.[183] Perhaps from this perspective it is most understandable, first, that it is "only with respect to those 'privileges' and 'immunities' bearing on the vitality of the Nation as a single entity that a State must accord residents and nonresidents equal treatment"[184] and, second, that the clause is inapplicable to corporations.[185] These two doctrinal elaborations concentrate the focus, although perhaps unduly, on the political unification and personal liberty concerns of the clause. That the equal right to work in the private sector of another state is, and always has been, accepted as one of those core privileges and immunities,[186] may make some aspects of economic integration a constitutionally derivative norm of political integration and personal interstate equality rights, but the not wholly peaceful coexistence of those rights with congressional power to authorize state discrimination against interstate commerce in nonpersonal forms must also be acknowledged.

Consider, in this connection, the power of Congress to interfere with free interstate migration. One might ask at least three different types of questions represented by three different restraints previously imposed on state power to burden interstate travel. First, could Congress have authorized the statute criminalizing the bringing of indigents into the state that was struck down in *Edwards v. California*?[187] Insofar as the right of indigents to migrate from state to state was based on the commerce clause, the question left open in *Edwards* of the scope of congressional power to deal with mass migrations of the needy[188] arguably might be answered by reference to the admitted power of Congress to authorize state discrimination against interstate commerce. But later developments tending to rest the right of interstate migration on personal rights of national citizenship and the inherent implications of political unification make it unlikely that this would be the result. It is difficult to imagine that in exercising the commerce power Congress could itself, or through authorization of the states, constitutionally adopt such measures as requiring students to attend universities in the states in which they reside, restricting the migration of physicians, or limiting the number of times a family might move from state to state. The right of interstate migration is simply too fundamental to permit such severe federal restrictions on the right to choose to relocate in a new state.[189]

Second, could Congress authorize the states to impose durational residence requirements as a condition of receiving vital government benefits? That issue has been resolved. Although two members of the Supreme Court would have held in *Shapiro v. Thompson*[190] that ''Congress, acting under one of its enumerated powers, [may] impose minimal nationwide residence requirements or authorize the States to do so[,]''[191] the majority of the Court invalidated federal as well as state one-year waiting periods as prerequisites to the receipt of welfare assistance. It held that ''Congress may not authorize the States to violate the Equal Protection Clause''[192] and that ''the Due Process Clause of the Fifth Amendment forbids Congress from denying public assistance to poor persons otherwise eligible solely on the ground that they have not been residents of the District of Columbia [over which Congress has exclusive legislative power] for one year at the time their applications are filed.''[193] Here the explicit use of intrastate equality and individual rights guarantees to protect the right of interstate migration solidified the right against federal, as well as state, interference. A distinction between new and old residents, although theoretically just an intrastate distinction, rests sufficiently on the distinction between residents and former nonresidents to implicate the values of interstate migration.[194]

Third, could Congress authorize the states to exclude nonresidents from the legal or other professions or to favor resident access to such professions without showing a special justification for discriminating against nonresidents? As a matter of enforcing the interstate equality guarantees of Article IV, the Supreme Court very recently has begun to strike down unjustified unequal treatment of otherwise qualified nonresidents seeking to establish a professional practice within the state.[195] These protections are not for the right to choose to resettle permanently in a new state, or if allowed to migrate, to be treated equally with those residents who arrived earlier, but to protect the right to reside in one state and work in another on equal terms with those who also reside there. It is true, as the Chief Justice argued in dissent in *Supreme Court of Virginia v. Friedman*,[196] that equality might be restored by making qualification to practice the profession more difficult for residents, as well as by making it less difficult for nonresidents, with the consequences that higher qualification standards for all might increase the burden on the choice to resettle permanently in a new state. Residents are likely to effectively resist this method of equalization, however, and in any event, what is protected is a more flexible system of daily interstate connections between work and home that increasingly reflects the nature of modern life. Whether Congress, if not the states, could choose to authorize a reverse ordering of priorities is an open question,[197] but again, given the political unification and personal rights grounding of Article IV, §2, that power seems doubtful. If Congress cannot authorize states to discriminate among different classes of their residents, one would not expect that Congress could authorize discrimination between residents and nonresidents either. Congress should no more be able to prevent the residents of one state from holding property in another or seeking medical services or recreation there, than can the states.

CONSTITUTIONAL LIMITS ON FEDERAL IMPAIRMENT OF STATE POLICY AUTONOMY: THE LIMITS OF PREEMPTION

The power of Congress to impair integration is at least somewhat circumscribed, while its power to promote integration is extremely broad. But does the Constitution, in the interest of state autonomy, limit the scope of congressional power to further integration? Most prominently, are there limits on Congress' power to compel or induce uniform regulation among the states to further a completely integrated economy?

Judicial enforcement of constitutional[198] state policy autonomy limits on federal power has had its ups and downs, but at present the Court takes the view that the states are largely remitted to their representational power in the Congress and the selection of the president to enforce these limits.[199] In *Garcia v. San Antonio Metropolitan Transit Authority*,[200] the Court held that the commerce power extended to imposition of uniform minimum wage and maximum hour regulations that state, as well as private employers, must respect. Although leaving open the possibility that there might be some narrow ''affirmative limits the constitutional structure might impose on action affecting the States under the Commerce Clause,''[201] the sharply divided Court reasoned that judicial protection of state autonomy in the name of the Constitution was inappropriate because ''[t]he political process ensures that laws that unduly burden the States will not be promulgated.''[202] Recently, in *South Carolina v. Baker*,[203] the Court followed the same approach in upholding a provision of the federal tax laws that it construed as equivalent to a prohibition against state issuance of bonds in bearer, rather than registered, form. The Court left open the possibility that congressional regulation of state activities might be held invalid under the Tenth Amendment if a state were ''deprived of any right to participate in the national political process or . . . was singled out in a way that left it politically isolated and powerless,''[204] but generally closed the door on substantive protection for core elements of state policy autonomy.

The possible limitation for Congress singling out particular states for burdensome unequal regulation is akin to the explicit provisions of Article I, §9, that bar various forms of congressional discrimination among states. To these limitations should be added those that stem from the special case of the Twenty-first Amendment, which authorizes state import controls of alcoholic beverages and seems to make such state regulation immune from federal interference, although the scope of the power to control importation may be limited to restrictions aimed at preventing consumption of liquor and not protectionist measures aimed at assisting local liquor merchants.[205] Moreover, the Court also held recently that even if, under the Twenty-first Amendment, Congress lacked the power to regulate a national minimun drinking age directly (a question it did not decide), it was well within Congress' power to exercise its spending power to withhold federal highway funds from states that allowed purchase of liquor by persons under twenty-one.[206]

Apart from these few limitations on federal power, the regulatory autonomy of the states is for now left to the not inconsiderable tradition and continuing attachment in the federal government for state policy diversity. But the way is wide open for Congress, if it wishes, to integrate the economy by imposing uniform regulations on both private and state enterprises.

That Congress seemingly can preempt the entire regulation of the private sector as it relates to interstate commerce, and can include similar regulation of the public sector as a means of ensuring the effectiveness of its private sector regulation, does not necessarily mean that it is as equally free to displace state spending and taxing autonomy with requirements of uniformity as it is to displace state regulatory autonomy with uniform federal regulation. The constitutionality of federal minimum wage provisions as applied to state labor expenditures[207] does, of course, recognize at least some power to interfere with state funding decisions, but in theory, at least, that power did not deprive the states of doing what they wished if they were prepared to pay for it. Would that power extend to federal restrictions on what the states might choose to subsidize, in particular to a federal ban on state subsidies to local business in the interests of a federal policy of favoring competition undistorted by government action of any kind? Would it, even more broadly, extend to equalization of tax rates and policies and spending priorities among the states in order to integrate the economy and make differing state policies irrelevant to decisions about migrating from one state to another?[208]

The broader questions, at least, may never have to be faced, but posing them does suggest that there are limits to federal power to integrate the economy and make local government policy an irrelevant factor in commerce and migration. We *do* have a federal system, and it assumes policy autonomy elsewhere than in Washington. Diversity of some policies is a constitutional virtue, and integration must occur with that virtue as something of a limit. When it comes to more realistic possibilities, at least in the near future, such as forbidding local business subsidies, the issue is harder because state spending autonomy exercised in this positive fashion is designed to directly affect interstate commerce and this is the domain in which Congress' direct regulatory power is at its strongest. Given the fact that some justices would have been prepared to hold subsidies favoring resident business inconsistent with the dormant commerce clause,[209] it seems highly likely that the Court would at least allow Congress to forbid them if it decided they were too great a burden on interstate commerce.[210] But as state spending choices and state tax policy move away from the purpose of affecting interstate commerce and are not necessary to control private sector interstate commerce, federal power to restrain state autonomy should become more questionable.

CONCLUSION

In an excellent examination of the constitutional law of interregional migration in the United States, presented in connection with a conference devoted to interstate commerce and movement in the United States and the European Economic Community, Gerald Rosberg cautioned that "changes in the social and economic milieu over the past two hundred years frustrate the effort to draw meaningful comparisons between the early experience in the United States and the early experience in the EEC."[211] That wise caution about generalizing from one effort at integration to another, based on recognition that one began at a much earlier and very different stage of the world's political economy than the other, should be supplemented by a somewhat different caution about generalization: Even if two efforts at economic integration of a diverse group of sovereign states were to begin at roughly the same historical era with similar levels of industrialization and economic development, the legal character of those efforts might well be expected to differ depending on whether, and to what extent, the economic integration objective was to be carried out in a context that included both political unification and centrally defined and enforced personal freedoms extending far beyond commercial freedom.

The precise level of economic integration and interregional migration legislatively pursued and constitutionally protected in the United States, both in its reach and its qualifications, does reflect the influence of the political unification and personal liberty goals of the Constitution. Somewhat more surprisingly, perhaps, in the search for an appropriate balance between state policy autonomy and national commercial integration, strong constitutional protection for political unification and personal freedom may ironically have led, at certain times and in certain ways, to a tilt in favor of state autonomy at the expense of commercial integration. That stronger political bonds among states may create greater room for preservation of local autonomy, somewhat in the way that stronger personal bonds may make accommodating individual differences in interpersonal relationships easier, could be an important lesson for those who fear that unification and centralization inevitably mean conformity.

However counterintuitive the idea may seem at first glance, experience in the United States seems to reflect this occasionally inverse correlation between the degree of constitutional enforcement of political unification and free interstate migration and the degree of constitutional promotion of economic integration. Perhaps when political integration is absent, greater emphasis on economic integration may be thought necessary.[212] Local political loyalties, as well as divergences in political outlook, account for local regulatory and wealth distribution policies that sacrifice economic common market values. A sense of political solidarity with other states, a common political attachment, may in fact reduce to some degree the impulse to act without regard for the economic consequences to their citizens. That should reduce a little the need for centralized regulation to combat local protectionism.

Conversely, absent the self-restraint of common political community, economic protectionist impulses will be more inclined to have their way. Moreover, diverse economic policies among states may be perceived as more legitimate, despite their actual adverse effects on interstate commerce, to the degree that they are attributed, not to protectionist motivations, but to policy choices that might be made by any state within the common political structure. Perhaps this accounts, at least in part, for the fact that subsidies by individual states limited to in-state businesses are considered acceptable in the United States, but unacceptable in the European Economic Community.[213] Political integration may thus produce relatively fewer anti–Common Market policies in fact *and* the relatively more frequent perception that those anti–Common Market policies that are adopted are acceptable costs of local autonomy. In short, economic diversity with limited political friction may be more likely to occur in a politically unified nation than in an economically unified one.

These observations are deliberately suggestive and tentative. The aim here has been to demonstrate with more definitiveness that economic integration as an independent value has been left in significant measure in the United States to discretionary policy, subject to very few state autonomy limitations, and that, although it does have important constitutional dimensions, economic integration has not been as strongly embraced as an independent constitutional mandate as has political integration and the people's freedom to move among the states, permanently or temporarily, as they choose.

NOTES

1. The most general and authoritative statement of these purposes is set forth in the Preamble to the U.S. Constitution:

We the People of the United States, in Order to form a more perfect Union, establish Justice, insure domestic Tranquility, provide for the common defence, promote the general Welfare, and secure the Blessings of Liberty to ourselves and our Posterity, do ordain and establish this Constitution for the United States of America.

2. Id.

3. The structure of the Constitution is built on this assumption, and the Tenth Amendment is declarative of its existence. That Amendment provides: "The powers not delegated to the United States by the Constitution, nor prohibited by it to the States, are reserved to the States respectively, or to the people." U.S. CONST. amend. X.

4. The original Constitution delegated significant powers to the national government, the exercise of which inevitably would call state power into question, especially given the Supremacy Clause, which renders the "Constitution, and the Laws of the United States which shall be made in Pursuance thereof . . . the supreme Law of the Land[.]" U.S. CONST. art. VI, cl.2. The political integration stemming from these grants of national power to adopt uniform regulations directly binding on the nation's inhabitants

was supplemented in an important integrative manner by the provisions of Article IV, especially the interstate Privileges and Immunities Clause, which provides: "The Citizens of each State shall be entitled to all Privileges and Immunities of Citizens in the several States." U.S. CONST. art. IV, §2, cl.1.

The tension between state authority and national integration only grew following the Civil War with the constitutional revolution in federalism wrought by the adoption of the Thirteenth, Fourteenth, and Fifteenth Amendments. These amendments, and their eventual judicial and congressional enforcement, established uniform nationally guaranteed norms of personal liberty and equal treatment among each state's own residents with which the states, and to a large degree even the federal government, may not interfere. In doing so, they both limited independent state prerogatives and fostered social, legal, political, and even economic union.

5. See Andrzej Rapaczynski, "From Sovereignty to Process: The Jurisprudence of Federalism after *Garcia*," 1985 *Supreme Court Review* 341, 395–405 (1985); Lewis Kaden, "Politics, Money, and State Sovereignty: The Judicial Role," 79 *Columbia Law Review* 847, 853, 855–56 (1979).

6. See Kaden, supra note 5, at 854; Michael McConnell, "Federalism: Evaluating the Founders' Design," 54 *University of Chicago Law Review* 1484, 1493–94, 1509 (1987).

7. See Rapaczynski, supra note 5, at 380–95; McConnell, supra note 6, at 1504–07. Even while arguing in favor of the expansion of national power in the proposed Constitution, James Madison noted the liberty-preserving aspects of retained authority in the states. See *Federalist* 46 (Madison) (Clinton Rossiter ed. 1961) [all subsequent references to *The Federalist* are to the Rossiter edition].

8. The classic statement is set forth in Justice Brandeis' dissenting opinion in New York Ice Co. v. Liebmann, 285 U.S. 262, 311 (1932): "It is one of the happy incidents of the federal system that a single courageous State may, if its citizens choose, serve as a laboratory; and try novel social and economic experiments without risk to the rest of the country." See Kaden, supra note 5, at 854; McConnell, supra note 6, at 1498. For a more skeptical view, see Rapaczynski, supra note 5, at 408–12.

9. See Kaden, supra note 5, at 854–55.

10. See McConnell, supra note 6, at 1498–1500, 1503–04.

11. See, e.g., *Federalist* 3, 4, 5 (Jay), 6, 7, 9, 14 (Hamilton).

12. Of course, political union also has often contributed to the ability to improve noneconomic welfare, especially in the area of equality and civil rights for the nation's minorities. One has only to ponder the connection between civil rights and national authority exemplified in the Civil War and its legal aftermath to appreciate the point. The power and responsibility for the protection of civil rights against interference by individual states, bestowed on Congress and the federal judiciary with the adoption of the Thirteenth, Fourteenth, and Fifteenth Amendments, certainly enlarged the possibilities for the promotion of nationwide equality and liberty, however long it may have taken— and may yet take—to realize that potential.

13. In *Federalist* 11, Hamilton promotes the concept of political union as a better means of dealing with foreign countries seeking access to American markets and of improving aggregate domestic commerce. Important as those advantages are, however, they are not as strongly emphasized as the concerns for survival against foreign and domestic military strife discussed in *The Federalist Papers* cited in the preceding footnote. See also *Federalist* 23 (Hamilton), at 153; No. 45 (Madison), at 288.

14. See Laurence Tribe, *American Constitutional Law* §15–14, at 1378–80 (2d ed. 1988).

15. See Jonathan Varat, "State 'Citizenship' and Interstate Equality," 48 *University of Chicago Law Review* 487, 518–19 (1981).

16. Id. at 519.

17. Tribe, supra note 14, at 1378–80.

18. E.g., *Federalist* 11 (Hamilton).

19. "Our system, fostered by the Commerce Clause, is that every farmer and every craftsman shall be encouraged by the certainty that he will have free access to every market in the Nation." *H. P. Hood & Sons, Inc. v. DuMond*, 336 U.S. 525, 539 (1949).

20. See *Federalist* 7 (Hamilton), at 62–63. See also Richard Collins, "Economic Union as a Constitutional Value," 63 *New York University Law Review* 43, 64 (1988). ("The framers sought economic union, but the focus of their concern was interstate commercial harmony rather than market efficiency.")

21. *Federalist* 22 (Hamilton), at 144–45; No. 42 (Madison), at 268. (An unrestricted state power to impose import and export duties on goods coming from other states that are passing through the imposing state "would nourish unceasing animosities, and not improbably terminate in serious interruptions of the public tranquillity.")

22. Compare generally Collins, supra note 20, with Donald Regan, "The Supreme Court and State Protectionism: Making Sense of the Dormant Commerce Clause," 84 *Michigan Law Review* 1091 (1986). Professor Regan urges a number of important themes, one of which is that "[g]enuine national interests for dormant commerce clause purposes are those interests, and only those, that, like the interest in preventing state protectionism, are fundamentally related to the existence and political viability of federal union."

23. For a general discussion of the preemption of state policy diversity by uniform federal regulation, whether complete preemption or preemption that permits supplemental state regulation, see Tribe, supra note 14, at §§ 6–25, 6–26, and 6–27. For a searching critique of the Supreme Court's efforts to delineate the proper jurisdictional boundary between (uniform) federal and (diverse) state regulation of securities exchange transactions, see Alison Grey Anderson, "The Meaning of Federalism: Interpreting the Securities Exchange Act of 1934," 70 *Virginia Law Review* 813 (1984). See also John Kozyris, "Corporate Takeovers at the Jurisdictional Crossroads: Preserving State Authority Over Internal Affairs While Protecting the Transferability of Interstate Stock Through Federal Law," 36 *U.C.L.A. Law Review* 1109 (1989).

24. E.g., Austin v. New Hampshire, 420 U.S. 656 (1975); Hale v. Bimco Trading, Inc., 306 U.S. 375 (1939); Welton v. Missouri, 91 U.S. 275 (1876); Ward v. Maryland, 79 U.S. (12 Wall.) 418 (1870).

25. E.g., Lewis v. BT Investment Managers, Inc., 447 U.S. 27 (1980); Philadelphia v. New Jersey, 437 U.S. 617 (1978).

26. E.g., Supreme Court of New Hampshire v. Piper, 470 U.S. 274 (1985); Hicklin v. Orbeck, 437 U.S. 518 (1978).

27. E.g., Commonwealth Edison Co. v. Montana, 453 U.S. 609 (1981); Minnesota v. Clover Leaf Creamery Co., 449 U.S. 456 (1981); Exxon Corp. v. Governor of Maryland, 437 U.S. 117 (1978).

28. See United States v. Pink, 315 U.S. 203, 233 (1942) ("Power over foreign affairs is not shared by the States; it is vested in the national government exclusively"); Zschernig v. Miller, 389 U.S. 429 (1968); The Chinese Exclusion Case, 130 U.S. 581 (1889). See also Graham v. Richardson, 403 U.S. 365, 378 (1971).

29. Long before the Constitution was adopted, the dollar was a common currency among the states. Under the Articles of Confederation it was true that the states had concurrent power with Congress to coin money and could emit bills of credit, two powers that the Constitution explicitly withdrew from state hands. Even under the Articles, however, Congress had the sole authority to regulate the value of coin, whether issued by state or congressional authority. See J. Willard Hurst, *A Legal History of Money in the United States, 1774–1970*, at 8–9 (1973).

30. U.S. CONST. art. I, §8, cl. 5. Briscoe v. Bank of the Commonwealth of Kentucky, 36 U.S. 257 (1837). The much more controversial issue, now also long settled in favor of federal power, was whether Congress is empowered to issue paper money that may be used as legal tender in payment of private debts. See generally Kenneth Dam, "The Legal Tender Cases," 1981 *Supreme Court Review* 367; Charles Fairman, *Reconstruction and Reunion 1864–88, Part One (VI History of the Supreme Court of the United States)*, 677–775 (1971).

31. See *Federalist* 42 (Madison), at 269. ("The proposed uniformity in the value of the *current* coin might be destroyed by subjecting that of foreign coin to the different regulations of the different States.")

32. In discussing the desirability of the proposed Constitution's withdrawal of power to coin money or to substitute paper money in place of coin, Madison emphasized both economic and political integration values. See *Federalist* 44, at 282. ("Had every State a right to regulate the value of its coin, there might be as many different currencies as States, and thus the intercourse among them would be impeded; retrospective alterations in its value might be made, and thus the citizens of other States be injured, and animosities be kindled among the States themselves.")

33. A common currency not only facilitated economic integration but social integration. See Kenneth Karst, *Belonging to America: Equal Citizenship and the Constitution* 178 (1989). In helping to provide "the language of how many, how much, how far," the common currency provided a "common vocabulary, a means of communicating the essence of their [Americans'] lives across the innumerable gaps that divided them." Robert Wiebe, *The Segmented Society: An Introduction to the Meaning of America* 41 (1975).

34. See Peter Hay and Ronald Rotunda, *The United States Federal System: Legal Integration in the American Experience* 169–81 (1982).

35. Such programs are commonplace today. Despite some early constitutional qualms about the power of Congress to foster such "internal improvements," Congress appropriated funds for building interstate transportation networks beginning at a very early stage of constitutional history. See Merrill Peterson, "Internal Improvements," in Leonard Levy and Kenneth Karst, 2 *Encyclopedia of the American Constitution* 991 (1986) [hereinafter cited as *Encyclopedia*]. Often interstate transportation facilities are "built or owned by states or localities though largely with federal funds." Hans Linde, "Transportation and State Laws under the United States Constitution: The Evolution of Judicial Doctrine," in I *Courts and Free Markets* 139, 147 (Terrence Sandalow and Eric Stein eds. 1982) [hereinafter *Courts and Free Markets*].

36. See South Dakota v. Dole, 107 S. Ct. 2793 (1987). (Whether or not Congress could directly regulate a national minimum age of 21 to drink alcoholic beverages, it may withhold federal highway funds from states that do not prohibit drinking under the age.)

37. See Harry Scheiber, "Cooperative Federalism," in 2 *Encyclopedia*, supra note

35, at 503–04; Richard Stewart, "Pyramids of Sacrifice? Problems of Federalism in Mandating State Implementation of National Environmental Policy," 86 *Yale Law Journal* 1196 (1977).

38. For indications of the respective realms of federal and state power in each of these fields, see Perez v. Campbell, 402 U.S. 637 (1971) (bankruptcy); Sturges v. Crowninshield, 17 U.S. (4 Wheat.) 122 (1819) (same); Goldstein v. California, 412 U.S. 546 (1973) (copyright); Bonito Boats, Inc. v. Thunder Craft Boats, Inc., 109 S. Ct. 971 (1989) (patents); Kewanee Oil Co. v. Bicron Corp., 416 U.S. 470 (1974) (same); Ex parte Jackson, 96 U.S. (6 Otto) 727 (1878) (postal power).

39. See, e.g., Carter v. Carter Coal Co., 298 U.S. 238 (1936); Hammer v. Dagenhart, 247 U.S. 251 (1918).

40. See, e.g., Russell v. United States, 471 U.S. 858 (1985); Perez v. United States, 402 U.S. 146 (1971); Wickard v. Filburn, 317 U.S. 111 (1942).

41. Id.

42. For an introductory sampling of the scope of federal regulation of the electronic media, see Marc Franklin, *Mass Media Law: Cases and Materials* 704 et seq. (3d ed. 1986).

43. See Daniel Brenner and Monroe Price, *Cable Television and Other Nonbroadcast Video*, ch. 3 (1989).

44. See Garcia v. San Antonio Metropolitan Transit Authority, 469 U.S. 528, 550–51 (1985); Herbert Wechsler, "The Political Safeguards of Federalism: The Role of the States in Composition and Selection of the National Government," 54 *Columbia Law Review* 543 (1954). The structural idea was acknowledged at the outset, see *Federalist* 45, at 291 (Madison).

45. Commission of the European Communities, *Completing The Internal Market: White Paper from the Commission to the European Council* 21 (1985).

46. For a useful discussion, see American Law Institute, *Study of the Division of Jurisdiction Between State and Federal Courts* 99–108 (1968).

47. See Paul Bator, Daniel Meltzer, Paul Mishkin, and David Shapiro, *Hart & Wechsler's The Federal Courts and the Federal System* 883–84 (3d ed. 1988).

48. See William Cohen, "Congressional Power to Define State Power to Regulate Commerce: Consent and Pre-emption," in II *Courts and Free Markets*, supra note 35, at 540–41.

49. 41 U.S. (16 Pet.) 1 (1842).

50. See William Fletcher, "The General Common Law and Section 34 of the Judiciary Act of 1789: The Example of Marine Insurance," 97 *Harvard Law Review* 1513 (1984).

51. See Edmund Kitch, "Regulation and the American Common Market," in *Regulation, Federalism, and Interstate Commerce* 25–26 (A. Dan Tarlock ed. 1981); Carl B. Swisher, *The Taney Period, 1836–64, V History of the Supreme Court of the United States* 327–32 (1974); Robert Wiebe, *The Opening of American Society* 303 (1985).

52. David Shapiro, "Federal Common Law, Civil," in 2 *Encyclopedia*, supra note 35, at 689.

53. The Supreme Court also acted to foster economic integration in the early years of the republic by broadly interpreting the powers of Congress to regulate interstate commerce and by acknowledging that Congress possessed wide-ranging implied powers to use any appropriate means of achieving the objectives encompassed in its enumerated powers. See Chief Justice Marshall's classic opinions in McCulloch v. Maryland, 17 U.S. (4 Wheat.) 316 (1819), and Gibbons v. Ogden, 22 U.S. (9 Wheat.) 1 (1824). One

of the most dramatic instances of judicial encouragement of the use of federal legislative power in the pursuit of economic integration involved President Monroe's veto of an appropriation bill for repair of the Cumberland Road. Monroe reluctantly concluded that Congress lacked constitutional power to authorize expenditures for internal improvements and sent a copy of his views to each of the justices. Justice Johnson wrote back indicating that the Court found no constitutional objections with the internal improvements bill. See Edward Barrett, William Cohen, and Jonathan Varat, *Constitutional Law: Cases and Materials* 184–85 (8th ed. 1989).

    54. See David Shapiro, "*Swift v. Tyson,*" in 4 *Encyclopedia*, supra note 35, at 1841–42.

    55. 304 U.S. 64 (1938).

    56. Compare Carter v. Carter Coal Co., 298 U.S. 238 (1936), with NLRB v. Jones & Laughlin Steel Corp., 301 U.S. 1 (1937). See also Barrett, Cohen, and Varat, supra note 53, at 212–24.

    57. Even from the perspective of uniform federal common law, the late Judge Friendly commented positively on the replacement of *Swift* by *Erie*:

In one of his last essays Judge Clark expressed the belief that the Erie decision ran counter to the "trend of nationalism [that] was happily developing in 1938" and that it caused an "extreme resurgence of state law in the federal courts." My view is that, by banishing the spurious uniformity of Swift v. Tyson—what Mr. Justice Frankfurter was to call "the attractive vision of a uniform body of federal law" but a vision only—and by leaving to the states what ought to be left to them, Erie led to the emergence of a federal decisional law in areas of national concern that is truly uniform because, under the supremacy clause, it is binding in every forum, and therefore is predictable and useful as its predecessor, more general in subject matter but limited to the federal courts, was not.

Henry Friendly, "In Praise of Erie—And of the New Federal Common Law," 39 *New York University Law Review* 383, 405 (1964).

    58. United States Steel Corp. v. Multistate Tax Commission, 434 U.S. 452 (1978).

    59. Id. Professor Kitch believes "[t]he Court's construction of the Compact Clause [in that case] was strained, clearly influenced by the Court's awareness of the value of coordination in this area and the failure of Congress to act on the problem." Kitch, supra note 51, at 36. More generally, his view of the requirement of congressional consent to interstate compacts is that "[t]he relative unavailability of a binding interstate agreement under constitutional law has significantly restricted the ability of the states to coordinate their commercial policies." Id. at 21.

Professor Kitch generally holds the unorthodox view that "the existence of paramount, national political integration has not demonstrably furthered free internal trade." Id. at 10. Instead, he argues that "[f]ree trade among decentralized [state] authorities will result [and often has resulted] from voluntary cooperation, motivated by the fact that free trade will produce greater wealth for all to share." Id. at 13–14. His position is that "in the long run, this system may provide more free trade than centralized authority because it places stronger incentives on each jurisdiction to promulgate efficient rules for both its internal and external commerce." Id. at 14. In this view, interstate compacts, being voluntary agreements among states, are more likely to produce free trade than is imposed by national regulation.

To a considerable extent, Kitch treats economic integration and free trade as synonymous notions, however. Economic integration might better be thought of as coordinated or uniform rules in the different jurisdictions making up the economic union. Whether the coordination is imposed by union-wide authority or is the product of voluntary efforts by the union's constituent authorities, a coordinated or uniform rule need not lean toward a regime of laissez faire. Moreover, that interstate compacts may further economic integration does not mean they are a better mechanism for doing so than is congressional regulation. In any event, the Court's interpretation of the compact clause makes clear the priority of political over economic union, however valuable such compacts may be for economic integration when they are not inconsistent with political unity.

60. See generally Hay and Rotunda, supra note 34, at 185–95.

61. See James Day, "The National Conference of Commissioners on Uniform State Laws," in *The Life of the Law* 324 (John Honnold ed. 1964). See generally Hay and Rotunda, supra note 34, at 310–24.

62. See Hay and Rotunda, supra note 34, at 313–15, 324. See also Kitch, supra note 51, at 42.

63. A compilation of the uniform acts and the status of their legislative adoption in each state is set forth in Hay and Rotunda, supra note 34, at 314–23.

64. See id. at 324–37.

65. Jerome Hafter, "Toward the Multistate Practice of Law Through Admission by Reciprocity," 53 *Mississippi Law Journal* 1, 4, 15, and n.44 (1983). For an argument that under the Commerce Clause the twelve states with "retaliatory reciprocity" requirements are acting unconstitutionally, see Jonathon Chase, "Does Professional Licensing Conditional Upon Mutual Reciprocity Violate the Commerce Clause?" 10 *Vermont Law Review* 233 (1985). The article by Chase lists the states that have such requirements for professions other than law as well. Id. at 233 n.3.

66. See Hafter, supra note 65.

67. Barnard v. Thorstenn, 109 S.Ct. 1294 (1989); Supreme Court of Virginia v. Friedmann, 108 S.Ct. 2260 (1988); Supreme Court of New Hampshire v. Piper, 470 U.S. 274 (1985).

68. Hafter, supra note 65, at 43.

69. Allied Stores of Ohio, Inc. v. Bowers, 358 U.S. 522 (1959).

70. See generally Tribe, supra note 14, at 403–68. For a very brief discussion of the basic justifications for the Court's practice, see Varat, supra note 15, at 488 n.4. A good, brief discussion of the constitutional sources for so limiting state authority is presented in Vincent Blasi, "Constitutional Limitations on the Power of States to Regulate the Movement of Goods in Interstate Commerce," in I *Courts and Free Markets*, supra note 35, at 174–76.

71. Professor Kitch contends that this conventional account is a misreading of the nation's experience under the Articles of Confederation and of *The Federalist Papers*. See Kitch, supra note 51, at 15–19. A similar view is expressed in George Carpinello, "State Protective Legislation and Nonresident Corporations: The Privileges and Immunities Clause as a Treaty of Nondiscrimination," 73 *Iowa Law Review* 351, 367–69 (1988). Professor Regan retorts persuasively that however interesting a review of the actual state of trade warfare at the time might be, the framers responded to the perception that there was a serious problem and thus it is what they did in response to that perceived problem that matters. See Regan, supra note 22, at 1114 n.55 (1986). For a fuller rejoinder to the Kitch position, see Collins, supra note 20, at 51–60.

72. U.S. CONST. art. IV, §2, cl. 1.

73. 334 U.S. 385, 395 (1948).

74. E.g., Paul v. Virginia, 75 U.S. (8 Wall.) 168, 177–82 (1869); Bank of Augusta

v. Earle, 38 U.S. (13 Pet.) 519, 586 (1839). A wide range of commentators, myself included, have argued that this doctrine is anachronistic and should be overturned. See, e.g., Varat, supra note 15, at 499 n.47; Carpinello, supra note 71, at 378–411. Professor Carpinello collects the citations to other scholars who share this view, id. at 353 n.17. The Supreme Court as yet has shown no inclination to move in this direction, however. See, e.g., Western & Southern Life Insurance Co. v. State Board of Equalization, 451 U.S. 648, 656 (1981).

75. Toomer v. Witsell, 334 U.S. 385 (1948).

76. Supreme Court of Virginia v. Friedman, 108 S.Ct. 2260 (1988).

77. Varat, supra note 15, at 499–501.

78. Id.

79. Boston Stock Exchange v. State Tax Commission, 429 U.S. 318 (1977).

80. Tyler Pipe Industries, Inc. v. Washington Dept. of Revenue, 483 U.S. 232 (1987).

81. Baldwin v. Montana Fish & Game Comm'n, 436 U.S. 371, 388 (1978). In *Baldwin* the Court held recreational elk hunting to be insufficiently basic in these senses to come within the protection of the privileges and immunities clause. For a critical analysis of the fundamentality doctrine, see Varat, supra note 15, at 509–16.

82. As the Court said in United Building and Construction Trades Council of Camden County and Vicinity v. Mayor and Council of the City of Camden, 465 U.S. 208, 219 (1984), where it found the right to seek employment on a city construction project fundamental under the privileges and immunities clause:

Certainly, the pursuit of a common calling is one of the most fundamental of those privileges protected by the Clause. Baldwin v. Montana Fish and Game Comm'n, 436 U.S. 371, 387 (1978). Many, if not most, of our cases expounding the Privileges and Immunities Clause have dealt with this basic and essential activity. See, e.g., Hicklin v. Orbeck, 437 U.S. 518 (1978); Austin v. New Hampshire, 420 U.S. 656 (1975); Mullaney v. Anderson, 342 U.S. 415 (1952); Toomer v. Witsell, 334 U.S. 385 (1948); Ward v. Maryland, 79 U.S. 418 (1871).

83. Alexander Hamilton considered this clause "the basis of the Union." *Federalist* 80, at 478.

84. See cases cited supra note 82.

85. See William Cohen, "Federalism in Equality Clothing: A Comment on *Metropolitan Life Ins. Co. v. Ward*," 38 *Stanford Law Review* 1 (1985).

86. Shapiro v. Thompson, 394 U.S. 631, 630 n.8 (1969).

87. 19 *Journals of the Continental Congress* 214–15 (Galliard Hunt ed. 1912).

88. E.g., Zobel v. Williams, 457 U.S. 55, 73–74 (1982) (O'Connor, J., concurring in judgment); United States v. Wheeler, 254 U.S. 281, 297–98 (1920); Paul v. Virginia, 75 U.S. (8 Wall.) 168, 180 (1869); Corfield v. Coryell, 6 Fed. Cas. 546, 552 (C.C.E.D. Pa. 1823) (No. 3230) (Washington, J.).

89. Crandall v. Nevada, 73 U.S. (6 Wall.) 35, 43–44 (1868).

90. Edwards v. California, 314 U.S. 160 (1941); The Passenger Cases, 48 U.S. (7 How.) 283 (1849).

91. Twining v. New Jersey, 211 U.S. 78, 97 (1908).

92. See Williams v. Fears, 179 U.S. 270, 274 (1900).

93. E.g., Attorney General of New York v. Soto-Lopez, 476 U.S. 898 (1986); Zobel v. Williams, 457 U.S. 55 (1982); Shapiro v. Thompson, 394 U.S. 631 (1969).

94. 314 U.S. 160 (1941).

95. Id. at 173.

96. Id. at 176.

97. Id. at 177–81 (Douglas, J., joined by Black and Murphy, JJ., concurring); id. at 180–86 (Jackson, J., concurring).

98. Id. at 177.

99. Id. at 182.

100. Shapiro v. Thompson, 394 U.S. 618 (1969).

101. Memorial Hospital v. Maricopa County, 415 U.S. 250 (1974).

102. Dunn v. Blumstein, 405 U.S. 330 (1972). But see Sosna v. Iowa, 419 U.S. 393 (1975), upholding a one-year durational residency requirement as a condition to obtaining a divorce from the state's courts.

103. 394 U.S. at 629.

104. 405 U.S. at 339.

105. 415 U.S. at 261.

106. As to goods, see e.g., New England Power Co. v. New Hampshire, 455 U.S. 331 (1982); Hughes v. Oklahoma, 441 U.S. 322 (1979); Pike v. Bruce Church, Inc., 397 U.S. 137 (1970); H. P. Hood & Sons v. Du Mond, 336 U.S. 525 (1949); Foster-Fountain Packing Co. v. Haydel, 278 U.S. 1 (1928). As to people, see Rosberg, "Free Movement of Persons in the United States," in II *Courts and Free Markets*, supra note 35, at 298.

107. Preferential access requirements for in-state consumers was at one time permitted with respect to game birds killed in the state, Geer v. Connecticut, 161 U.S. 519 (1896), overruled Hughes v. Oklahoma, 441 U.S. 322 (1979), and with respect to restrictions on the exportation of water, Hudson County Water Co. v. McCarter, 209 U.S. 349 (1908). Similar preferences with respect to natural gas were invalidated from the beginning but not without taking the states' claims seriously: Pennsylvania v. West Virginia, 262 U.S. 553 (1923); West v. Kansas Natural Gas Co., 221 U.S. 229 (1911). The Court has become more skeptical even of export restrictions on water but has left open the possibility that some such state power remains. See Sporhase v. Nebraska, 458 U.S. 941 (1982). See also Blasi, supra note 70, at 192–97.

108. As to goods, see, e.g., Great Atlantic & Pacific Tea Co., Inc. v. Cottrell, 424 U.S. 366 (1976); Polar Ice Cream & Creamery v. Andrews, 375 U.S. 361 (1964); Dean Milk Co. v. City of Madison, 340 U.S. 349 (1951); Baldwin v. G.A.F. Seelig, Inc., 294 U.S. 511 (1935); Schollenberger v. Pennsylvania, 171 U.S. 1 (1898); Brown v. Maryland, 25 U.S. (12 Wheat.) 419 (1827). See also Regan, supra note 22, at 1119. As to people, see Rosberg, supra note 106, at 279–95.

109. See generally Collins, supra note 71; Julian Eule, "Laying the Dormant Commerce Clause to Rest," 91 *Yale Law Journal* 425 (1982); Regan, supra note 22; Rosberg, supra note 106, at 314–44; Robert Sedler, "The Negative Commerce Clause as a Restriction on State Regulation and Taxation: An Analysis in Terms of Constitutional Structure," 31 *Wayne Law Review* 885 (1985); Gary Simson, "Discrimination Against Nonresidents and the Privileges and Immunities Clause of Article IV," 128 *University of Pennsylvania Law Review* 379 (1979); Mark Tushnet, "Rethinking the Dormant Commerce Clause," 1979 *Wisconsin Law Review* 125 (1979); Varat, supra note 15.

110. See the cases discussed in Blasi, supra note 70, at 211–18.

111. Compagnie Francaise v. Louisiana Board of Health, 186 U.S. 380 (1902); Morgan's Steamship Co. v. Louisiana Board of Health, 118 U.S. 455 (1886). See the discussion by Rosberg, supra note 106, at 291–94. That there has been no recent reconsideration of this issue reflects the absence of modern attempts at this kind of exclusion,

not an acceptance of the power to exclude. It seems highly unlikely that such power would be reaffirmed today.

112. 477 U.S. 131 (1986).

113. Id. at 138.

114. Id. at 143.

115. Id. at 152.

116. See Varat, supra note 15, at 540–48. It is more problematic if a state conditions a grant of funds to a private party on the recipient's agreement to bias its decision in favor of in-staters. Id. at 560–64. See also South-Central Timber Development, Inc. v. Wunnicke, 467 U.S. 82 (1984).

117. Varat, supra note 15, at 522–23. See also Regan, supra note 22, at 1193.

118. Martinez v. Bynum, 461 U.S. 321 (1983). See Varat, supra note 15, at 552–54. But see Simson, supra note 109, at 395–97.

119. See White v. Massachusetts Council of Construction Employers, 460 U.S. 204 (1983); McCarthy v. Philadelphia Civil Service Comm'n, 424 U.S. 645, 646–47 (1976); Varat, supra note 15, at 546–48.

120. American Yearbook Co. v. Askew, 409 U.S. 904 (1972), aff'g 339 F. Supp. 719 (M.D. Fla. 1972); Hughes v. Alexandria Scrap Corp., 426 U.S. 794 (1976); Reeves, Inc. v. Stake, 447 U.S. 429 (1980); White v. Massachusetts Council of Construction Employers, Inc., 460 U.S. 204 (1983); South-Central Timber Development, Inc. v. Wunnicke, 467 U.S. 82 (1984).

This doctrine has been analyzed from a number of perspectives. See, e.g., Varat, supra note 15, at 503–08; Collins, supra note 71, at 98–105; David Pomper, "Recycling *Philadelphia v. New Jersey*: The Dormant Commerce Clause, Postindustrial 'Natural' Resources, and the Solid Waste Crisis," 137 *University of Pennsylvania Law Review* 1309, 1317–28 (1989); Regan, supra note 22, at 1193–1200; Sedler, supra note 109, at 1011–26.

121. See Reeves, Inc. v. Stake, 447 U.S. 429, 436–39 (1980).

122. Varat, supra note 15, at 522–40. See also Pomper, supra note 120, at 1320–22.

123. Collins, supra note 71, at 102–03; Regan, supra note 22, at 1194.

124. This is the basic premise of the lengthy, insightful article by Professor Regan, supra note 22. See, e.g., id. at 1192: "Genuine national interests for dormant commerce clause purposes are those interests, and only those, that, like the interest in preventing state protectionism, are fundamentally related to the existence and political viability of federal union."

125. Id. at 1194.

126. Id. at 1194–95.

127. Compare Mark Gergen, "The Selfish State and the Market," 66 *Texas Law Review* 1097, 1134–43 (1988), and Collins, supra note 71, at 98–104, with Regan, supra note 22, at 1194–96, and Varat, supra note 15, at 541–45.

128. See Varat, supra note 15, at 530 n.175; Collins, supra note 71, at 102–03. Professor Gergen would go further. He is critical of my position that state policy autonomy includes the authority to prefer residents in the disposition of state-created resources and to enlarge the public sector to do so if the state's voters so choose. Gergen, supra note 127, at 1142–43 and n. 247. The point may be somewhat academic in the United States, given the ideological and financial resistance to publicly owned and operated enterprise on any large scale. More fundamentally, however, I do not share Professor Gergen's view that free trade is valued primarily because it serves "the cause of efficiency or

utility maximization." Id. at 1107–16. Accord, Regan, supra note 22, at 1177; Eule, supra note 109, at 429–35, 444–46. See also Pomper, supra note 120, at 1313–17. Rather, I believe state autonomy is a more powerful constitutional value when local democracy is employed to act in pursuit of interests other than efficiency, so long as political integration and personal freedom of interstate migration are not impaired.

129. See Regan, supra note 22, at 1195–96.

130. See Varat, supra note 15, at 491.

131. Compare sources cited supra notes 117–19 with sources cited supra note 127.

132. The "free-rider" justification for resident preference in welfare assistance programs is discussed in Varat, supra note 15, at 522–23.

133. See id. at 527–30. There are difficult problems here concerning the rights to resident preference of commuters who work but do not live in the state and are asked to pay income taxes and of nonresidents seeking access to courts, highways, and other public goods that may not be rationed on the basis of residence. Discussion of these is beyond the scope of this paper, but attention is paid to them in the article just cited.

134. See Collins, supra note 71, at 68; Gergen, supra note 127, at 1112–16.

135. See cases cited supra notes 100–102.

136. 460 U.S. 204 (1983).

137. 465 U.S. 208 (1984).

138. Id. at 221.

139. Compare White v. Massachusetts Council of Construction Employers, Inc., 460 U.S. 204 (1983), with South-Central Timber Development, Inc. v. Wunnicke, 467 U.S. 82 (1984). See Tribe, supra note 14, at 432–34.

140. But see Sedler, supra note 109, at 1018–20 (arguing that the state should have the right to reserve for residents the benefits of its collective wealth, without restriction under *either* the commerce clause *or* the privileges and immunities clause). Compare Regan, supra note 22, at 1199–1200 (arguing that *Camden* does not really reject the relevance of the "state-as-market-participant idea . . . to the privileges and immunities clause").

141. For a useful discussion of various national interests that might be considered candidates for constitutional values, see Regan, supra note 22, at 1177–82.

142. See text accompanying notes 124–26 supra.

143. See Michael Smith, "State Discriminations Against Interstate Commerce," 74 *California Law Review* 1203, 1239–52 (1986). For different perspectives on this subject and the relevant principal cases, see Collins, supra note 71, at 75–85; Eule, supra note 109, at 456–74; Regan, supra note 22, at 1233–44.

144. 449 U.S. 456 (1981).

145. 437 U.S. 117 (1978).

146. Id. at 127–28.

147. Tribe, supra note 14, at 417.

148. Great Atlantic & Pacific Tea Co., Inc. v. Cottrell, 424 U.S. 371, 379 (1976).

149. Id. at 380. See also Sporhase v. Nebraska, 458 U.S. 955, 957–98 (1982), holding unconstitutional a mandatory reciprocity requirement for the exportation of groundwater.

150. The Court articulates its general standard of review as follows:

Where the statute regulates even-handedly to effectuate a legitimate local public interest, and its effects on interstate commerce are only incidental, it will be upheld unless the burden imposed on such commerce is clearly excessive in relation to the putative local benefits. If a legitimate local purpose is found, then the question becomes one of degree. And the extent of the burden that will be tolerated will of course depend on the nature of the local interest involved and on whether it could be promoted as well with a lesser impact on interstate activities.

Pike v. Bruce Church, Inc., 397 U.S. 137 (1970).

For a review of the development of the "burdens" doctrine that concludes that, although continually articulated, the standard is not applied in practice, see Sedler, supra note 109, at 941–68. For a review that explains and defends that doctrinal branch, see Collins, supra note 71, at 61–109.

151. See Martin Redish and Shane Nugent, "The Dormant Commerce Clause and the Constitutional Balance of Federalism," 1987 *Duke Law Journal* 569, 594; Thomas Anson and P. M. Schenkkan, "Federalism, The Dormant Commerce Clause, and State-Owned Resources," 59 *Texas Law Review* 71, 84 (1980); Daniel Farber, "State Regulation and the Dormant Commerce Clause," 3 *Constitutional Commentary* 395, 411–12 (1986); Regan, supra note 22, at 1152–53. But see Jesse Choper, "The Scope of National Power Vis-a-Vis the States: The Dispensability of Judicial Review," 86 *Yale Law Journal* 1552, 1586 (1977) ("Congress seems especially unsuited to the task of determining . . . the compatibility of isolated local ordinances with the broad demands of the federal system. This task . . . is the traditional work of adjudicative, not legislative, organs"); Eule, supra note 109, at 442.

152. See Farber, supra note 151, at 407–10. But see Collins, supra note 71, at 128 n.496.

153. Professor Kitch is of the view that there should be no review under the dormant commerce clause, because it too often leads to anticompetitive federal regulation, and because trade barriers among states are likely to be lowered more efficiently through voluntary negotiations among them than through judicial supervision. Kitch, supra note 51. But see Collins, supra note 71, at 124–26 (finding Kitch's position flawed).

154. See Eule, supra note 109, at 442–43; Farber, supra note 151, at 402–04. See also Regan, supra note 22, at 1153 ("[I]t is especially inappropriate for any body other than Congress to attempt to evaluate from a national point of view effects that we have specifically chosen, by having a federal system, to leave to varying state evaluations in the normal course").

Professors Redish and Nugent would go even further. They argue not only that the Court should refrain from invalidating state laws as "undue burdens" on interstate commerce (Redish and Nugent, supra note 151, at 598) but more generally that the Court should abandon dormant commerce clause review entirely. They base their position primarily on an asserted lack of support in constitutional text or history for the practice and, more fundamentally, on the view that federalism's structural valuing of state autonomy was intended to leave federal oversight of state regulation in Congress, where the states would have political power to attempt to block uniform federal regulation, and not the courts, where the states cannot assert political pressure.

155. See, e.g., Eule, supra note 109, at 430–31, 439–43, objecting to judicial substitution of free-trade, laissez-faire values for evenhanded policy decisions made by electorally accountable state legislators. See also Farber, supra note 151, at 401–02; Anson and Schenkkan, supra note 151, at 78–79. See also Sedler, supra note 109, at 986–91.

Professor Gergen takes a somewhat contrary view and urges attention to economic efficiency as a primary basis for controlling state interference with interstate commerce, although he apparently would temper that view by incorporating attention to administrability and respect for tradition. Gergen, supra note 127, at 1107–16. He would, moreover, shift review on this basis to the privileges and immunities clause, although he is troubled by "the clause's inability to correct evenhanded measures that pose an intolerable burden on interstate commerce." Id. at 1118.

156. I tend to agree with Professor Collins that, despite the ambiguity of some of the language in Supreme Court opinions, "economic efficiency is [not] the essential national value arrayed against state autonomy." Collins, supra note 71, at 63. Instead, "[t]he framers sought economic union, but the focus of their concern was interstate commerce harmony rather than market efficiency." Id. at 64. He later asserts, moreover, that the dormant commerce power doctrine "does not in any meaningful sense impose laissez faire as a substantive value." Id. at 114–15.

See also Sedler, supra note 109, at 964–68; Regan, supra note 22, at 1177–78.

157. Professor Regan, generally an opponent of judicial balancing under the dormant commerce clause, acknowledges that invalidating undue local burdens imposed on an effective national transportation system may be an appropriate judicial task. Regan, supra note 22, at 1177, 1182–85. That is so, he argues, only because "an effective transportation network is essential to genuine political union just as the suppression of protectionism is essential to political union (and as economic efficiency, unlimited access to potential markets, and the actual movement of goods are not)." Id. at 1184.

Professor Collins would approve balancing/burdens analysis of somewhat more generous scope than Professor Regan, but he, too, is not interested in balancing to enforce a fundamental value of "free trade." Collins, supra note 71, at 122–24. Rather, he argues for a basic national interest in "interstate commercial harmony" (id. at 123) as the national interest that appropriately is to be weighed against local tax or regulatory burdens.

The common ground between them should not be overlooked, however. Burdens analysis is acceptable when there is a special national interest other than uniformity or laissez faire that is affected by local policies.

158. See, e.g., Bendix Autolite Corp. v. Midwesco Enterprises, Inc., 108 S.Ct. 2218, 2224 (1988) (Scalia, J., dissenting); Southern Pacific Co. v. Arizona, 325 U.S. 761, 784, 794–95 (1945) (Black, J., and Douglas, J., dissenting); McCarroll v. Dixie Greyhound Lines, 309 U.S. 176, 188–89 (1940) (Black, Frankfurter, and Douglas, J. J., dissenting); Gwin, White & Prince, Inc. v. Henneford, 305 U.S. 434, 455 (1939) (Black, J., dissenting).

159. See generally Collins, supra note 71, at 85–98.

160. See Eule, supra note 109, at 446–55; Redish and Nugent, supra note 151, at 605–12; Gergen, supra note 127, at 28.

161. Barnard v. Thorstenn, 109 S.Ct. 1294 (1989); Supreme Court of Virginia v. Friedman, 108 S.Ct. 2260 (1988) (residency requirement for admission to law practice "on motion"); Supreme Court of New Hampshire v. Piper, 470 U.S. 274 (1985) (residency requirement for admission to law practice on examination).

162. See authorities cited supra note 44.

163. For useful discussion, see Cohen, supra note 48, at 523–27; Hay and Rotunda, supra note 34, at 197–200; Sedler, supra note 109, at 1000–02.

164. See Prudential Insurance Co. v. Benjamin, 328 U.S. 408 (1946). But see Metropolitan Life Ins. Co. v. Ward, 470 U.S. 869 (1985).

165. See Northeast Bancorp, Inc. v. Board of Governors, 472 U.S. 159 (1985).

166. Clark Distilling Co. v. Western Maryland R. Co., 242 U.S. 311 (1917) (Congress may prohibit the interstate shipment of intoxicating liquors); Hipolite Egg Co. v. United

States, 220 U.S. 45 (1911) (impure food and drugs); Champion v. Ames, 188 U.S. 321 (1903) (lottery tickets).

167. See United States v. Darby, 312 U.S. 100 (1941), overruling Hammer v. Dagenhart, 247 U.S. 251 (1918), and upholding the power of Congress to prohibit interstate shipment of goods manufactured by employees paid less than a minimum wage or kept at work beyond a maximum number of hours per week.

168. Caminetti v. United States, 242 U.S. 470 (1917). (Congress may prohibit transporting women interstate for immoral purposes.)

169. In addition to the authorities cited supra notes 30–31, this is the strong implication of the fact that the Constitution's explicit injunction against state coining of money, emitting bills of credit, or making anything but gold or silver coin a tender in payment of debts (U.S. CONST. art. I, §10, cl. 1) is expressed as an unconditional prohibition, in sharp contrast to the bar against state imposition of "Imposts or Duties on Imports or Exports" and the bar against state imposition of "any Duty of Tonnage," both of which are conditional limits subject to "the Consent of the Congress," id. at §10, cls. 2–3. See Redish and Nugent, supra note 151, at 591.

170. U.S. CONST. art. I, §8, cl.1 (taxation), 4 (bankruptcy). An indirect tax is a sales or excise tax, or, as Hamilton defined it in *Federalist* 36, at 219, "duties and excises on articles of consumption."

171. United States v. Ptasynski, 462 U.S. 74 (1983) (taxation); Regional Rail Reorganization Act Cases, 419 U.S. 102 (1974) (bankruptcy); Head Money Cases, 112 U.S. 580 (1884) (same). See generally Tribe, supra note 14, at 318, 324–26.

172. U.S. CONST. art. I, §9, cl.6.

173. See Cohen, supra note 48, at 534–36.

174. U.S. CONST. art. IV, §1.

175. Id. at §2, cl.1. See supra notes 81, 82. In the context of the interstate equality requirements of the privileges and immunities clause, in sharp contrast to the context of the intrastate equality requirements of the equal protection clause, voting is not fundamental. See Varat, supra note 15, at 520–21.

176. U.S. CONST. art. IV, §2, cl.2.

177. U.S. CONST. art. IV, §1. Congress has exercised this power since 1790, and together with Supreme Court interpretations that have recognized an expansive authority for Congress in this respect, the power has been employed as a strong force for national unity. See Willis Reese, "Full Faith and Credit," in 2 *Encyclopedia*, supra note 35, at 823–25.

178. U.S. CONST. art. IV, §3, cl.1.

179. Id. at §4.

180. Pacific States Tel. & Tel. Co. v. Oregon, 223 U.S. 118 (1912). See Arthur Bonfield, "The Guaranty Clause of Article IV, §4: A Study of Congressional Desuetude," 46 *Minnesota Law Review* 513 (1962); Tribe, supra note 14, at 98–100.

181. Moreover, I tend to agree with Professor Tribe that "it need not follow from the unavailability of the guarantee clause as a textual source of protection for *individuals* that the clause confers no judicially enforceable rights upon *states as states*." Tribe, supra note 14, at 398 (emphasis in original).

182. See note 177 supra.

183. See Varat, supra note 15, at 569–71; Tribe, supra note 14, at 525. But see Cohen, supra note 48, at 531–34, finding no functional reason to treat congressional power to consent to state impairment of interstate privileges and immunities any differently than

congressional power to consent to state discrimination against interstate commerce, at least as to instances where the limitation on state power that would be applicable absent congressional consent was "designed to preserve paramount Congressional power to promote a national common market." My disagreement with Professor Cohen arises, of course, because of my view that the privileges and immunities clause was designed primarily to protect political, rather than economic, union. As such, even Congress should not be able to consent to political disintegration of the union. See also Rosberg, supra note 106, at 344–45.

184. Baldwin v. Montana Fish & Game Comm'n, 436 U.S. 371, 383 (1978).

185. See supra note 74.

186. See supra note 82.

187. 314 U.S. 160 (1940).

188. See text accompanying notes 94–99 supra.

189. Accord, Rosberg, supra note 106, at 301–03 (discussing whether Congress could authorize Hawaii to restrict in-migration in order to keep its population limited).

190. 394 U.S. 618 (1969).

191. Id. at 644 (Chief Justice Warren, with whom Justice Black joined, dissenting).

192. Id. at 641.

193. Id. at 642.

194. See the concurring opinions of Justices Brennan and O'Connor in Zobel v. Williams, 457 U.S. 55 (1982). See also Tribe, supra note 14, at 542–43.

195. See cases cited supra note 161.

196. 108 S.Ct. 2260, 2267–68. (1988).

197. See White v. Massachusetts Council of Construction Employers, 460 U.S. 204, 215 n.1 (1983) (Blackmun, J., concurring in part and dissenting in part).

198. The Supreme Court may often require Congress to be quite explicit about its invasion of state policy autonomy in the interpretation of federal statutes and construe the reach of federal legislation more narrowly when that autonomy is at stake as a means of nonconstitutional protection. E.g., United States v. Enmons, 410 U.S. 396 (1973); United States v. Bass, 404 U.S. 336 (1971); Rewis v. United States, 401 U.S. 808 (1971). See generally Tribe, supra note 14, at 316–17, 383.

199. For an insightful account of these developments, see Tribe, supra note 14, at 400.

200. 469 U.S. 528 (1985).

201. Id. at 556.

202. Id.

203. 108 S.Ct. 1355 (1988).

204. Id. at 1361.

205. See Bacchus Imports, Ltd. v. Dias, 468 U.S. 263 (1984). See generally Tribe, supra note 14, at §6–24.

206. South Dakota v. Dole, 197 S.Ct. 2793 (1987).

207. Garcia v. San Antonio Metropolitan Transit Authority, 469 U.S. 528 (1985).

208. In *Federalist* 32, at 197–98, Hamilton gave critics of the proposed Constitution the following unconditional assurances:

I am willing here to allow, in its full extent, the justness of the reasoning which requires that the individual States should possess an independent and uncontrollable authority to raise their own revenues for the supply of their own wants. And making this concession, I affirm that (with the sole exception of duties on imports and exports) they would, under the plan of the convention, retain that authority in the most absolute and unqualified sense; and that an attempt on the part of the national government to abridge them in the exercise of it would be a violent assumption of power, unwarranted by any article or clause of its Constitution.

See also *Federalist* 33, at 204–05; No. 34, at 205–06.

209. See Hughes v. Alexandria Scrap Corp., 426 U.S. 794, 817–32 (1976) (Brennan, J., joined by White and Marshall, JJ., dissenting).

210. This would be especially true with respect to certain kinds of "impure" or "conditional" subsidies that raise troublesome issues under the current contours of the dormant commerce clause. See Gergen, supra note 127, at 1134–45; Saul Levmore, "Interstate Exploitation and Judicial Intervention," 69 *Virginia Law Review* 563, 577–89 (1983); Varat, supra note 15, at 541–45.

211. Rosberg, supra note 106, at 277.

212. See, e.g., Donald Kommers and Michel Waelbroeck, "Legal Integration and the Free Movement of Goods: The American and European Experience," in Vol. I, Book 3 *Integration Through Law: Europe and the American Federal Experience* 165, 223–24 (Mauro Cappelletti, Monica Seccombe, and Joseph Weiler eds. 1986).

213. See Gergen, supra note 127, at 1137–38, especially nn.209, 220.

3

Preservation of Cultural Diversity in a Federal System: The Role of the Regions

GIANDOMENICO MAJONE

INTRODUCTION

A striking feature of contemporary Europe is the parallel movement toward greater political and economic integration on the one hand, and toward regional decentralization on the other. The successive enlargements of the European Community (EC), the renewed drive toward completion of the internal market by 1992, and the continuous expansion of Community regulation in all domains of economic and social life are clear signs that essential functions of modern government can no longer be carried out effectively in a purely national context. At the time, the strength of the regionalist movement proves that if the European nation-state is too small for certain functions, it is also too large to carry out other functions.

What has to be explained is how the same process that pushes toward economic and political integration also produces regional consciousness and a growing desire for identification and membership in a community more distinct and culturally homogeneous than national society. This process is not peculiar to Europe but it may find here its most advanced expression.

The reemergence of ethnic and cultural regionalism in many parts of the world has been explained (for example, by the American sociologist S. M. Lipset) as a form of resistance to modernizing trends in postindustrial society. This is certainly not true in the case of Europe. Here the current fascination with cultural distinctiveness is not due to a rejection of the imperatives of modernity but to the enormous increase in the intensity of exchange among European countries that forces each European to better understand his or her cultural roots in order to understand other cultural identities. The driving force behind the regionalist movement is not the desire to reject all that unites Europe culturally, but rather the wish to preserve cultural diversity in the presence of economic, scientific, and technological internationalization processes that are largely neutral with respect to cultural differences.

A growing number of Europeans hope that the existing nation-states will eventually be displaced by a federation that would allow full expression to their cultural diversity while at the same time uniting all Europeans in a larger European nation. This is not going to happen soon, yet the logic of a "Europe of regions" cannot be easily refuted. The idea persists and continues to grow because it is based on the correct insight that cultural diversity is the very essence of the European identity.

The notion of a Europe of regions was perfectly familiar to the people of the Middle Ages, of the Renaissance, and even of the Enlightenment—up to the time of the French Revolution. If the idea has to be rediscovered today, it is only because we still live in the shadow of nationalist ideologies and suffer from the historical amnesia imposed on us by the nation-state.

"ONE STATE, ONE CULTURE"

For liberal historians of the last century, the principle "one state, one culture" was not only normative but also was descriptively an essential element, if not the driving force, in the process of formation of the nation-state in Western Europe. According to this principle, Western European nations constituted culturally homogeneous communities that inevitably strived to bring into being territorial states congruent with these communities. When necessary, political boundaries were redrawn to ensure the requisite congruence.

Present-day students of nation-building in Europe argue that cultural homogeneity within a territory strongly facilitated the emergence of a durable state, that its absence significantly limited the capacity of any state to mobilize its resources, and that the successful European states generally engaged in a deliberate program of cultural homogenization.[1] Taken together, these three propositions do not seem to be mutually consistent. If cultural homogeneity was an important precondition for the emergence of the nation-state, why was a deliberate policy of homogenization at all necessary?

In reality the liberal interpretation of national history is not well supported by the historical evidence. For example, the fact that the France of the *ancien régime* had a highly centralized administration has been wrongly interpreted to mean that cultural homogeneity had in fact been achieved. But then, how can one explain that the provincial identities of French elites played an important role throughout the Revolution or that the denial of official recognition to the historical provinces—replaced by the new *départements*—raised such fierce opposition? The White Terror of 1815 had as strong a regional, even autonomist, character as did some of the revolutionary movements in 1848 and 1870. As

Eugen Weber informs us, in 1863, according to official figures, about a quarter of France's population spoke no French. In twenty-four of the country's eighty-nine *départements*, more than half the communes did not speak French, and in six others a significant proportion of the communes were in the same position. In short, Weber concludes, French was a foreign language for a substantial number of "the French," including almost half the children who would reach adulthood in the last quarter of the century.[2]

French regionalism remained a political factor of some significance in the period between the two world wars, and regionalists joined Henri Pétain's national revolution in the hope of obtaining from him the regionalization that the Republic had refused them. Thus, as Aristide Zolberg points out, the ethnic and cultural regionalism that came to light in France in the 1950s was less of a revival or a reversal than a resumption of normal politics after a decade of interruption.[3]

What is true of France is a fortiori true of other European societies. The task of nation-building continued to be regarded as problematic and remained on the agenda of almost every Western European society throughout the nineteenth century. In countries like Belgium, Ireland, Spain, Yugoslavia, and for different reasons, the two Germanies, that task is still problematic. Here, too, present-day tensions between ethnic-cultural regionalism and established nation-states represent historical continuity rather than change. If this continuity seems surprising, especially in the case of old nation-states like France, it is only because national history in the nineteenth century has been largely written from the point of view of the winners. Attention to cultural diversities that continued to challenge the nationalist dogma of "one state, one culture" became the province of writers and intellectuals outside the mainstream of official culture.[4]

The Historical Amnesia of the Nation-State

It is the great merit of Ernest Renan to have perceived the historical reality hidden by the slogan "one state, one culture." In his *Qu'cest-qu'une Nation?* (1882), the French historian singled out collective amnesia and anonymity of membership as the two crucial characteristics of the modern nation-state. According to Renan, a shared forgetfulness is at least as important as common memories of a shared past for the emergence of a nation. If culturally homogeneous communities are regarded as the only legitimate repositories of political authority, internal differentiations within the politically sanctified culture must be suppressed or at least minimized. Hence the main goal of educational policy in nineteenth-century Europe, no less than in the United States, was not only that each citizen should learn the standardized, centralized, and literate language in primary school but also that he should forget or at least devalue the dialect spoken at home.[5] The magnitude of the task of cultural standardization, of making the state congruent with the politically recognized culture, can be appreciated if we remember that as late as the 1860s about one-half of the school children of

France did not speak or at least could not write standard French, and the proportion was much higher in most other states.

Collective amnesia is closely related to what Renan identifies as the other characteristic of the modern nation-state, that is, anonymity of membership. If a nation is defined as a collection of people such that its members identify with the collectivity without identifying in any important way with sub-groups of that collectivity, then linguistic and other links with groups predating the emergence of the nation must be treated with suspicion or even open hostility. This hostility toward cultural diversity pervades the social and political history of Europe since the French Revolution. The ideals of the Revolution lay in uniformity and the extinction of particularisms. The Jacobins insisted that "the unity of the Republic demands the unity of speech. . . . Speech must be one, like the Republic."[6]

As Ernest Gellner writes, what distinguishes areas like Western Europe, within which nationalism has become the crucial political principle, is that "some . . . profound change has taken place in the way in which society is organized—a change which makes anonymous, internally fluid and fairly undifferentiated, large-scale, and culturally homogeneous communities appear as the only legitimate repositories of political authority."[7] Gellner argues that this change is not only deep but also permanent. As this chapter attempts to show, there are good reasons for doubting the permanence of the change; but as historical reconstruction, the analysis is quite convincing.

It would be wrong to assume that the process of cultural and social homogenization took place only in centralized nation-states like France, Italy, Spain, or Britain. Even in the various (con)federal structures of nineteenth-century Germany, there was very little correlation between the existing states and the actual diversity in German economic and cultural life. The vast majority of these states did not reflect the national past, but rather the success of some of the latter units (and especially of centralized states like Prussia and Saxony) in becoming great or small European powers, and the relative success or failure of various small and medium-states to absorb the territory of their neighbors during the Napoleonic wars.[8] The effort to minimize the cultural distinctiveness of the historical provinces (for example, of the Catholic Rhine provinces of Prussia at the time of Bismarck's *Kulturkampf*) was as determined in Germany as in the centralized nation-states.

Indeed, the central problem of German federalism throughout the nineteenth century was that although hardly anybody denied that federal organization was necessary in view of the great cultural diversity of the country, the existing states (with the possible exception of Bavaria) did not correspond to that diversity. Hence they could not represent that cultural variety that the legislators of the Frankfurt assembly of 1848 desired to preserve. However, the existing states did represent a political reality that had to be accepted in shaping a federal constitution.

In this respect, the situation had not changed at the time of the Weimar Constitution. In the words of Rudolf Schlesinger, "[T]here were many arguments in favor of German federalism, but hardly any rational grounds for basing that federalism on the conglomeration of states which Bismarck had preserved."[9] Hugo Preuss, the father of the Weimar Constitution, thought that the existing states, and above all Prussia, should be replaced by a new organization based upon the great cultural diversity of the national life. In the end, the opposition of provincial leaders, state bureaucracies, and the parties of the left proved too strong. The traditional states, whose origin, as Preuss argued, was in dynastic quarrels rather than in cultural and social individuality, continued to exist under the new federal constitution.[10]

INDUSTRIALIZATION AND CULTURAL STANDARDIZATION

Historically, cultural homogenization, nation-building, and industrialization have been closely interrelated processes. If we follow Gellner's argument, there are two main types of society, both marked by great complexity and size but which differ radically in the manner in which they make use of culture. One of these, represented by an advanced agrarian society, allows great cultural diversity and uses that diversity to mark out, economically and politically, the different positions and roles of the various subpopulations found within it.

The other type, the growth-oriented industrial society, is strongly impelled toward cultural homogeneity, since people can efficiently cooperate on complex tasks involving high technology only on the basis of a shared, homogeneous, and school-inculcated culture. In this type of society,

a man's culture, the idiom within which he was trained and within which he is effectively employable, is his most precious possession, his real entrance-card to full citizenship and human dignity, to social participation. The limits of his culture are the limit of his employability, his world, and his moral citizenship. . . . So culture, which had once resembled the air men breathed, and of which they were seldom properly aware, suddenly becomes perceptible and significant. The wrong and alien culture becomes menacing . . . The age of nationalism is born.[11]

The impulse toward a shared, homogeneous, school-inculcated culture is also fed by other factors not explicitly mentioned by Gellner. One such factor is, to use William McNeill's phrase, the "industrialization of war," a process already well advanced under the old regime but which finds its most complete realization in the nationalist idea of every man a soldier. The entire nation is now viewed as "an army marching by divisions, composed of thousands of men all moving in the same step, inspired by the same thought, as if they formed a single entity."[12]

Cultural and especially linguistic homogeneity could also become an important element of strength in the relations of the nation-state with other members of the international system. For example, in the international system created by the

Congress of Vienna, some states were not organized around the principle of nationality. Hence a country like France could pursue a policy of "universalistic nationalism," to encourage the formation of national states in Europe in order to weaken the position of a multinational state such as Austria.

We may conclude that cultural homogeneity has been an important, perhaps even an essential precondition for developing the productive and security structures of the modern nation-state. The important question today is: what are the cultural implications of the increasing globalization of production and technology, and of the gradual, uneven, but apparently inexorable transfer of important functions from the European nation-state to supranational institutions?

Since the end of the Second World War, the traditional nations of Western Europe have lost their credibility as relevant security communities, while their markets and macroeconomic policies have come to be increasingly dominated by the world economy. At the same time, their political monopoly has been seriously eroded by the creation of the European Community and its institutions and by an expanding network of bilateral and multilateral agreements of cooperation and policy coordination. The resurgence of regionalism since the end of the war can only be understood against this background. At a time when it becomes evident that the European state is too small for certain essential tasks, such as military security and economic management, it also becomes possible to argue that the nation-state is too large for other purposes. Hence many regionalists view the movement toward greater European unity and decentralization of state functions to the regional level as complementary trends.

It used to be thought that economic underdevelopment, associated with certain cultural distinctions, was the main cause of regionalism; with increasing affluence, regionalism would lose its raison d'être. But the examples of Catalonia and the Basque country in Spain, South Tyrol in Italy, and the Flemish region in Belgium show that regional nationalism can also flourish in economically favored regions. As Albert Hirschman has observed, since both underdevelopment and superior economic performance are invoked as grounds for complaining about the center, one must conclude that the economic argument is subsidiary to the main grievance of the regions, which is usually to be found in more basic matters such as linguistic and cultural differences.[13]

In fact, state-imposed cultural standardization loses much of its legitimation when national economic elites are being superseded by a transnational managerial class whose members resemble each other more than they resemble state officials or corporate managers who operate only in a national framework. Even national languages seem to lose some of their significance as English becomes the chosen language, not only of business, but of science, technology, and popular culture as well. The apparent paradox of a simultaneous movement toward integration and transnational cooperation on the one hand, and toward decentralization on the other—a phenomenon evident not only in Western Europe but throughout the industrialized and industrializing world—may be explained in terms of the distinction between culture and civilization. *Culture* designates what is singular and specific in a given society; *civilization* designates what can be generalized and hence acquired and transmitted from one society to another. As western civilization—in its economic and social dimensions no less than in its scientific and technological aspects—becomes the common civilization of the industrial- ized world, people rediscover those specific cultural traits that alone can preserve the identity of their subgroup against the rising tide of standardization. In many parts of the world the search for cultural roots has led to the revival of ethnicity and religious fundamentalism. In Europe the search for cultural, and sometimes ethnic, distinctiveness has found its main expression in the many regionalist movements that today dot the political map of the continent.

A EUROPE OF REGIONS?

In view of these developments it is not so surprising that regionalist leaders frequently talk about a "Europe of regions." They hope that the existing nation- states will gradually be displaced by the supranational institutions of the European Community and by regional institutions whose jurisdictions would be determined by historical, cultural, linguistic, and ethnic factors. In such a future Europe, regions like Catalonia, the Basque country, Corsica, and South Tyrol would take their place beside the other regions in a federation that would allow full expression of their cultural distinctiveness while at the same time uniting all Europeans in a large European nation. In this view, the nation-states of Europe would not disappear altogether, but they would become much less important than they are now and would lose much of their power to shape policy.[14]

This does not mean that the nation-states are ready to abdicate their historical role. On the contrary, they continue to delay both the regionalization process and the process of European integration, for example, by limiting as much as possible the powers of regions in the field of external relations. Thus, Italian regions are not allowed to establish direct contacts with the institutions of the European Community even in areas that the constitution has entrusted to their exclusive jurisdiction. This means that they are denied the possibility of directly influencing Community policymaking precisely in the areas that affect them most: the common agricultural policy, the European regional development fund, the European social fund. At the same time, the central authorities use their monopoly over external relations to recover some of the powers that the con- stitution transferred from the center to the regions.

The restrictions imposed on the Italian regions in their relations with the institutions of the European Community are by no means unique; on the contrary, they exemplify the situation prevailing in most member states. It should be noted that, though imperfect, the process of integrating states into a supranational organization such as the European Community should logically imply that the relations of the member states, and also of their regions, with the organization are not foreign relations but internal relations within the organization. Hence, if the organs of the Community can enter into relations only with states, even when dealing with matters of regional or local interest, this constraint can be attributed only to the reluctance of the central authorities to transfer power to the regions on the one hand and to the Community on the other. It is not by chance that within the Community the Commission and the Parliament have up to now shown themselves much more accessible than the Council of Ministers, which represents the interests of the member states, as far as contacts with regional and local authorities are concerned.[15]

Another European institution, the Council of Europe, has always shown great sensitivity to regional problems, especially in their cultural aspects. The Conference of Local and Regional Authorities of Europe, organized within the framework of the Council, has developed a substantial body of doctrine concerning the regionalization of the process of European integration. Important elements of this doctrine are the affirmation that the regions of Europe represent the true cultural dimension of European society and the demand that regions be granted the right of direct representation in European institutions and of cooperation across national frontiers. Concrete steps in the latter direction were taken with the treaty of Madrid on transfrontier cooperation that came into force in 1981. The aim of the convention is to allow local and regional authorities to cooperate across frontiers under conditions similar to those applying to cooperation among regions of the same country. Transfrontier regional cooperation is particularly intense in the fields of research, technology transfer, cultural exchange, and education and training.

The title of a recent project sponsored by the Cultural Fund of the Council of Europe, ''Cultural Dynamics of Regional Development,'' expresses well the continuing interest of the council in the framing of cultural policies at the regional level and in the interdependence between cultural policies and other policies of economic and social development.

CONCLUSION

Both the process of regionalization and that of Europe integration reflect the slow but continuous loss of legitimacy of the traditional nation-state. The process of integration is fed by constant reminders that the basic political and economic problems of European societies cannot be adequately formulated, let alone solved, in a purely national context. The main appeal of regionalism is less economic (in fact, a strong central state is needed to redistribute resources from rich to poor regions) than cultural: the rediscovery of the deeper roots of European culture and the growing aversion toward internal anonymity and cultural standardization imposed from above. These two processes are not only mutually consistent but also mutually supportive. In the debate between central and regional authorities, integration introduces new interlocutors that are not weighed down by the conflicts and misunderstandings of the past. The mere existence of this enlarged forum tends to strengthen the position of the region. At the same time, with integration, and with the subsequent loss of power of the central state, even the more extreme exponents of regional autonomy find that separation from the nation state is no longer necessary; they too want to belong to the larger community.

On the other hand, the European Community, which does not have its own enforcement agencies, must in the final analysis rely on the regions for the implementation of many of its policies. Direct contacts with the local authorities would significantly increase both the speed and the precision of the implementation process. Hence, the growing attention toward the regional dimension of Community policies. The convergence of interests between the Community and the regions—the institutional embodiments of local lore and traditions—is the best guarantee for the preservation of cultural diversity in the wider European society in formation.

It is tempting to close the paper on this optimistic note. However, it would be disingenuous not to mention that the increasing regionalization of Europe and the rediscovery of local cultures and traditions also present a serious danger. Just as the completion of a unified European market embracing 330 million consumers raises in the minds of many non-Europeans the specter of a "Fortress Europe"—a powerful but inward-looking and protectionist block—so one must consider the possibility that a Europe of regions may lead to forms of cultural protectionism even more exclusive and bigoted than those practiced by the nation-states.

The danger is particularly acute in the case of non-European cultures. Present demographic trends tell us clearly that in a few decades European society will become multiracial to an extent unknown since the fall of the Roman Empire. How to preserve and invigorate this new kind of cultural diversity is the real challenge for the next generation of Europeans. The experience of the United States shows that the problem is difficult but not insoluble.

NOTES

1. Stein Rokkan, "Dimensions of State Formation and Nation-Building: A Possible Paradigm for Research on Variations within Europe," in *The Formation of National States in Western Europe* (Charles Tilly ed. 1975), at 562–600.

2. Eugen Weber, *Peasants into Frenchmen* (1979), at 67.

3. Aristide R. Zolberg, "Ethnic Regionalism in Europe," in *The State in Europe* (Arthur Cyr ed. 1975), at 23–42.

4. Id. at p. 27.

5. Ernest Gellner, *Nationalism and the Two Forms of Cohesion in Complex Societies* (1983), pp. 165–87.

6. Quoted by Weber, supra note 2, p. 72.

7. Id. at pp. 168–69.

8. Rudolf Schlesinger, *Federalism in Central and Eastern Europe* (1970, reprint of 1945 edition).

9. Id. at 91.

10. Hagen Schulze, *Weimar* (1982), at 86–104.

11. Gellner, supra note 5, at 175.

12. Cited in Stanley Hoffman, *Sur la France* (1976), at 172.

13. Albert O. Hirschman, "Three Uses of Political Economy in Analyzing European Integration," in *Essays in Trespassing* (1981), at 280.

14. John F. Coverdale, "Regional Challenges to the Nation State: The Case of Spain," in *The State in Europe*, supra note 3, at 43–65.

15. Luigi Condorelli, "The Powers of Regions in the Field of External Relations: The Italian Experience," in *Regionalism in European Politics* (Roger Moran ed. 1986), at 144–54.

4

Putting Up and Putting Down:
Tolerance Reconsidered

MARTHA MINOW

One of the paradoxes of liberal societies arises from their commitment to tolerance.[1] A society committed to respecting the viewpoints and customs of diverse people within a pluralistic society inevitably encounters the challenge posed by those who themselves do not agree to respect the viewpoints or customs of others. Paradoxically, the liberal commitment to tolerance required, at some point, intolerance for those who would reject that very commitment.

Imagine this paradox, however, from the perspective of the member of a group who rejects the liberal commitment to respect the viewpoints or customs of others yet lives in a liberal society. This person may see toleration for variety a threat to the integrity and coherence of his or her community's way of life.[2] This perspective is perhaps made even more understandable when a further assumption of liberal societies is brought to view. Liberalism treats the proper unit for concern as the separate and distinct individual, who bears rights to develop and express viewpoints that then deserve tolerance, and who is obliged to tolerate others. A contrasting assumption, however, identifies the individual as importantly located within a group of shared traditions.[3] Someone proceeding with this contrasting assumption could argue that true tolerance requires recognition and respect for this contrasting mode of group identity. A diverse society would include some subcommunities that do not embrace the attitudes of liberal society and instead make commitments contrary to tolerance. Tolerance then would require respect even for a subcommunity that inculcates attitudes that are inconsistent with—indeed, intolerant of—the liberal commitments to individual rights and to obligations of tolerance. Unless the larger society respects such a subcommunity, it threatens the latter's very viability and existence.[4] Paradoxically, perhaps, this subcommunity views liberal tolerance as intolerance. Indeed, to the subcommunity, tolerance that stops short of accommodation is in effect intolerance, and tolerance that imposes routes of access to the larger society for each individual inside the subcommunity represents an invasion of the subcommunity's values and ways of life.

Tolerance without accommodation perpetuates assumptions that those who put up with others are actually superior to those others. Yet from another perspective, the very injunction to put up with others may be experienced as putting down some ways of life.

Now consider the debate between these two perspectives on tolerance in the context of another debate—the debate over allocating political and legal authority among local, state, national, and international levels of government. One might suppose that allocation of primary political power to local authorities would preserve cultural diversity and increasing grants or concessions of authority to centralized or coordinated authorities would risk interference with the cultural diversity. A closer look at the actual worldwide experience of cultural diversity demonstrates many contrary patterns. Often, increased centralization affords new protection for minority subgroups that otherwise face intolerance by local authorities.

Centralized rather than decentralized authority may be more protective of subgroups because local governmental units seldom correspond to homogeneous communities. Thus, even with the most decentralized form of official authority, potential conflicts among cultural groups and tensions between majorities and minorities arise and persist. Centralized authorities may be more likely to pursue norms of tolerance because of pressures to solicit respect and maintain legitimacy among a broader array of interest groups and communities.

Perhaps the only conclusion to be drawn is that the content of the norms adopted by a government, at whatever level, will be more relevant to the question of tolerance for diverse cultures than will the actual level of government entrusted with final authority on the question. A local, state, national, or transnational authority could embrace a policy of respect for the practices adopted by a minority subcommunity. Similarly, any level of governmental authority could adopt a rule that is intolerant of cultural practices of deviations from the rules applicable to the majority.

In sum, like the paradox of tolerance itself, a related paradox arises in the choices from among competing models of relationships between and among local, regional, national, and international political units—and even nongovernmental units, such as designated religious institutions. A commitment to respect diversity may seem to support respect for the more immediate levels of government through which policies tailored to particular communities may be developed. Yet minority groups in any given community may find greater support for their different needs and interests in a strong political authority that announces protections for minorities and restricts the prerogatives of local authorities. A political commitment to diversity may require, at some point, regulation of the self-determination processes of local authorities in order to protect subgroups within their midst, even though the local authorities themselves may assert the goal of diversity in order to preserve their own autonomy.

There is still another twist to the problem. Development of centralized authority structures that recognize and implement rights contrary to the preferences of local authorities may create avenues for individuals to challenge practices of subgroups and may thereby pose a threat to the autonomy and vitality of distinctive cultures. Cultural subcommunities thus may clash with the prerogatives of local authorities, the preferences of centralized authorities, and the commitments of any governmental authority to respect rights of individuals to leave or reject aspects of a subcommunity. The creation of centralized authorities empowered to protect subgroups may itself threaten the viability of subgroups by elaborating rights for individuals to escape subgroups. Centralized authority may challenge cultural diversity in other ways as well, especially in pursuing goals that are insensitive to, or disruptive of, some forms of cultural practice and identity.

These issues are vital as various nations and continents struggle with relationships among subgroups in their midst. Will adoption of national and international conceptions of individual rights promote the ideals of tolerance or impose one from among competing perspectives about individuality, group identity, and fundamental values? As the European Community heads toward 1992 and promotes harmonization of economic and regulatory arrangements, the treatment of ethnic and religious subgroups will surface even if not intended as a subject for concern. As the United States and Canada struggle with new waves of immigrants, old issues about the treatment of subgroups will be posed in the context of evolving legal rights. Similar issues in India, Sri Lanka, the Soviet Union, and other parts of the world have inspired scholarly and political attention.[5]

The disparity between solutions that emphasize the rights of each distinct individual and solutions that recognize a realm of self-governance for subgroups becomes especially salient when women's rights, pronounced by central governments, conflict with deference to distinctive cultural groupings that operate on contrary assumptions about women, families, and communities. With the potential conflict between women's rights and respect for cultural differences as a recurring concern, this chapter examines the issues of tolerance, first by discussing definitions and assumptions, then by exploring the challenges to cultural diversity that arise across a range of contemporary societies. The final section turns to the potential threats to cultural diversity posed by varied relationships among levels of government through a contrast between the United States and Canada. The discussion offers a distinction between threats to cultural diversity posed by failures of respect and threats posed by the creation of individual rights reaching within the traditional cultural subgroups, although this distinction may not be meaningful to members of subgroups confronting a challenge to their self-determination. The chapter also develops arguments for maintaining cultural diversity while articulating a conception of oppression to set the boundaries of tolerance. Consequences of these arguments for models of governmental authority are suggested, with special attention to developments emerging in Europe. Finally, the presentation recommends, and attempts to exemplify, a recognition of the long-standing tensions and paradoxes of tolerance, centralization, and decentralization, and respect for individuals and groups.

PRELUDE: STARTING POINTS

The very terms used to discuss the issues addressed here embody the ambiguities and disagreements engendered by the topics rather than the tools for sorting them out. At the risk of seeming didactic and the probably greater risk of proving inconsistent over the course of the discussion, this section offers some basic definitions for the chapter's central concepts. No claim is made to resolve persistent disputes over the meanings of contested terms, but here are working definitions, subject to modification in light of the ensuing discussion.

Culture refers to a way of life shared by a group; the way of life may be constituted by daily habits of meals and dress, by habitual assumptions that are shared (often without discussion), by a shared language, by shared religious beliefs or practices, by a shared way of making life meaningful, or by a shared heritage or tradition or a collective intent to create one. There may be conflict and disputes within a culture; membership is determined by the culture and its own rules and customs regarding membership.[6]

Subgroup refers to a group living or working within a larger group and having members who identify themselves as a distinctive enclave or as otherwise collectively different from others in the larger group; a subgroup may itself represent a culture of members of one culture that have moved to another country or society where other culture(s) also exist or predominate.[7]

Tolerance is a political and psychological stance toward varieties of viewpoints, customs, and behaviors that signals passive acceptance and that allows that variety to exist without interference or disapproval.[8]

Respect for cultural diversity is a more active demand than tolerance, for it may call for accommodation of subgroup practices and therefore changes in dominant institutions.[9]

Federalism refers to a structure of governmental relationships that permits integration among different levels of authority without absorbing local authorities into a centralized, superior or higher authority; it represents simultaneously the diffusion of power and its concentration in order to achieve common or shared ends, including continued respect for the diffusion of power.[10]

Even with these definitions as starting points, we are not likely to understand how and where we agree and disagree without further statements of assumptions. Let me start by explaining my assumption that preserving distinctive cultural groups is a worthy social and political goal. I understand that this is not obvious. Some may argue a contrary view on the grounds that many of the groups that concern me are "traditional" and outdated, especially since their origins in preindustrial societies predispose them to frequent clashes with the economic and social practices of an industrialized and even postindustrialized world. Other critics may emphasize the constant risk of conflict posed by distinctive culturaland ethnic groups. From their perspective, integration and assimilation are important goals as well as important means to promote peace. Why, then, should we even seek to protect cultural minorities?

From the vantage point of a cultural minority, preserving cultural diversity is a matter of self-preservation. Diversity here becomes a code word for allowing minority groups to retain some autonomy. From the vantage point of majorities, why should cultural diversity be valued? Perhaps it should be enough for them that members of minority cultures advocate preserving cultural diversity, but this argument has never been enough, practically or even theoretically. Nor is the goal of preserving cultural diversity defensible solely in terms of a liberal commitment to tolerance, for there are considerable shortcomings in such a commitment as a means to advance the goal of preserving opportunities for potentially intolerant subcommunities to exist and grow.

One can think of three reasons why majorities that are not part of traditional subcultures should be interested in preserving cultural diversity. The first matches the challenge put by many defenders of traditional cultures and by many contemporary advocates of republicanism, feminism, and communitarianism who criticize political systems that prize only individual liberty without valuing primary group identities.[11] They argue that diverse subcultures provide settings in which individuals can develop a sense of themselves through their membership in groups joined by common histories and common commitments. For many people who define themselves, at least in part, in terms of a group identity, that identity is as much chosen as found; the group's "existence and relations one experiences as always having been."[12] Such a sense of self, constituted in membership that is both prior to the self and chosen or reaffirmed, provides a basis for psychological and social stability.

Second, multiple communities of meaning also provide some check against a kind of absolute authority structure that could suppress alternatives, thereby posing grave risks of totalitarian power as well as poor judgment.[13] De Tocqueville was not the first or the last to note how intermediate organizations provide important buffers between the individual and the state and diffuse that potential tyranny of a centralized government, as does a federal system of government and the separation of powers.[14]

Third, in a real sense, tolerance and equality depend upon the very preservation of differences that could become subject to tolerance and equal treatment. The presence of the "other" is also critical for oppressing them, as Hegel so powerfully explored in his discussion of the master's need for the slave.[15] There is no "other" to oppress if the master destroys the slave. But a more subtle need for the "other" arises in commitments to respect differences as well, even in the course of articulating one's own values.[16]

Despite these reasons for preserving cultural diversity, doing so faces increasing challenges, explored in the next section.

THEMES OF VARIATION: CHALLENGES TO CULTURAL DIVERSITY

> [T]he more perceptive [critics of liberalism] recognized in its espousal of tolerance the principal threat to the traditional society of shared values and community integration.
>
> —Robert Paul Wolff[17]

> We are both on to our oppression and tricked by it.
>
> —Kate Bartlett[18]

Intolerance by official governmental acts presents obvious threats to cultural diversity. When the Supreme Court of the United States directed the enforcement of state laws against polygamy, it manifested "implacable hostility" to the Mormon religion and community.[19] Even more virulent forms of governmental hostility appeared in the U.S. Internment of Japanese-Americans during World War II,[20] and U.S. and Canadian disregard for the land claims of their native peoples. The history of slavery in the United States presents a tortured strain in the treatment of minorities, not only because of the legacies of state-supported oppression, but also because of the legacies of racial separatism advocated by whites who sought to preserve their prerogatives.

Less obvious threats to cultural diversity arise in some governmental programs that espouse tolerance, in others that ostensibly pursue aims unrelated to either promoting or harming cultural diversity, and in still others that pursue policies against discrimination or domination even where embedded within historic cultural practices.

Threats to Cultural Diversity from Limited Views of Tolerance and Equality

Governmental programs embracing a commitment to equality may appear to implement tolerance for persons with varied religious, ethnic, and linguistic backgrounds. The actual interpretation of equality used in designing school programs and employment conditions, however, may impose one set of cultural norms that fail to respect and may even undermine other cultural traditions. An employer may seek out employees with varied cultural practices in pursuit of equality and yet impose rules for the workplace governing dress, diet, hours, or language that burden the practices or beliefs of members of a cultural minority. Legal challenges to such rules may sometimes secure judicial protection for the minority, although usually without the result of changing the workplace rules.

For example, a series of decisions by the Supreme Court have required state unemployment commissions to make unemployment benefits available to members of religious minorities who lost their jobs because the workplace rules were incompatible with their religious practices or beliefs.[21] These decisions could indirectly convince employers to change their practices in order to avoid increased levies to support unemployment benefits, but the decisions do not themselves directly alter the employers' prerogatives to structure the workplace in ways that burden the practices and beliefs of minority groups. When the government itself has been the employer—in the perhaps sui generis situation of the federal military—requests to accommodate minority groups have proved unavailing.[22] Failures of accommodation are hardly neutral when the rules that differently burden members of minority groups are constructed without them in mind. A form of intolerance, along with disrespect for cultural diversity, may arise in the simple adoption and enforcement of rules designed by and for members of a dominant group that in effect exclude or constrain members of minority groups.[23]

The guise of tolerance may accompany school programs that actually implement disrespect for cultural differences. A school dress code may lead school officials to bar a student who wears headgear and long hair in violation of the regulations, but what should happen when the student's appearance reflects his membership in a subgroup, such as the Sikhs?[24] Failure to accommodate such subgroup differences from the vantage point of the minority student, would be a real interference with group membership. It also would matter little to that person if the school officials and governing legal authorities announce that discrimination in such contexts is permissible if exercised on bases other than racial difference.[25]

From the vantage point of some religious and culturally conservative subcommunities, many school programs advance a liberal social philosophy promoting tolerance for varied lifestyles and beliefs at the cost of undermining the traditional values preferred by those subcommunities. In the United States, this conflict between "secular humanism" and "fundamentalist" subcultures has crystallized around the treatment of the topic of evolution in public school classrooms. In the 1920s fundamentalists pushed for and obtained state legislation prohibiting the teaching of evolution in schools receiving tax revenues. The prosecution of a teacher named John Scopes under the Tennessee statute produced a dramatic lawsuit that later became the basis for books, plays, and movies.[26] When the Supreme Court heard a similar case some forty years later, it found a state statute forbidding the teaching of evolution to violate the First Amendment's ban against the establishment of religion.[27] The Court reasoned that the statute adopted a particular religious viewpoint and its enforcement would put state power behind that viewpoint, in violation of the constitutional requirement to separate church and state. Fundamentalists, however, believe that school instruction in evolution and silence about the biblical story of creation amount to unconstitutional interference with their own beliefs and practices.

During the 1970s and 1980s, members of these groups lobbied for the passage of laws directing any teacher who instructs students in the theory of evolution to also provide instruction in "creation science," a curriculum developed by fundamentalists to challenge the theory of evolution from their perspective while studiously avoiding explicit discussion of the Bible or a divine role in creation. Court challenges to these statutes in Arkansas and Louisiana have produced judicial decisions rejecting "creation science" as religious in purpose and there-fore in violation of the establishment clause of the First Amendment.[28]

This entire story may seem an oddity produced by the combination of the United States' constitutional commitment to separate church and state and the use of state-supported schools rather than religious schools by some members of religious minorities.[29] Yet it illuminates the conflict between ostensible tol-erance, advanced by members of a secular, liberal community, and perceptions of intolerance by members of religious, conservative subcommunities. "Secular humanism," from the vantage point of certain religious subcommunities, is not a solvent of tolerance for all points of view but a conflicting belief system that threatens the integrity and viability of their own culture.[30]

Moreover, these debates highlight the contexts in which such conflicts may be most pronounced: schooling and family prerogatives about raising children. When it comes to issues surrounding the acculturation of the next generation, even traditional liberals express doubts about the ideal of tolerance. Perhaps they assign their doubts to the view that children are not the sorts of individuals entitled to toleration for their own judgments; children instead are presumed to lack the capacity and competence to form their own views and need the guidance of adults. The child cannot be the individual accorded respect because the lack of confidence in the child is the starting point for this problem. But what adults should be entrusted with the power to choose for a child? Deference to any adults already departs from the liberal commitment to tolerate unique individual dif-ferences. Parents provide the obvious group to be entrusted with power to decide about their child's schooling and upbringing. Yet if the parents seem disinclined to provide the child with the preparation for participation in the tolerant, liberal society, traditional liberals may be reluctant to extend complete toleration for whatever the parents select for the child.

Some advocates of liberal tolerance go so far as to criticize fundamentalists for their intolerance toward science, toward modernity, and toward the variety of viewpoints respected by liberals. Of course, this problem looks quite different to fundamentalist parents. They view the position of secular liberals as threatening to—and intolerant of—their ways of life. They would not claim to be neutral but instead they seek to announce and protect particular values.[31] Governmental policies to promote the preparation of children for participation in the dominant society, then, may appear to run counter to the beliefs and practices of minority groups who disapprove of qualities in the dominant society. Even decisions to require literacy in a language used by a majority in the country could be seen by some minority groups as a threat to their cultural integrity.[32]

In light of these examples, it is valuable to reconsider the meaning of tolerance and intolerance. Intolerance surely means interference with a given viewpoint or practice; it also means a refusal to accept that viewpoint or practice as some-thing that a person should be able to adopt and express. Does intolerance, though, also mean disapproval of, or disagreement with, that viewpoint or practice? That cannot be the case, because then tolerance would require the suspension of all judgments and all disagreements. Yet mere noninterference seems inadequate to convey the idea captured by tolerance, especially where noninterference occurs within a context in which the viewpoint or practice does not conform to the majority practices. The majority may stigmatize, deride, or chill the adoption of minority group viewpoints or practices. The majority may undermine the conditions subgroups need to preserve in order to flourish. Apparently equal policies that nonetheless fail to accommodate the differences of a minority culture edge toward intolerance if those policies make expression or maintenance of the minority culture's views or practices difficult or costly to members of that group. Thus, some governmental policies that aspire to equality and neutrality may be expressed by members of majority groups in ways that minority groups find threatening and intolerant of their culture.

Even where centralized authorities set out to protect a notion of group rights, such as the rights of families, the very conception of the group adopted by those authorities may depart from the group's own self-conception and impose considerable burdens as a result. For example, the European Commission and European Court have largely construed family to mean nuclear units of parents and children. This approach neglects or undervalues assertions of human rights that concern different family formations and that reflect the sincere sentiments of the parties to live together as a family, to enter or remain in a country where family members reside, to obtain custody of children, or to define family in ways that depart from the majority's practices.[33]

Threats to Cultural Diversity Due to Centralized Governmental Policies

Some governmental policies designed to secure goals quite remote from the treatment of culturally diverse communities may nonetheless threaten minority groups. For example, a government plan to develop natural resources may run counter to the cultural or religious practices of a minority group.[34] Cultural subgroups may be disturbed by policies designed to promote general economic development by encouraging geographic and social mobility for workers and the skills necessary to promote such mobility. The European Community has embraced such policies to promote both the greatest possible freedom of movement for the factors of production and the greatest opportunities for success for individuals.[35] Accompanying such policies are commitments to guarantee individuals against any infringements by member states. The Community therefore bans discrimination on the basis of nationality in employment, pay, and working conditions[36] and also declares the right of individuals to move freely across the territories of member states and to reside in any of the member states to pursue employment. Further, the Community establishes rights for the spouses of such workers to set up homes in such member states, and rights for their children to be admitted to "general education, apprenticeship, and vocational courses."[37] And the Community establishes in considerable technical detail methods for aggregating time worked and benefits earned under social security systems in member countries.[38]

Promotion of free mobility of workers may appear to respect diversity, yet this set of policies represents two kinds of potential threats to cultural diversity. The first, already discussed above, can arise when the interpretation of equality excludes accommodation for differences between people or groups. If the commitment to treat workers who have traveled from Italy the same as local German workers involves no accommodation for the linguistic, religious, or ethnic differences of the Italians, "equality" will provide a sham guarantee of mobility rights. Requiring the workers to be proficient in German, for example, could be characterized as treating all workers the same, but its differential impact on Italian and German workers will undercut the vision of equality opportunity. And even if a given Italian worker is proficient in German, prohibiting the use of Italian on the job would also represent a burden on that individual and on the cultural integrity of his group.

This very refusal to accommodate group differences has been approved in the United States. A federal court of appeals ruled that an employer has the power to establish English as the language that must be used on the job, despite a worker's claim that Spanish was not only his native language but also the language used by seven out of eight of his co-workers and by 75 percent of his customers.[39] The employer allowed the workers to use Spanish when speaking with Spanish-speaking customers, but not when speaking with Spanish-speaking co-workers. The worker, Hector Garcia, had been discharged for violating the English-only rule after a Mexican-American co-worker asked about the availability of an item requested by a customer and Garcia replied in Spanish. At trial, Garcia introduced testimony that the Spanish language is the most important aspect of ethnic identification for Mexican-Americans. Despite a federal law forbidding employment discrimination on the basis of national origin, the court concluded that there is no right to speak any particular language while at work and that there was no evidence to establish that an atmosphere of racial or ethnic oppression prevailed at that workplace.

This decision might be construed as part of a larger pattern of rules designed to promote national unity even if that means subordinating linguistic diversity. If similar kinds of decisions are reached in Europe, problems may arise both in terms of unequal burdens on individuals who are linguistic minorities in the nation where they work and in terms of dangers to the cultural integrity of linguistic minority groups.[40] Failure to accommodate differences can implement a kind of intolerance even if accomplished under overarching goals, such as national unity or mobility of labor. Similar failures of accommodation for the spouses and children of workers from other countries could carry large threats to the viability of their distinct cultural identities.

A second danger arises from the sheer inducement to dislocate individuals and nuclear families from larger family and community networks. The encouragement of labor mobility will itself disrupt patterns of family and community ties that cannot be reconstituted once disassembled. The devastation of cultures by natural disasters and by wars gives us much evidence of the dependence of cultural identity on geographic and intergenerational stability. A lawsuit brought by members of a community devastated by a natural disaster successfully convinced an American court that the loss of community ties itself supported enormous damages, despite the extremely modest monetary value of the property destroyed.[41]

During the past century, the United States has witnessed economic policies that induce dislocations of families and individuals. Some corporations actually direct their employees to relocate in order to achieve promotions. Periods of economic difficulties, such as the Depression of 1929 and the contemporary period of factory closings, have forced many relocations of families and individuals. Upwardly mobile Americans typically move to new areas. Often higher education causes family and cultural groups to become dispersed. How much, if at all, do these patterns reflect deliberate policies?

Some have argued that the framers of the American Constitution contemplated a reduction of local and regional loyalties, even as they expected individuals to continue partial, lesser affiliations based on family and local community ties.[42] The framers no doubt imagined that people would remain closely attached to religious and regional identities and would secure a sense of personal and communal stability on that basis. But suspicious of groups with values distinct from the values of the whole nation and distrustful of strong political affections in general, the framers sought to fragment loyalties by creating multiple sources of authority that could each properly lay claim to the attention of individuals.[43] The framers probably never imagined the continued challenges to the balance they sought between personal attachments to subcommunities and individual citizenship in the national community.

As a nation of immigrants who displaced the native communities, the United States has undergone repeated migrations with some ethnic and cultural subcommunities developing niches in particular cities. Indeed, the initial immigrations of families from countries outside the United States produced gatherings within metropolitan and rural areas of people from the same home country or even home town. Major American cities thus developed enclaves known as Chinatown, Andersonville, or other names based on the national or ethnic origins of the group. For those who maintained their subgroup identities, a route toward a sense of national identity could be found precisely because so many other Americans could claim some subgroup identity that distinguished them from some unidentified majority.[44] Yet, after a first generation spent in urban enclaves, the second generations within many ethnic and religious groups tended to assimilate in the larger culture and move away from the cultural enclave.[45] Deliberate programs of "Americanization" designed by those already settled in the United States pushed newer immigrants to assimilate, to join the "melting pot," in which individual and group differences merged into a stew softening or even dissolving those differences.[46] The emerging public culture emphasized both individualism—rather than religious, ethnic, or other group affiliations—and conformity to practices and values cutting across all groups with the help of mass commercial markets.[47] Economic centralization reduced individual attachments to local neighborhoods and communities. People pursued job opportunities even if that meant moving across the state or across the country.

In the second half of the twentieth century, a large proportion of the population who attend college or university programs leave their families and communities and do not return because of the economic opportunities available in other locations. The explicit creation of retirement communities for elderly people in locations removed from their families and homes further scatters families. That children and grandchildren shed ethnic and religious identities of their families is a familiar white American story.[48] The story includes a sense of yearning for what was lost and a search for some replacement community or group affiliation, sometimes leading to fierce but short-term attachments to charismatic figures or popular trends, or an effort to revive what the last generation gave up. In addition, critics locate sources of anomie and alienation in the creation of "shopping mall cultures" and the replacement of local customs by a homogenized television culture.[49] Even ethnic identities may in part be taught by the mass media to people who lack more personal experiences with their different heritages.

European patterns, until recently, have been quite different. True, parts of European history surely demonstrate the extreme cruelties of discrimination and oppression motivated by animosities by some ethnic groups toward others. But the significance of place, of locale, to most Europeans is persistent; the importance of one's identity as a Sicilian, or as someone from Turin, stems from a sense of family, history, and continuity unlikely to change for most Europeans even in the face of growing economic centralization. It may be worth considering, nonetheless, how the policies promoting free mobility of workers could push toward some resemblance with the experience in the United States. Economic practices and policies have recruited workers from various countries to leave their homes and work elsewhere in Europe. One observer comments that "[the] result was to create polyethnic hierarchies on European soil, analogous to similar hierarchies which had existed in European colonial empires before the wars, and in lands of European overseas settlement from the moment of initial immigration. Thus we can say that Europe's proudest nations were catching up with the rest of the world, willy-nilly—or sinking to its level, if one values ethnic unity and cultural cohesiveness more highly than wealth and power."[50] In this way, governmental programs that ostensibly pursue aims unrelated to either promoting or harming cultural diversity, such as policies in favor of economic development and coordination, may disturb patterns of cultural diversity.[51]

Threats to Cultural Subgroups Posed by Individual Rights

A final challenge to cultural diversity arises from governmental policies that directly assault practices internal to distinctive cultures by forbidding discrimination or domination on the basis of gender, race, religion, or disability even where such practices are embedded within cultural traditions.[52] Here, centralized governmental policies directly implement the liberal vision of the individual as the proper unit of analysis and proper locus for rights and tolerance, despite contrary cultural traditions that treat the family or the social group as the proper unit of analysis and locus for tolerance. One conflict between a liberal norm against gender discrimination arose where the government authority offered jobs to women as school bus drivers, but members of a religious community refused to ride the bus on the grounds that their community would not allow women to hold such jobs. Another arose where a religiously sponsored university faced the loss of its tax-exempt status under federal law because it refused on religious grounds to permit interracial dating among its students.[53] Yet another conflict occurred where a health club, owned by a religious organization, dismissed an employee who had lapsed from religious observance. The statute forbidding employment discrimination on the basis of religious identity would have prevented any other kind of employer from using religious observance in a dismissal decision, but the Supreme Court found an exemption for religious organizations from this ban against discrimination compatible with the Constitution.[54]

In each of these cases a direct tension arises between respect for the practices and preferences of a subgroup (organized around cultural identity or voluntary affiliation) and commitment to liberal value of nondiscrimination on the basis of gender, race, religion, or other immutable traits.[55] Here, a threat to cultural integrity may accompany enforcement of antidiscrimination principles, yet arguments for enforcing those principles may be weighty and even sponsored by many who otherwise favor sensitivity to cultural differences.[56] Enforcement of antidiscrimination principles should not be endorsed, however, without at least noting and weighing the cost to the preexisting cultural communities whose self-determination and integrity may be damaged or undermined.[57] Especially where intergenerational issues appear, as in the education and care of children, there may arise direct collisions between the priorities of a subcommunity and a liberal concern for individuals, apart from their subgroup identities.

In sum, threats to the preservation of distinctive cultures thus may arise in insensitive applications of equality norms that burden members of minority groups by treating them as though they were the same as members of majorities. A different source of threat occurs as centralized authorities pursue goals, such as national unity or international harmonization, that devalue cultural differences or prompt geographic dislocation. A final threat accompanies enforcement of antidiscrimination norms that challenge the contrary rules developed within some cultural traditions. In each instance the conflicts arise in part when governments treat individuals as individuals, rather than as members of extended families and cultural and religious groups. And in each instance what may seem justified on a theory of liberal tolerance may, to a minority group, seem severe disrespect for cultural diversity.

INTERRUPTION AND DISRUPTION FROM ANOTHER PERSPECTIVE: WHO MIGHT BE OPPRESSED BY PRESERVING DISTINCTIVE CULTURES?

> You will also have to come to terms with the sense of alienation, of not belonging, of having your world thoroughly disrupted, having it criticized and scrutinized from the point of view of those who have been harmed by it, having important concepts central to it dismissed, being viewed with mistrust, being seen as of no consequence except as an object of mistrust.
> —Maria Lugones and Elizabeth Spelman[58]

I have tried up to this point to imagine how liberal norms of tolerance may seem disrespectful and even threatening to minority subgroups. This risks taking that subgroup's perceptions, not just as a starting point, but as the endpoint for analysis. It also risks implying that members of the subgroups are in agreement and, together, view all threats to cultural integrity the same way. The last set of threats, posed by central governmental commitments against discrimination on the basis of race, gender, religion, and other characteristics, may well seem as harmful to some members of cultural subgroups as do any other external challenges. Threats to cultural integrity due to antidiscrimination policies, however, stand on a different footing and we need to change course in the analysis here. Tolerance, as defined earlier, is a political and psychological stance toward varieties of viewpoints, customs, and behaviors that signals acceptance and that allows that variety to exist without interference or disapproval. If the burden of the previous section was to show that tolerance, so defined, often requires more than mere noninterference, the burden of this section is to suggest that tolerance is not an unqualified good, and should be limited in the case of viewpoints, customs, and behaviors that systematically oppress members of the group.

In general, it is often useful to contrast a subcommunity's desire to export to the rest of the society its values that contradict the broader society's own commitments with its desire to secure space free from intrusion to develop and perform its own practices.[59] The subgroup is often more able to persuade the majority to allow it separate space than to accept and implement its rules— perhaps about marriage, childrearing, or diet—for everyone else. Therefore, accommodations that exempt the subgroup from societal rules or that devolve authority to the subgroup for self-governance over particular matters are familiar measures to implement tolerance while leaving the dominant culture unchanged.[60] The subgroup may thus secure greater deference in the name of autonomous self-governance than it would if it sought to influence or control the larger society.

This distinction does not work well when the group seeks to exercise its autonomy in ways that can be seen to discriminate against or oppress members of its own group who would be protected by antidiscrimination principles embraced by the larger society.[61] When a religious subgroup implements practices that systematically subordinate some of its members, such as women and children, deference to the self-government and autonomy of the group is obviously not well placed. Indeed, this situation elicits several questions: Should the centralized government's guarantees of individual rights against discrimination be available to challenge those practices? Should the secular courts, for example, hear a dispute brought by a woman member of a religious community who claims that her employment contract with a church school violates the law against sex discrimination by requiring her to resign if she becomes pregnant? And should the state's courts be available to hear an Indian woman who challenges her tribe's rules about property, inheritance, and the tribal status of children for denying to women rights accorded to male members?[62]

The problem is not unusual. Collisions between norms against gender discrimination and commitments to cultural diversity arise over marriage and divorce rules that in many subgroups disadvantage women.[63] Some subgroup views about abortion collide with women's rights of reproductive choice.[64] Some groups perform clitoridectomies on their infant girls despite state laws deeming such practices child abuse. Others promote as a religious rite the self-sacrifice of a widow when her husband is buried, again despite governmental laws prohibiting such practices. And cultural traditions justifying physical abuse of women and children clash with emerging public policies punishing such conduct.

There are several options for the secular public authority. It can permit, with varying degrees of affirmative assistance, access to its courts and agencies and application of its general antidiscrimination rules. If this is the option selected, however, the state officials should address whether pursuing this route in effect requires the complainant to leave her community and face its rejection of her because of her disloyalty.[65] If so, this option becomes largely subsumed by a second option: The state could work to ensure the possibility of exit for any member of a subcommunity who seeks it. This would be no minor matter, especially since communicating the possibilities for exit could inject the state into the educational system of the subgroup, and because simply providing the option of exit already changes the meaning of the group and of group membership if the group has used metaphors of family, natural origins, or divine command to explain itself.[66] At the same time, the exit option may seem so drastic that it provides little aid to any member who views that as too great a sacrifice to be traded against an individual right.

As a third option, the state could require the subgroup to establish procedures internal to the group to permit individuals to bring claims of unfair treatment. The state could even impose certain substantive norms, such as a ban against gender discrimination, while leaving it to the subgroup's own governance mechanisms to implement those norms. This approach can be attacked as both too intrusive and not intrusive enough. By dictating requirements of participatory processes, individual hearings, and norms of equality, the centralized authorities would be invading and could be changing the core elements of a subgroup's self-governance. At the same time, by leaving interpretation and enforcement to those already in charge, the centralized authorities may be consigning the individual complainant, not only to inevitable failure, but to the status of a resented renegade purveying the outside threat to the subgroup's integrity. This option is worth considering, however, at least as an effort to acknowledge that "preserving distinctive cultures" does not mean preserving them in amber but instead allowing them to grow and change in light of the struggles of their members and the pressures from outside challenges.

Together, these options explore what Hirschman has identified as "exit" and "voice."[67] They appear against a backdrop of presumed loyalty by subgroup members to their group, yet the very discussion of options like exit or voice makes loyalty merely another option, rather than the necessary state of affairs, and elevates the individual and her choices as the important unit of analysis. This may be precisely what the subgroup's practices are designed to avoid. Thus, if we remain in the framework of tolerance and ricochet between the perspectives of the dominant societal groups and the subgroups, there seems to be no answer, and no winning solution.

That cannot be right. What is missing is an acknowledgement that it is impossible to be neutral in the struggle between points of view and a normative commitment. What is missing is a substantive theory, a theory of oppression. I suggest this notion of oppression because it raises the issue of power implicit in the competition between points of view about tolerance; the very idea of tolerance as "putting up with" those one does not like depends, implicitly, on the view that those who "put up" have the power not to, in fact, have the power to reject, or stigmatize, or oppress the others. The notion of oppression enables a meeting ground between a commitment to preserve distinctive cultures and a commitment to implement laws against gender discrimination. Both commitments are efforts to resist what otherwise would be the likely course of events by dint of the distribution of power: The subgroups would risk domination by the majority, and women, given their historical treatment by multitudes of cultural and religious groups, risk degradation or misuse by men.[68]

In a recent article Iris Marion Young offers an elaboration of oppression as a concept to be applied to actual social situations.[69] "Oppression is the inhibition of a group through a vast network of everyday practices, attitudes, assumptions, behaviors, and institutional rules."[70] She also suggests five possible dimensions of oppression. Because they enable contrasting insights into the collisions between preservation of distinctive cultures and norms against gender discrimination, I examine them here in detail.

First, Young identifies exploitation as the "domination [that] occurs through a steady process of the transfer of the results of the labor of some people to benefit others."[71] One of the intriguing qualities of this dimension is its ambiguity about the scope of labor: Does it include, as feminist theorists have advocated, reproductive activities? If not, the concept may systematically devalue women's contribution to a family; if so, the concept may be useful in evaluating a problem such as the patrilineal rules of an Indian tribe or the restrictions on reproductive choice imposed by a particular subgroup contrary to the dominant society's position.

Second, Young discusses marginalization, which denotes the ways that an individual or group may be expelled from useful participation in social life, citizenship, and productivity.[72] If the subgroup systematically excludes women from participation in its social life, in its governance, and in its productive activities, should we conclude that it oppresses women? This, too, is a complicated question. The very definition of social life and of people's roles in it may vary by subgroup, and gender-based roles are so familiar in social activities that notions of equality have proved slippery and divisive. The Jewish requirement that a husband grant a wife a religious bill of divorcement before she may be considered properly divorced under religious law could be interpreted as a gender-based exclusion, especially if it means that women are systematically excluded from remarriage within the religion simply because their husbands refuse to follow this religious law while securing a secular divorce. On the issues of political governance and productive activities, gender-based exclusions could well be examined, and if demonstrated, a case for gender-based oppression could be supported.[73]

Young's third dimension of oppression is powerlessness; she defines it with a special focus on the contrast between professionals and nonprofessionals in societies that accord to professionals much greater autonomy and opportunity for creativity in their work.[74] A more general meaning of powerlessness could also be pursued in exploring the possibilities of oppression against women by subgroups. A sophisticated study of the practice of Sati (the self-sacrifice by a widow at the funeral of her husband) suggests that this practice offers a venerated position for the woman who chooses it; she is deemed to escape the lowly spiritual status usually assigned to women and to offer spiritual benefits to her family and her community by choosing this act.[75] Indeed, the practice can be considered oppressive only in light of the larger question: What kind of society would create so few options for veneration for women that suicide upon the death of the husband would be a desired opportunity?

Young then introduces the notion of cultural imperialism[76] as "the experience of existing with a society whose dominant meanings render the particular perspectives and point of view of one's own group invisible at the same time as they stereotype one's group and mark it out as the Other." Young expressly cites women as likely to be subjected to this experience, and contemporary debates about women's status in cultural forms, academic disciplines, and political discourse may support the charge of imperialism against women by the dominant society. Assessment of the treatment of women's experience in subgroups may reveal that women are not oppressed by the Amish or other culturally distinctive groups, and it will be difficult to determine whether any outsider can fully understand women's experiences in such subgroups. The concept of oppression on this basis may still be relevant, however, if women who are members of a subgroup themselves claim that their experiences are rendered invisible or stereotyped by their own group.

Young's final dimension of oppression is systemic violence, directed on the basis of group membership.[77] Feminist analyses of rape and pornography in dominant Western culture maintain that these are instances of oppression as systemic violence against women. Some also argue that efforts to regulate and restrict abortion represent systemic violence against women by exposing women to risks of illegal and dangerous abortions or by constraining women's own control over their own bodies. These are challenging arguments that redefine violence, and perhaps, instead, a different quality than oppression should be articulated to convey the point.

Indeed, Young's conception of oppression is only one initial point of departure in what one hopes will be a sustained scholarly effort to give meaning to the concept. Studies of the sources of oppression from economic and social structures would be important for this effort. Work by scholars on these subjects seldom enters the discourse of lawyers and judges. Devising ways to talk about oppression will be critical to any effort by law to take tolerance seriously, from everyone's point of view. Part of this effort must include a search to resist becoming party to oppression in the very critique of oppression. As Susan Griffin has written, theories of liberation begin as efforts to articulate feelings of oppression, and they restore

to the oppressed a belief in the self and in the authority of the self to determine what is real. . . . But when a theory is transformed into an ideology it begins to destroy the self and self-knowledge. . . . It organizes experience according to itself, without touching experience. . . . It is annoyed by any detail which does not fit into its world view. Begun as a cry against the denial of truth, now it denies any truth which does not fit into its scheme. Begun as a way to restore one's sense of reality, now it attempts to discipline real people, to remake natural beings after its own image. All that it fails to explain it records as dangerous. All that makes it question, it regards as its enemy. Begun as a theory of liberation, it is threatened by new theories of liberation; slowly, it builds a prison for the mind.[78]

The very method of inquiry into oppression, then, must not become intolerant of challenges. If only because the tension between admirable tolerance and despicable oppression undoubtedly remains even in the construction of theory, it should not be surprising that I cannot here recommend the optimal public policy to resolve the tension. Indeed, it is because of my conviction that the struggle to give content to the criteria of oppression will require participation by people who experience it in countless ways and varied settings that I turn now to the procedural, but no less important, questions of the allocation of governmental powers and its impact on dilemmas of tolerance.

FEDERALISM AND CULTURAL DIVERSITY

> [T]he viability of a federal society depends upon the capacity of citizens to have recourse to principles of constitutional choice in organizing concurrent communities of interest for solving problems arising from the inconveniences that neighborhood brings.
>
> —Vincent Ostrom[79]

> Lo and behold, here in our midst is dissimilarity that simply could not be squelched, and that now is insisting on its right to flourish.
>
> —Jane Jacobs[80]

The problems of tolerance and intolerance are familiar and enduring. Perhaps any group of people will find some distinctions among the people in their midst that pose risks of discrimination and that invite majorities to interfere with minorities. But the problems of tolerance and intolerance increase with the lack of coincidence between territorial boundaries and cultural boundaries. Geographical boundaries fail to match up with cultural boundaries as nation states form and reform with boundaries that encompass members of many different cultural groups, and as members of different cultural groups move to nation-states where they have not previously lived. One observer commented that "[t]here are thousands of ethnic, tribal, racial, lingual and ethno-religious communities" while "there are only about 150 'nation' states, within which heterogeneous groups coexist."[81]

Given this diversity of cultural groupings within nation-states, there are historic and persistent demands for self-governance by local and regional authorities that claim greater identification with, and responsiveness to, their particular cultural groups. Some groups remain minorities even at the local and regional levels. They may find more protection for their interests—more promise of tolerance— if a centralized national government retains control. Still other groups may believe that international accords better ensure tolerance, perhaps because they represent cultures that are minorities in their own country of residence but majorities elsewhere, or perhaps because the norms developed in international accords better recognize their rights or needs.[82] Some groups may discover that no particular form of official policy within a nation provides protection for cultural autonomy, self-governance, or basic human rights; they may find more promising assistance in the sphere of international human rights. The experience of Native Americans in the United States may provide such an example. Perhaps no greater variety of federalism theories has appeared in American jurisprudence than here; from coordinate sovereigns, to dependent nations, to wards protected by the nation-state, to individuals with some special claims, Native Americans have seen the range of legal statuses and witnessed the inventive interpretation of these statuses by administrators and judges to repeatedly deny the power and entitlements of these culturally distinctive groups.

The variety of governmental relationships connecting local, regional, national, and international authorities carries both promise and threats to cultural diversity. In the abstract, it is not obvious that any particular allocation of responsibility among levels of government will ensure more tolerance for cultural diversity than any other. Contextual, historical inquiries can provide some illumination of the consequences of varied patterns of relationships among local, regional, national, and international authorities for the preservation of cultural diversity.[83] In part, such inquiries replay the contrast between the liberal conception of individual rights and alternative notions of group identity. Different cultural groups, at different times, have found more help through one of these conceptions over the other, and different levels of governmental authorities have similarly found varied reasons for adopting one rather than the other. The intersection of pluralism and federalism problems appears in two historical examples in the United States. These examples help to explain the support for centralized, national governance in the United States as part of the campaign to protect cultural diversity. Yet a contrasting set of examples, drawn from the Canadian experience, identifies a context in which decentralized control has been more effectively linked to the preservation of distinctive cultures and highlights particular traits of the United States experience that warrant caution before emulation.

Two Stories from the United States

The first story arises from the presence, in the United States, of minority groups that have sought a refuge. Such groups sought space within which to construct their own community and preserve their own culture. What chance do such groups have, given the overlapping and concurrent sovereign authorities of local, state, and national governments? The facts behind the United States Supreme Court decision in *Wisconsin v. Yoder*[84] illuminate the problem and demonstrate the intersection between issues of tolerance for cultural differences and choices among levels of governmental control. A law adopted by the state of Wisconsin required all children to attend school until they reached the age of sixteen; otherwise, their parents would be subject to a fine. Members of the Amish community, who opposed schooling for their children past the eighth grade,[85] challenged this law as an intrusion on their rights to exercise their religion freely, as guaranteed by the First Amendment to the Constitution. They argued that their religion called for a way of life tied to the local farming activities and deliberately shielding community members from the industrial and heterogeneous world. They demonstrated, to the satisfaction of the Court, that these beliefs were religiously motivated and thus protected under the Constitution.

Wisconsin maintained, however, that it represented the interests of the broader community and the children themselves in ensuring that all of its children received the same minimum amount of educational instruction. As pursued in a separate opinion by one Supreme Court justice, concern for the children's interests should include a commitment to the future and preserve options for individual children who might wish to leave the Amish community as adults—and who then could well need the extra years of school instruction required by the state.[86] The majority on the Court concluded that the burdens placed on the religious freedoms of the Amish could not be justified by the state's espoused interests, especially because, in the Court's view, the Amish already fulfilled many of the state's purposes by ensuring that its children become self-sufficient and productive individuals.

The case presents in sharp relief the potential conflict between and among subcommunity cultural traditions, state-level public demands, and federal constitutional guarantees of toleration for religious diversity. The case also presents the tension between a conception of the group, in which adults speak for children, and the individual as the focus for concerns about tolerance. A critic of the decision could argue that the Court failed to protect the rights of individual Amish children to develop the abilities and experiences that would enable free choice about how to live;[87] a defender could celebrate the Court's willingness to sacrifice a liberal value of individual choice through respect for the subcommunity's choice about how to raise their children.[88]

For yet another layer of complexity, the enforcement of a commitment to diversity by a tribunal or legal structure that is maintained by the state, national, or transnational authority, itself already represents a considerable intrusion on the cultural practices of a subgroup forced to try to persuade people outside of itself. From the subgroup's perspective, complete tolerance may require recognition of that group's own right to self-determination and self-governance, beyond the control or even direct permission of state, national, or international authorities. This concept involves a recognition of the plurality of sources of legal authority, rather than an assumption that all sources of legal authority fit together in one united whole.[89] The spheres of authority, in this view, are not nested in a hierarchy, with each successive level subsuming the more local and intimate ones, but instead, the subcommunity provides a reference point for its members that sets them outside the structures of governmental authority. It is quite plausible that if the Amish had lost in the Supreme Court, they would have left Wisconsin, and indeed, left the United States, for their allegiance to these sovereign political authorities remains overshadowed by their religious and cultural identities.

For individuals and subgroups, then, the choice from among competing levels of authority includes options outside the scheme of a coordinated federal structure devised within one constitutional framework, or even within one international federation. Decisions reached within such structures do not end the matter for members of subgroups who are themselves tolerating the secular political arrangement only as long as it remains compatible with their own sense of alternative authorities. The pilgrim groups who helped to settle America, and lent their stories to the myths of America's founding, represent just this sort of migration to the new locale due to conscientious objection to the political choices in their home state.

For groups that have migrated to the United States from another country, persistent conflicts among levels of government in governing their affairs etch the results of interest-group politics and of larger political tides in the country. Here is a second story about United States federalism and pluralism: the story of bilingual education. A local community may decide to provide within its schools classes conducted in the language spoken by a majority of its students, even though that is not the official language of the state within which the local community exists.[90] The state may argue that this local decision violates the state's own commitment to promote literacy in the official language and mobility for individuals who seek success beyond their local communities. The nation-state may, in turn, articulate basic rights for each student to receive an education that accommodates his or her own language background. Indeed, the federal government has done so in both a decision by the Supreme Court,[91] and in federal statutes.[92]

A federal agency took the lead in developing the acceptable forms of education for children whose primary language is not English. Those forms are designed to foster proficiency in English on a transitional basis: They include instruction in the student's native language in classroom subjects until the attainment of English proficiency, and they also emphasize literacy in the native language and respect for the children's cultural heritage.[93] Shifting political tides, however, produced a federal administration that disagreed with this approach and instead decided to return discretion to state and local authorities in the selection of programs for students lacking proficiency in English.[94] This shift of authority to state and local officials allows the adoption of programs such as "structured immersion" in which teachers primarily use English while structuring the curriculum to ease assimilation for students lacking extensive familiarity with English. Another program that local school officials can adopt is English-as-a-second-language: Linguistic minority students spend most of their school day in the regular classroom, taught in English, but they also spend part of the day receiving intensive instruction in the English language. Many advocates for the rights of language-minority students fear that increased state and local discretion will produce programs that are unresponsive to those students' needs and disrespectful of the goal of preserving their native languages and cultures.[95]

Which level of government should be entrusted with making the final decision about the language to be used in school instruction or the form of instruction? Recognition of cultural diversity may require greater authority at the national level to check the state-level effort to override local choices. The minority group's interest in national authority may be even more pronounced where it lacks the political power to secure control of the school programs at the local level—or to require self-governance powers—and finds only in the national government's intervention an ability to challenge local, as well as state, decision-making. Yet this preference for centralized authority depends on substantive commitments at that level to respond to the minority cultures' needs and preferences. Absent those commitments, the choice of federal authority may provide no greater protection for the minority groups than would state or local authorities. Perhaps, for this reason, advocates of cultural diversity have argued in favor of multiple and overlapping jurisdictions and governmental authorities. The very presence of more than one authority provides some chance for minority groups to seek a second opinion, some free space in the tension and gaps between layers and competing sovereigns, and some opportunity to correct errors made by one through recourse to another.[96] Most important will be the room to develop nonpublic norms—subcommunity values that may then be advocated at any favorable level of government.

Contrasts Between Canada and the United States

The very example of linguistic subcultures in the United States highlights an important contrast with Canada, a contrast that many observers link to differences in the two nations' experiences with federalism. Although the United States is a nation composed of people who are members of numerous linguistic communities,[97] the United States primarily employs English, and public and private authorities are authorized to implement a preference for English.[98] In contrast, Canada reflects its historical settlement by primarily two linguistic groups: English and French. Despite British rule for the early part of the Canadian history, the French communities remained powerful. The British North American Act of 1876 recognized this power by guaranteeing the political integrity of French language, civil law, and culture. Separate French-language schools maintain this cultural distinctiveness, and demands by Francophones for control over their own communities have increasingly challenged the traditional centralized structure of Canadian government.[99]

Yet an imbalance between the two language groups exists, both in terms of the numbers of people originally involved in each group and in the preferences of new immigrants to learn English and send their children to English-speaking schools, as most perceive English as the language of mobility.[100] This pattern has in some senses strengthened the Francophone resolve to pursue a separate political base in order to ensure a future for the French culture in Canada.[101] As a result, Quebec has adopted rules forcing non-Anglophone immigrant children to attend the French language schools within the province.[102] And many Canadians expressly oppose the notion of "the melting pot" that for so long dominated American attitudes toward cultural diversity.[103] These conflicts over bicultural and multiculturalism have largely been fought, in Canada, in the arena of federal-provincial relations. Some have identified the preoccupation with federalism as pivotal to Canadian identity.[104]

Ronald Watts, a professor of political studies at Queen's University in Ontario, Canada, has developed an intriguing comparison of federalism in the United States and Canada.[105] He noted first that Canada is moving from centralization toward greater regionalism, while the United States has moved from regionalism (with a constrained central government) toward greater national governmental powers.[106] He acknowledges some countertrends, such as the push toward greater decentralization in the United States in policies like Richard Nixon's and Ronald Reagan's "new federalism," and in the Canadian Charter of Rights and Freedoms of 1982, which is producing some protection at the federal level for the rights of individuals and minority groups.[107]

Watts also observes the contrasting "territorial concentration" of the most significant minority groups in each country. In Canada the French-speakers are a minority of 26 percent across the country, but their concentration in Quebec gives them an 80 percent majority in that province. In contrast, the blacks in the United States constitute 11 percent of the total population and have no majority in any state.[108] While the Francophones in Quebec push for regional power to enable greater self-governance, blacks have pursued centralized federal protection to guard against local and intolerant majorities.[109] Actually, even more may be made of this contrast than Watts affords. The unique circumstance of blacks in the United States due to the history of slavery means that blacks have for the most part lacked the political or economic power to articulate and preserve a distinctive culture, although much that is original in United States music and oratory is directly traceable to the contributions of blacks. The Francophones may have lacked a dominant economic position during many periods of Canadian history, yet historically, they had considerably more power to create their own cultural institutions than did African Americans in the United States.

Watts offers several other suggestions for the contrasting development of intergovernmental relations in Canada and the United States. He notes that the United States economy since World War II has become largely national while the Canadian economy remains largely organized at the regional level.[110] Furthermore, the United States often assigns concurrent authority to state and federal entities, prescribing supremacy for federal law and at the same time reserving to the states powers not granted to the national government.[111] Canada, in contrast, historically created areas of exclusive provincial control and areas of exclusive federal control.[112] Further, the Canadian parliamentary system and the United States checks-and-balances system provide contrasting pressures on federalist structures.[113]

Unlike the United States system, Canadian federalism has been characterized as a community of communities, the centralized, federal government is simply one of these communities, albeit a big one.[114] Perhaps, as some suggest, the significance of "a sense of place" to Canadians accompanies a self-consciousness about hyphenated (or multiple) identities,[115] unlike the United States cultivation of outside identities.[116]

As Canada struggles to interpret its Charter of Rights and Freedoms, these hypotheses about Canadian federalism will have practical tests and challenges. The decision by the Supreme Court of Canada in *Ford v. Quebec*[117] and the response of Quebec to that decision provide evidence of an experiment still unfolding. The case posed the question whether the Quebec Charter of French Language, which required all public signs and commercial advertising to use only French, infringes upon the freedom of expression guaranteed by the Canadian Charter.[118] The court reasoned that language is so intimately related to expression that "there cannot be true freedom of expression by means of language if one is prohibited from using the language of one's choice." Yet this very phrase, "one's choice," conflates the potential conflict between individual rights unavoidably presents. The opinion in essence acknowledges this contrast: "Language is not merely a means or medium of expression; it colours the content and meaning of expression. It is, as the preamble of the Charter of the French Language itself indicates, a means by which a people may express its cultural identity. It is also the means by which the individual expresses his or her personal identity and individuality." The court interpreted the guarantee of freedom of expression to extend beyond political expression to commercial speech, or, more precisely, held that the right of individuals to use the English language persists even when exercised through signs that have a commercial purpose. This decision could be characterized as the imposition by the central government of a conception of individual rights on a province that sought to protect a group against cultural domination; it could also be characterized as the search for a national common denominator of basic respect through the concept of individual freedoms despite regional differences.

If this decision were reached by the United States Supreme Court, and premised on the federal Constitution, it would be the last word, absent, that is, a constitutional amendment or a reversal by the Supreme Court itself. But under the distinctive conception of centralized and provincial powers in Canada, the decision in *Ford v. Quebec* simply served as a volley in a continuing process of centralized/provincial struggle. Quebec responded by exercising its right to override a Supreme Court decision.

This array of factors differentiating Canada and the United States helps to portray how complicated are the relationships between alternate federalist structures and cultural diversity. The particular appeal of decentralized versus centralized governmental control within a generally federalist system depends upon particular historical circumstances and the relative power and geographic concentration of cultural minorities. A federal structure with greater centralization can be used to strengthen rights for individuals, which seems to be the trend in both the United States and Canada. Assessed simply in light of experiences in Canada and the United States, asking whether a centralized government can do much to preserve distinctive cultures actually yields inconclusive results, and a demand for contextual assessments.

CONCLUDING A BEGINNING

> We have to learn to tolerate questions.
>
> —Susan Griffin[119]

This chapter began by advocating commitments to preserve distinctive cultures. This means reconceiving tolerance to include the vantage point of members of traditional subgroups that do not share the dominant liberal commitments to individual choice, experimentation, and value relativism. An argument has also been made in favor of gender equality, although in many instances, this runs counter to the practices of traditional cultures and religious groups. Together, these arguments pose a question: What mix of concerns for group rights or cultural preservation, on the one hand, and individual rights and freedoms, on the other, should a given society pursue if it hopes to respect cultural diversity without colluding in the domination or oppression of some of its own members?

Even this question makes the problem look too simple. There remain urgent needs for larger structures of political organization, economic coordination, communication, and ideology for ordering relationships among subgroups and methods for articulating and resolving conflicts. Global markets drive political centralization and coordination efforts. Nations within large sectors of the world have come together for mutual support, in part to counter competition across such sectors and in part to provide larger contexts within which to order relationships among subgroups and to define and handle the kinds of conflicts that could spell war. The allocation of governmental powers between levels and among branches of governments, and between nations and continents, poses a difficult enough question when economic and military concerns are most salient. When combined with the paradoxes and dilemmas of tolerance, these central questions of political design are enormously complicated, and comparisons of historical experiences suggest no determinate mix of powers is particularly better than another to preserve distinctive cultures or to enforce individual rights.

In short, the tensions and paradoxes explored in this chapter do not suggest solutions. Indeed, one purpose here is to argue that solutions are likely to neglect the multiple perspectives on issues of tolerance, cultural diversity, and allocation of governmental power. The search for an answer is often stymied by the faulty assumption that the right question has been asked. What questions are right profoundly reflects the point of view of the inquirer, and this fact can bedevil efforts to get beyond the acknowledged limits of one point of view. "How can a society promote tolerance?" is an inadequate question, not only because tolerance leads to passive acquiescence in existing power arrangements rather than accommodating or respecting differences, but also because tolerance risks undermining subgroups committed to particular values inconsistent with majority practices. Yet there are comparable faults in a question such as, "how can a society respect and preserve cultural diversity?" for that formulation obscures the potential tension between preserving some subcultures and promoting individual rights that may be undermined by those very groups. It is also no solution, for a complex society, simply to embrace an existing point of view in order to address questions about tolerance and cultural diversity. The challenge is to formulate an inquiry from a point of view that can be attentive to other points of view, that can acknowledge them and their differences. Once pursued, such an inquiry cannot be neutral. It is for that reason that I advocate explicit attention to the concept of oppression, even though that concept will inevitably draw debates over its meaning and its application. I suggest that respecting cultural diversity while pursuing basic liberal freedoms and individual rights must be an ongoing struggle among people who disagree about many things. In the spirit of such a struggle, scholarly and political efforts to define the notion of oppression must be pursued by people coming from different points of view.[120]

What combination of large structures and primary group identities can provide latitude for individual freedoms, respect for historically different subcommunities, and coordination of economic and political institutions and activities across locales, regions, states, and nations? Varied versions of federalism—relationships that simultaneously recognize the demands for centralization and the needs to decentralize—provide promising models for responding to this large question. At the same time, there is nothing peculiar to a federal system that exacerbates or eases problems of preserving cultural diversity. Within particular historical moments, within particular constellations of relationships among levels of government and between cultural groups, arguments for and arguments against greater centralization or greater decentralization provide avenues for both protecting and undermining cultural diversity.[121] Centralized governmental authority, historically, has been linked to the development and articulation of individual rights that may become corrosive to particular cultural traditions while advancing the freedom and self-realization of each person. There may be ways, however, that centralized governments can protect subgroups from intolerant policies of local authorities. But whatever level of government retains control on any given issue, there will persist a tension between basic rights of individuals to be free from discrimination on the basis of immutable traits and respect for subgroups so that cultural traditions may be preserved.

What may be most important is simply the existence of multiple levels of governmental authority. For it is the presence of multiple authorities that, paradoxically, gives minority groups the opportunity to seek alternatives to a singular answer. Robert Cover's work on the values of jurisdictional redundancy provides an eloquent defense of the multiple court systems in the United States as increasing the chances that errors will be corrected, and then less powerful voices will ultimately have a chance to be heard.[122] Thus, governmental powers should be allocated to multiple sources of authority in an effort to enhance the avenues for challenging public and private intolerance.

The challenge, from this vantage point, is to devise modes of inquiry that can solicit multiple perspectives rather than suppress them. At the same time, the challenge is to construct structures of governance that can acknowledge "legal pluralism"—the variety of sources of authority that include religious and cultural practices outside of the governmental hierarchy of local-national-international authority—and still retain some ability to govern with coherence.[123] What mix of respect for multiple authorities and demands for singular authorities can provide for the conflicting demands of order and freedom and also elicit respect and solicit assent from people with differing backgrounds and assumptions?[124]

I close with three images that may assist future discussion of these issues.

The first comes from Marge Piercy's novel *Woman on the Edge of Time*. The book combines two stories. The first tells of a poor woman of color who, through a series of misfortunes, finds herself in a mental hospital where she is subjected to repeated shock treatments. The second story is either the delusions of this woman—or the utopia she periodically escapes to, only to return to the mental hospital. In the utopia, the main character finds many intriguing contrasts with contemporary American society. For example, children are born only through test tubes; parents sign up for the opportunity, and in that way, parents and children are commonly of different races and backgrounds. Upon reaching adolescence, every individual changes parents and goes to stay with a new guardian, who shepherds the person through that transition to adulthood. In addition, equality on the basis of gender is unhampered by gender differences in child-bearing and child-rearing.

More to the point of the topic of tolerance, this utopian society confronted the issue of how to preserve distinctive cultures while avoiding the historical stigmas and status differentials associated with groups that were less powerful. This society decided to preserve traditional groups and promote the development of new groups, but to make group membership entirely voluntary. An adult could choose to join any group, such as a group devoted to preserving the traditions of the Iroquois Indians or another group interested in exploring and revising Reformation Protestantism. A child would participate in the group chosen by his parent or the multiple groups chosen by his multiple parents. Upon reaching adolescence, he or she could try any group joined by the guardian or any other group for that matter. In this way, the society maximized exit options by maximizing entry options. Thus, the society avoided converting all cultural traditions into mere museum artifacts or shopping-mall displays of fashions and foods.

The second image comes from an intriguing book by R. Laurence Moore called *Religious Outsiders and the Making of Americans*.[125] The book explores how each religious group in America helped to forge American history; and how each group, through time, has cultivated the idea of itself as an outsider to American culture. Thus, leaders of the Mormon Church explicitly elaborated narratives of oppression in part to strengthen a sense of group identity. American Jews did too, building on long traditions of external oppression and internal stories of chosen uniqueness. American Catholics decided to preserve the ethnic and national differences of immigrant Catholic groups and thereby ensured multiple meanings of outsider status in American culture. As Moore explores this theme in the history of Christian Scientists, Black Protestants, Fundamentalists, and early Protestant settlers, he suggests how "[r]eligious struggles engage people in elaborate strategies that on each side entail affirmation and denial, advancement and repression, of a set of cultural options."[126] And most Americans gained a sense of being American "by turning aspects of a carefully nurtured sense of separate identity against a vaguely defined concept of mainstream or dominant culture."[127] Although he does not claim that the creation of these stories about marginality explains the relative peace among enormous religious heterogenity in the United States, Moore suggests that some forms of tolerance may be promoted if everyone feels somewhat marginal.[128]

The final image, parochial as it may be, is of a law school. Imagine a law school that has celebrated its commitments to tolerance, demonstrated by its inclusion of people of varied backgrounds and political viewpoints as students and faculty. It has representatives of racial, religious, and ethnic minorities, and as large a percentage of women as any other law school. Imagine that some of its more "unusual" faculty members begin to write articles and teach courses that are deliberately not the mainstream. Some talk of feminism, some talk of multi-culturalism; some talk of economics; others of semantics and semiotics. Some of the more traditional members describe their feelings of rejection as the newer faculty members deprecate traditional work. Some of the traditionalists talk increasingly about the danger that standards are declining, and it may be necessary to deny someone tenure. Indeed, in a spectacular and prolonged battle, a woman is denied tenure. In such a context, what does tolerance mean? How can it be that a traditionalist may say, "We tolerated them, after all we appointed them, but they don't tolerate us," when a newcomer says, simultaneously, "Where's their tolerance, really?" and "I think traditional doctrinal work is bunk"? Who is putting up and who is putting down? There are more important struggles out there than what goes on in law schools. Yet if we can't make sense of tolerance and pay attention to who is oppressed by what we do in its name or in despite of it, how can we expect anyone else to?

NOTES

Thanks to Joe Singer, Brenda Cossman, Mary Ann Glendon, Lance Liebman, Frank Michelman, Judith Resnik, and members of the Stanford Legal Theory Workshop and Harvard Law Governance Seminar for suggestions and challenges. This article was originally published in the Osgoode Hall L. J., May 1990.

1. See Robert Paul Wolff, Barrington Moore, Jr., and Herbert Marcuse, *A Critique of Pure Tolerance* (1965).

2. See also Joshua Halberstam, "The Paradox of Tolerance," 14 *Philosophical Forum* 190 (1982–1983). (Tolerance cannot even arise as a question unless the two people or groups disagree with one another, and traditional orthodoxies require commitments that are deliberately intolerant, in the sense of rejecting the possibility that their tenets could be wrong.)

3. Wilson Carey McWilliams, "American Pluralism: The Older Order Passeth," in *The Americans* 293, 297 (Irving Kristol and Paul Weaver eds. 1976). (Traditionalists see humans as naturally dependent, social, and political and as requiring strong bonds to family, church, and community for the very development of personal identity; for them, virtue is more important than freedom.)

4. In particular, demands that each individual remain open to multiple viewpoints and that the community preserve rights for each individual to choose where and how to live threaten grave intolerance toward the community, its identity, and its needs. See text accompanying notes 85–89 infra.

5. See generally Donald Horowitz, *Ethnic Groups in Conflict* (1985).

6. See generally Clifford Geertz, *Local Knowledge* (1983).

7. There are many different dimensions of subgroup identity, and different subgroups differ in the particular constellation of such features as shared history, shared language, shared religion, shared geographic location, shared social status, and shared treatment by others.

8. See generally the *Oxford English Dictionary*.

9. For cogent statements of contrasting position in the contemporary debate over accommodation in the context of United States constitutional law and religion, see Michael McConnell, "Accommodation of Religion," 1985 *Supreme Court Review* 1; Mark Tushnet, "The Emerging Principle of Accommodation of Religion (Dubitante)," 76 *Georgetown Law Journal* 1961 (1988).

10. See generally *Federalism and Political Integration* (Daniel Elazar ed. 1979).

11. See generally Frank Michelman, "Law's Republic," 97 *Yale Law Journal* 1493 (1988); Suzanna Sherry, "Civic Virtue and the Feminine Voice in Constitutional Adjudication," 72 *Virginia Law Review* 543 (1986).

12. See Iris Young, "Five Faces of Oppression," 19 *Philosophical Forum* 270, 274 (Summer 1988).

13. Cf. Paul Chevigny, *More Speech* (1988) (arguing for justifications for free speech and due process on the basis of the philosophic, psychological, and political needs for dialogue).

14. See Alexis de Tocqueville, *Democracy in America* (Henry Reeve trans. 1838). De Tocqueville also warned against the tyranny of the majority, and subsequent observers have commented on the intolerance enforced by pressure to conform. See Louis Hartz, *The Liberal Tradition in America* 55–56 (1965). See also Deborah Jones Merritt, "The Guarantee Clause and State Autonomy: Federalism for a Third Century," 88 *Columbia Law Review* 1 (1988) (discussing values of federalism).

15. For a contemporary elaboration of his analysis, see Jessica Benjamin, *The Bonds of Love: Psychoanalysis, Feminism, and the Problems of Domination* 31–42, 51–84 (1988).

16. See id., at 183–224 (exploring ways to promote mutual recognition between men and women rather than patterns of domination); Judith Resnik, "Dependent Sovereigns: Indian Tribes and the Federal Courts," *University of Chicago Law Review* (forthcoming). In discussing respect for the sovereignty of Indian tribes by federal courts, Resnik notes that "[t]he degree of toleration of the 'other sovereigns' decisions enables the federal government to make plain what its own values are" in a dialectic interaction.

17. "Beyond Tolerance," in *A Critique of Pure Tolerance* 34 (1968).

18. "Book Review: Catharine MacKinnon, *Feminism Unmodified: Discourses on Life and Law*, and Susan Estrich, *Real Rape*," 13 *Signs* 879, 885 (Summer 1988).

19. Jill Norgren and Serena Nanda, *American Cultural Pluralism and Law* 81 (1988) (discussing Reynolds v. United States, 98 U.S. 146 (1879); Davis v. Beason, 133 U.S. 333 (1889); Romney v. United States, 136 U.S. 1 (1889)).

20. See Korematsu v. United States, 323 U.S. 214 (1944).

21. Sherbert v. Verner, 374 U.S. 398 (1963); Thomas v. Review Board of Indiana Employment Sec. Div., 450 U.S. 707 (1981); Hobbie v. Unemployment Appeals Comm'n, 107 S.Ct. 1046 (1987). Some Canadian cases indicate a demand for accommodation. Ont. Human Rights Comm'n v. Simpson Sears, Ltd., [1985] 2 S.C.R. 536.

22. Goldman v. Weinberger, 475 U.S. 503 (1986). (Free exercise clause does not

require an exemption from Air Force dress regulations for an Orthodox Jew who sought permission to wear a yarmulke while on active duty as a military psychologist.)

23. See generally Martha Minow, "The Supreme Court: 1986 Term—Foreword: Justice Engendered," 101 *Harvard Law Review* 10 (1987).

24. See Mandla v. Dowell Lee, [1983] All E. R. 1062 (H.L.); Benyon and Love, "Mandla and the Meaning of Racial Group," 100 *Law Quarterly Review of Public Law* 348. See also Bhinder and the Canadian Human Rights Comm'n v. Canadian National Railway Co., [1985] 2 S.C.R. 561.

25. See D. G. T. Williams, "Aspects of Equal Protection in the United Kingdom," 59 *Tulane Law Review* 959, 971 (1985).

26. See, e.g., Irving Stone, *Clarence Darrow for the Defense* (1969); *Inherit the Wind* (movie). The trial transcript was published as *The World's Most Famous Court Trial: State of Tennessee v. John Thomas Scopes* (1971). The Tennessee Supreme Court in essence reached a compromise decision in rejecting the fine against Scopes because of a procedural error but upholding the constitutionality for the statute forbidding instruction in evolution. See Norgren and Nanda, supra note 19, at 124.

27. Epperson v. Arkansas, 393 U.S. 97 (1968).

28. McLean v. Arkansas, 529 F.Supp. 1255 (E. D. Ark. 1982); Edwards v. Aguillard, 107 S.Ct. 2573 (1987).

29. Although the Constitution has been interpreted to require states to give parents the option to select private religious schools for their children, Pierce v. Society of Sisters, 268 U.S. 510 (1925), it would counter many principles to direct that families seeking to preserve their religious identities *must* use such schools, especially since the ban against state support for religion would place the entire financial burden of such education on the parents with no help from the state.

30. This challenge has been made even more explicit in recent lawsuits brought by fundamentalists who challenge the books and curricula used in public schools for implementing "secular humanism," which they charge is a religion. See Smith v. Board of School Commissioners, 655 F.Supp. 939 (S.D.Ala. 1987) (ruling that specified texts imposed religious ideas of secular humanism that offend the First Amendment rights of religious plaintiffs). This decision was reversed by the court of appeals, which reasoned that even if secular humanism is a religion, the textbooks at issue did not promote it. Smith v. Board of School Commissioners of Mobile County, 827 F.2d 685 (1987) (11th Cir. 1987). See also Mozert v. Hawkins County Board of Education, 827 F.2d 1058 (6th Cir. 1987); Engel v. Vitale, 370 U.S. 421 (1962) (state may not establish a religion of secularism that is hostile to traditional religions). For a defense of decisions to prefer liberal cultural values over the objections of fundamentalists, see Amy Gutmann, "Undemocratic Education" (unpublished paper presented to Harvard Law and Governance Seminar March 22, 1989).

31. Thus, when fundamentalists argue for "balanced treatment" of theories of evolution and theories of creation, they do not appeal to some abstract neutrality but instead seek recognition for their reference points—and a shift in the reference points used and promoted in the schools.

32. See text accompanying notes 90–96 infra.

33. Gillian Douglas, "The Family and the State Under the European Convention on Human Rights," 2 *International Journal of Law and the Family* 76 (1988). See also Moore v. City of East Cleveland, 431 U.S. 494 (1977) (plurality opinion rejecting city zoning ordinance defining family to exclude grandmother living with two grandchildren

who were offsprings of different sets of parents); Village of Belle Terre v. Boraas, 416 U.S. 1 (1974) (upholding zoning restriction that defined family to exclude a group of unrelated adults).

34. See Lyng v. Northwest Indian Cemetery Protective Ass'n, 108 S.Ct. 1319 (1988).

35. See Commission of the European Communities, *Thirty Years of Community Law* 285–286 (1981) (discussing articles 48–51, EEC Treaty, Foundations of the Community, dealing with the free movement of persons).

36. See Art. 48(2).

37. See *Thirty Years of Community Law* 290 (discussing Article 12).

38. Art. 51, EEC Treaty. See Keller v. Caisse regionale d'assurance vieillesse des travailleurs salaries de Strasbourg, European Court Reports, Case No.27/71; Laumann v. Landersversicherungsanstalt, European Court Reports, No. 115/77.

39. Garcia v. Gloor, 618 F.2d 264 (5th Cir. 1980).

40. Canada's current struggle over the treatment of linguistic differences provides an important set of contrasts. See text accompanying notes 117–18 infra.

41. See Kai Erikson, *Everything in Its Path* (1976); Gerald Stern, *The Buffalo Creek Disaster* (1976).

42. See McWilliams, supra note 3, at 296.

43. Id.

44. For an ingenious argument along these lines, combined with useful historical information, see R. Laurence Moore, *Religious Outsiders and the Making of Americans* (1986), and discussion of it, text accompanying notes 125–28 infra.

45. The experience of black people and native Americans in the United States in this respect, as in many other respects, requires a different narrative that would emphasize the persistent patterns of segregation and exclusion erected and maintained by succeeding generations of white immigrants.

46. See Robert Wiebe, *The Search for Order* (1967).

47. See McWilliams, supra note 3, at 303.

48. See generally Robert Bellah et al., *Habits of the Heart: Individualism and Commitment in America* (1985).

49. See Marshall Berman, *All That is Solid Melts Into Air: The Experience of Modernity* (1983). The original classic work on this subject is Emile Durkheim, *Suicide*.

50. William McNeill, *Polyethnicity and National Unity in World History* 69–70 (1986).

51. What kinds of policies could be devised to respect cultural differences or at least allow subgroups to retain some control over their own identities? Policies could promote geographic movement of cultural subcommunities as ensembles rather than as individuals. Especially since return to home nations is not always practicable or likely, the challenge for the host country is to devise modes for including newcomers without forcing assimilation.

52. These antidiscrimination norms appear in the United States Constitution and statutes such as Title VII, in the Canadian Charter, and to some extent, in current EEC law. Council Directive of the European Communities of Feb. 9, 1976 (76/207/EEC). See generally Council of Europe Committee of Ministers, Legal Protection Against Sex Discrimination (1985). See also European Convention of Human Rights (on gender discrimination).

53. Bob Jones University v. United States, 461 U.S. 574 (1983) (rejecting the university's claim to tax-exempt and tax-deductible status).

54. Corporation of the Presiding Bishop of the Church of Jesus Christ of Latter-Day Saints v. Amos, 107 S.Ct. 2962 (1987). Recently, in the United States, a similar set of tensions has appeared in challenges to the exclusion of racial minorities and women by private clubs under local or state laws protecting human rights. E.g., Board of Directors v. Rotary Club, 107 S.Ct. 1940 (1987); Roberts v. United States Jaycees, 468 U.S. 609 (1984). See generally Deborah Rhode, ''Association and Assimilation,'' 81 *Northwestern University Law Review* 106 (1986). Different, but related, challenges have been posed to all-female and all-black clubs and colleges. See Chai Feldblum, Nancy Fredman Krent, and Virginia Watkins, ''Legal Challenges to All-Female Organizations,'' 21 *Harvard Civil Rights–Civil Liberties Law Review* 171 (1986).

55. Similar issues arise when a company owned by citizens of a foreign nation refuses to hire women or insists on hiring only employees from the home country and then does business in a country that bans such discrimination.

56. See Nitya Duclos, ''Canada: Cultural Diversity Through Feminist Lens'' (LL.M. thesis, Harvard Law School (1989)).

57. See Robert Cover, ''The Supreme Court, 1982 Term—Foreword: Nomos and Narrative,'' 97 *Harvard Law Review* 47 (1983) (exploring the damage to private normative communities posed by governmental control).

58. ''Have We Got a Theory for You! Feminist Theory, Cultural Imperialism and the Demand for the 'Woman's Voice,' '' 6 *Women's Studies International Forum* (1983) (no.6). Although this essay was written to white feminists as a call to try understanding their exclusion from feminist theorizing, it suggests a method that could be used by other theorists who leave out certain people and their perspectives.

59. Carol Weisbrod has identified two types of legal rules sought by minority groups in search of protection for their religious interests. The first is a search for space to practice their own culture; the second is the effort to inject their preferred practice as the rule to govern everyone. See Carol Weisbrod, ''Family, Church and State: An Essay on Constitutionalism and Religious Authority,'' 26 *Journal of Family Law* 241 (1987–1988).

60. See text accompanying notes 84–89 infra.

61. A fortiori, the subgroup has even less likelihood of persuading the general society that it should be permitted to adopt practices that involve devaluation of some other members of the larger society, through caste systems or intolerance toward outsiders. See text accompanying notes 53–57 supra.

62. See Resnik, supra note 16 (discussing Santa Clara Pueblo v. Martinez). Santa Clara Pueblo v. Martinez, 436 U.S. 49 (1978), was a decision refusing jurisdiction sought by a woman member of that tribe who married a man out of the tribe and whose children were therefore deemed nonmembers by the tribe. She claimed that the federal statute called the Indian Civil Rights Act imposed limits on tribes similar to those imposed on the states by the Bill of Rights and the Fourteenth Amendment. The Supreme Court agreed but also concluded that federal imposition of remedies would undermine tribal autonomy and self-governance, so the Court declined to find any implied cause of action that would allow the individual complaint to obtain federal court review of the discrimination charge.

63. See Tanina Rostain, ''Note: Permissible Accommodations of Religion: Reconsidering the New York Get Statute,'' 96 *Yale Law Journal* 1147 (1987) (defending secular accommodation for observant Jewish women who require a religious bill of divorcement from their husbands to be lawfully divorced under Jewish rules but whose husbands may withhold such a document under the typical secular law).

64. See, e.g., Brief Amicus Curiae American Jewish Congress and 35 other religious groups, in William Webster, et al., v. Reproductive Health Services, et al., No.88–605 (U.S. Supreme Court).

65. See Albert Hirschman, *Exit, Voice, and Loyalty: Responses to Decline in Firms, Organizations, and States* 96 (1970).

66. Does this mandate universal exposure to educational materials prescribed by centralized authorities? Are there less intrusive ways to provide an exit option for individuals? Or could the commitment to protecting individuals within the subgroup involve the centralized government in prompting the subgroup itself to devise ways to change, ways devised by its own members?

67. Hirschman, supra note 65, at 3–5.

68. Interestingly, it is possible that some subgroups historically provided greater equality between men and women than does dominant Western society, and contact with this dominant society exacerbates gender inequality. See Sarah Deutsch, "Women and Intercultural Relations: The Case of Hispanic New Mexico and Colorado," 12 *Signs* 719, 737 (Summer 1987). (Hispanic men and women settling in the Anglo north suffered from narrowed opportunities, and women's opportunities suffered a decline compared to men's; women also became more marginal compared to men; women also became more marginal within the Anglo settings.)

69. Iris Young, "Five Faces of Oppression," 19 *Philosophical Forum* 270 (Summer 1988).

70. Id. at 275.

71. Id. at 278.

72. Id. at 281.

73. Internal challenges, brought through internal subgroup procedures, to the exclusion of women from positions as religious officials, already suggest how some subgroup governance and participation practices have been drawn along gender lines, to the disapproval of growing numbers of women who consider themselves loyal group members.

74. Young, supra note 69, at 283.

75. V. N. Datta, *Sati: Widow Burning in India* (1988).

76. Young, supra note 69, at 285.

77. Id. at 287.

78. "The Way of All Ideology," 7 *Signs* 641, 648 (Spring 1982).

79. "Federal Principles of Organization and Ethnic Communities," in *Federalism and Political Integration*, supra note 10, at 73, 80.

80. *The Question of Separatism: Quebec and the Struggle Over Sovereignty* 115 (1980).

81. Ivo Duchacek, "Federalist Responses to Ethnic Demands: An Overview," in *Federalism and Political Integration*, supra note 10, at 59.

82. Carol Weisbrod is writing a book that should remind us of the nongovernmental sources of authority that remain vital and in a superior competitive position for many cultural and religious groups that view secular governmental authority as simply one, and one inferior, source of rules.

83. See, e.g., J. M. Balkin, "Federalism and Conservative Ideology," 19 *Urban Lawyer* 459 (Summer 1987) (exploring historic, rather than inherent, links between the notion of states' rights and conservative ideologies in the United States); Richard Fallon, "The Ideologies of Federal Courts Law," 74 *Virginia Law Review* 1141, 1146–47 (1988) (noting political alignments and deep ideological structures of thought associated with

preferences for state sovereignty compared with preferences for national authority in United States jurisprudence of federal court power).

84. 496 U.S. 1526 (1972).

85. Usually, this means students attaining age 13 or 14.

86. See Wisconsin v. Yoder, 406 U.S., at 241 (Douglas, J., dissenting in part).

87. Similar criticisms can arise when respect for cultural diversity amounts to preservation of the subordination of some groups, such as women, by others within the subgroup.

88. Carol Weisbrod's two types of legal rules are well exemplified through the facts of the Yoder case. The first is a search for space to practice their own culture, as the Amish sought and obtained in the Yoder case. The second is the effort to inject their preferred practice as the rule to govern everyone, and this second mode would have arisen if the Amish had sought to forbid education beyond the eighth grade for all students, or if they had sought to require that even non-Amish students undergo the training and participation in the community required of Amish children. See Weisbrod, supra note 59.

89. See generally John Griffiths, "What is Legal Pluralism?," 24 *Journal of Legal Pluralism* 1 (1986); Marc Galanter, "Justice in Many Rooms: Courts, Private Ordering and Indigenous Law," 19 *Journal of Legal Pluralism* 1 (1981).

90. See generally "Note: 'Official English'—Federal Limits on Efforts to Curtail Bilingual Services in the States," 100 *Harvard Law Review* 1345 (1987).

91. Lau v. Nichols, 414 U.S. 563 (1974). See also Martin Luther King Junior Elementary School Children v. Ann Arbor School District Board, 473 F.Supp. 1371 (E.D. Mich. 1979).

92. For a discussion of the Bilingual Education Act and Equal Education Opportunity Act, see Rachel Moran, "Bilingual Education as a Status Conflict," 75 *California Law Review* 321 (1987). The European Court has confronted similar questions, but concluded that there is no obligation on a state to respect linguistic preferences. Belgian Linguistics case, Judgment, Series A, Vol. 48, discussed in Gillian Douglas, supra note 33, at 91–92.

93. Office for Civil Rights, Task-Force Findings Specifying Remedies Available for Eliminating Past Educational Practices Rules Unlawful Under Lau v. Nichols (1975), reprinted in *Bilingual Education* 213 (K. Baker and A. de Kanter eds. 1983).

94. See Rachel Moran, "The Politics of Discretion: Federal Intervention in Bilingual Education," 76 *California Law Review* 1249 (1988).

95. See id.

96. See Robert Cover, "The Uses of Jurisdictional Redundancy: Interest, Ideology, and Innovation," 22 *William & Mary Law Review* 639 (1986).

97. One estimate in the 1980s identified eighty-one languages spoken by school-age children in Los Angeles. Shirley Hufstedler, Speech, 1981.

98. There are some limited guarantees of accommodation for language differences where necessary for the exercise of fundamental rights. See, e.g., Arroyo v. Tucker, 372 F.Supp. 764 (E.D. Pa. 1974) (city of Philadelphia must provide information about voters' registration, registration forms, and ballots with Spanish as well as English).

99. See Ostrom, supra note 79, at 83–85.

100. Robert Harney, " 'So Great a Heritage as Ours': Immigration and the Survival of the Canadian Polity," 117 *Daedalus* 51, 62 (Fall 1988). Canada, like the United

States, has encountered some emerging pressures for a multilingual and multicultural society. See id. at 64–65.

101. Id. at 76.

102. Id. at 77.

103. Id. at 90.

104. See Lloyd Axworthy, "The Federal System—An Uncertain Path," 117 *Daedalus* 129 (Fall 1988). See also Jane Jacobs, supra note 80 (examining emergence of sovereignty as the central issue in Quebec's struggle for autonomy).

105. Ronald Watts, "The American Constitution in Comparative Perspective: A Comparison of Federalism in the United States and Canada," in *The Constitution and American Life* 109 (David Thelen ed. 1988).

106. Id. at 113–17, 131. See also Axworthy, supra note 104, at 130–31 (describing Canadian movement toward decentralization despite centralization in original constitutional scheme); Russell Chapin, "Reinvigorating Federalism," 19 *Urban Lawyer* 523, 527 (Fall 1987) (describing United States movement toward centralization despite decentralized constitutional scheme).

107. Watts, supra note 105, at 128. Canada also has a more developed tradition of respect for group identities than does the United States. See id.

108. Id. at 118. Blacks in the United States do have a majority in some cities, however, and some smaller geographic areas.

109. Id. at 118–19.

110. Id. at 119.

111. Id. at 124. Actually, the story is a bit more complicated; there are areas of United States law that specifically created exclusive federal power, e.g., federal patent law and federal tax law, and areas that created exclusive state power, for example, over the regulation of insurance, or superior state power, as when a state constitution may be more generous in protecting individual rights than the federal Constitution requires. As Watts later concludes, though, the larger patterns have been reinforced by judicial interpretation: "In the American case, with the federal and concurrent powers set forth explicitly but the state authority left to an unspecified residue, the tendency has been for the courts to interpret what is implicit in the specified federal powers as broadly as possible. In the Canadian case, where the provincial, as well as the federal, powers were explicitly enumerated in the Constitution, the courts have interpreted the specified provisional powers broadly and used them to define the limits on the federal exclusive powers." Id. at 129.

112. Id. at 125.

113. Id. at 123–24, 131.

114. See Axworthy, supra note 104, at 141.

115. See Eleanor Cook, " 'A Seeing and Unseeing in the Eye': Canadian Literature and the Sense of Place," 117 *Daedalus* 215 (Fall 1988).

116. See Moore, supra note 44.

117. Ford v. Quebec, [1988] 2 S.C.R. 712.

118. The case also raised the question of a conflict between the statute and the provincial Charter of Human Rights and Freedoms and discrimination based on language under the provincial Charter, and questions about Quebec's own relationship to the national charter.

119. "The Way of All Ideology," 7 *Signs* 641, 659 (Spring 1982).

120. The search is for a language to talk about pain and powerlessness while ac-

knowledging the incommensurability of experiences and, indeed, the impossibility of producing a language with universally shared meanings.

121. A compatible view is developed in Richard Cappalli, ''Restoring Federalism Values in the Federal Grant System,'' 19 *Urban Lawyer* 510 (1987). (''While federalism cannot be a power switch, perhaps it can be a fine-tuner within the politically determined structures and nation-state allocations of authority existing at any given moment.'')

122. Cover, supra note 96.

123. Some would argue in favor of recognition of legal pluralism and subgroup autonomy, because cultural subgroups within a country may provide a vehicle for better democracy, given limits of direct democracy. See Robert Paul Wolff, supra note 17.

124. See generally *Order, Freedom, and the Polity: Critical Essays on the Open Society* (G. Carey ed. 1986).

125. *Religious Outsiders and the Making of Americans* (1986).

126. Id. at xiii.

127. Id. at xi.

128. My experience representing diverse religious organizations in an abortion-rights case before the Supreme Court, Webster v. Reproductive Services, see supra note 64, similarly suggests that the common threat—state regulation—can bring otherwise disparate and mistrustful groups together.

5

Protecting Human Rights in a Federal System

A. E. DICK HOWARD

Federalism is an inescapable element of United States constitutionalism. Even during the colonial period, before 1776, the dynamics of the North American colonies' relations with the mother country instilled in Americans a federalist view of the political world. Distance and circumstance brought the colonists a considerable degree of de facto autonomy, whatever the view from London.

In drafting the nation's Constitution, the Philadelphia Convention of 1787 gave formal sanction to principles of federalism. To some extent, to be sure, federalism was the product as much of historical circumstance as of political theory; a result, in part, of compromises hammered out during the delegates' debates. But there is more to federalism's origins than politics. The Constitution's framers saw federalism—like separation of powers and checks and balances—as one of the institutional means by which to limit and disperse the powers of government.

Quite apart from its constitutional basis, federalism serves important purposes in advancing the polity's health and vitality. Ensuring a fair measure of local choice about important questions of policy and government tends to promote experimentation, diversity, and pluralism. There must, of course, be devices by which local and state governments are not allowed to frustrate legitimate national interests or to infringe individual liberties. Once those safeguards are in place, however, federalism can operate, as do the guarantees of freedom of speech and expression, to advance the principles of the open society and of self-government generally.

If we take diversity as such to be a value worth promoting, we may pose a question about the articulation and enforcement of rights in a federal system.

Should diversity apply to the defining and implementation of rights as it applies to shaping other public policy choices? For example, it may be argued that the needs of law enforcement may vary from one locale to another. Should that assumption be taken into account in deciding what constitutional limits should apply to police practices such as searches and seizures?

The question of diversity of rights in the United States federal system arises in more than one way. This chapter considers two ways in which the question is posed. It arises, first, when the courts—above all, the Supreme Court of the United States—decide when to apply and enforce national norms. It arises, second, when state courts, looking to state constitutions, recognize constitutional rights as being independent of, that is, going beyond, those recognized in federal constitutional decisions.

NATIONAL NORMS AND THE FOURTEENTH AMENDMENT

At the Philadelphia Convention in 1787, George Mason and Elbridge Gerry argued for the Constitution's having a bill of rights. Their proposal was rejected, and in the ratification contests that followed, the Antifederalists used the lack of a bill of rights as a key argument for rejection of the Constitution. So close were votes in states such as Virginia and New York that, in order to secure ratification, the Constitution's proponents undertook to propose a bill of rights.

At the first session of Congress in 1789, James Madison proposed amendments in the nature of a bill of rights. One proposal, protecting speech and the free exercise of religion, would have bound the states, but it failed adoption.[1] The amendments that went to the states for their ratification (ten of the twelve were ultimately ratified) were aimed at limiting what the federal government might do. In 1833, in *Barron v. Baltimore*, the Supreme Court rejected a litigant's claim that the Bill of Rights applied also to the states.[2]

The adoption in 1868 of the Fourteenth Amendment opened the door to a material change in the structure of the federal union. The amendment created, in particular, the basis for the nationalization of rights. One vehicle for that nationalization has been judicial interpretation of Section 1's language forbidding a state to abridge a citizen's privileges and immunities, to deny any person life, liberty, or property without due process of law, or to deny any person the equal protection of the laws. The other vehicle for nationalizing rights lies in Section 5's grant of power to Congress to "enforce" the amendment through appropriate legislation.

During most of the late nineteenth century and the first half of the twentieth century, neither Congress nor the courts made much use of the Fourteenth Amendment to shape individual liberties. In the *Slaughter-House Cases* (1873), the Supreme Court gave a narrow reading to the privileges and immunities clause, looking to the states to regulate civil rights.[3] In *Plessy v. Ferguson* (1896), the Court reacted to racial discrimination by saying that a regulation need only be "reasonable" and upheld the notion of "separate but equal" facilities (in *Plessy*, separate railway carriages for white and colored).[4] In the immediate wake of the Civil War, Congress used its Section 5 powers to enact such measures as the Ku Klux Klan Act of 1871.[5] But, thereafter, Congress turned its attention elsewhere; it was almost a century before Congress enacted another major civil rights statute (the Civil Rights Act of 1964).[6]

One should note a major exception to this generalization about the desuetude of the Fourteenth Amendment as regards personal liberties. Beginning around the turn of the century state and federal courts made frequent use of the Fourteenth Amendment to protect economic enterprise, the paradigm case being *Lochner v. New York* (1905).[7] Courts were activist in their intervention to invalidate social and economic measures, such as minimum wage laws, until the so-called "constitutional revolution" of 1937.[8]

As the Court after 1937 began to acquiesce in social and economic legislation, the justices became more active in hearing cases in which a litigant sought to invoke a national norm to protect noneconomic individual liberties. In the years after World War II, the debate over what norms should prevail in cases involving individual rights gathered force, reaching special intensity during the heyday of the Warren Court in the 1960s.

The Supreme Court may decide that a national norm does not apply, that the question is one to be decided by state law. However, when the Court does decide that national norms are to govern, its decisions reveal several modes of applying those norms: (1) The Court may apply national norms with general force, largely overriding competing traditions; (2) The Court may apply national norms to the states but then redefine, that is, dilute, those norms as they apply to government action generally, both federal and state; and (3) The Court may apply national norms but permit local standards, recognizing diverse, competing interests. I turn now to examples of each of these three modes of deciding on the operation of a national norm for rights.

Applying and Enforcing National Norms with General Force

The First Amendment declares that "Congress shall make no law respecting an establishment of religion . . . " The amendment's very language makes it clear that, when it was first adopted, it prohibited only federal action. Indeed, for decades after the First Amendment went into force, there were established churches in some of the states; for example, in Massachusetts the Congregational Church remained established until 1833.[9] And after the Supreme Court's *Barron* decision, rejecting the argument that the Bill of Rights applied to the states, the Court, in another case, explicitly reached the same result with regard to the religion clauses of the First Amendment.[10]

The advent of the Fourteenth Amendment was to provide, years after its adoption, the basis for the Court's bringing the states within the reach of the First Amendment's religion clauses. The stage was set in *Cantwell v. Connecticut*

(1940); there the Court looked to the First Amendment's speech clause to overturn the conviction of a Jehovah's Witness for breach of peace, while also considering, on the merits, Cantwell's claim that the conviction also violated his rights under the religion clauses.[11]

In 1947, in *Everson v. Board of Education*, the Court undertook its first extensive consideration of the First Amendment's establishment clause.[12] A New Jersey law permitted school boards to reimburse parents for the cost of transporting their children to parochial schools. Justice Hugo L. Black upheld the statute's constitutionality, but in sweeping language he declared the reach of the First Amendment over state actions that might be thought to aid religion.[13]

Justice Black's *Everson* opinion stakes out one side of a debate that still continues. The debate concerns the proper reading of the First Amendment's religion clauses, especially as they may be used to apply a national norm to what the states do. Black drew inspiration from Thomas Jefferson and James Madison. In 1802 Jefferson had written a letter to the Baptists of Danbury, Connecticut, in which he declared that the establishment clause was meant to erect "a wall of separation" between church and state.[14] In *Everson*, Black quoted Jefferson's letter almost as if it were part of the First Amendment's legislative history, certainly as if it were a definitive gloss on that amendment.[15]

Black also traced the events in Virginia in the 1780s, when Patrick Henry proposed to assess citizens to support ministers of religion. Responding to Henry, Madison drafted his famous Memorial and Remonstrance against Religion Assessments, and the General Assembly of Virginia enacted Jefferson's Bill for Religious Freedom.[16] Reviewing those landmark documents, Black concluded that the First Amendment was meant to provide "the same protection against governmental intrusion on religious liberty as the Virginia statute."[17]

Black's approach, a forceful insistence on separation, characterizes much of the Supreme Court's jurisprudence since 1947. Here and there one finds a decision in which the Court has taken a more modulated stand permitting government to accommodate or acknowledge religion, for example, in the Court's 1970 decision upholding tax exemptions for churches.[18] But the overall thrust of the Court's decisions through the eras of the Warren and Burger Courts was to police, with close scrutiny, state measures that might appear to support or favor religion. Thus one finds a long line of decisions, beginning with *Lemon v. Kurtzman* (1971), in which the Court struck down a variety of measures by which state legislatures have sought to channel public money or other assistance to church-related schools.[19]

The Court's separationist decisions have come under sharp attack. The critics argue that the First Amendment should be read as permitting states to be more accommodating of religious practices. The accommodationists argue that, in relying on the establishment clause, the Court too often has infringed on rights of free exercise of religion. Indeed, those who argue for accommodation often go beyond contending that it is permissible; they contend that it is mandated by the First Amendment.[20]

In briefs filed in Supreme Court cases, those who defend state practices, such as programs aiding church schools, often invoke pluralism and diversity as values to be served. When the Court heard arguments in *Wallace v. Jaffree* (reviewing an Alabama statute that authorized periods of silence in public schools for "meditation"), the solicitor general filed an amicus brief arguing that a government practice accommodating religious needs "makes an important point about toleration and pluralism."[21]

Accommodationists portray separationist judicial decisions as relying on speculation and will-o'-the-wisp abstractions to strike down state programs presenting no concrete dangers of the kind against which the establishment clause was meant to protect. These critics fault the Supreme Court for bad history. In its amicus brief in *Wallace*, the Center for Judicial Studies explores history at length. The center concluded that the Fourteenth Amendment was not intended to apply the establishment clause to the states and, even assuming the clause did apply, it was not intended "to prevent any government from encouraging religion and morality through prayer."[22]

Accommodationists look to legislative bodies to be more sympathetic than the courts have been. Noting in his *Wallace* brief that about half the states have thought it "appropriate" to have a moment of silence, the solicitor general declared: "How serious is the need for a particular religious accommodation (where not required by the Free Exercise Clause) is primarily a question of public policy, for legislatures to assess."[23] In his brief in another case (involving a Connecticut statute that forbade an employer to require an employee to work on whatever day of the week the employee chose to observe as his Sabbath), the solicitor general urged that, when it comes to accommodating religion, "there is a wide scope for legislative discretion."[24]

Accommodation may be about to have its day on the Supreme Court. During the era of the Burger Court (1969–86), there was no consistent working majority on the Court, no bloc of justices able to prevail on a predictable basis.[25] Only in criminal justices cases, especially cases involving police practices such as interrogations and searches and seizures, was the record of the Burger Court manifestly more conservative than that of the Warren Court.[26] In other areas, religion cases among them, a majority of the justices appeared willing to be activist in imposing national standards on the states.

In the early 1980s it looked as if the Court was beginning to respond to the pleas of the accommodationists. In *Marsh v. Chambers* (1983), Chief Justice Burger rejected an establishment clause challenge to Nebraska's practice of paying a chaplain to open legislative sessions. Burger found the practice to be "deeply imbedded in the history and tradition of this country."[27] The next year, in *Lynch v. Donnelly*, Burger once again wrote for the Court, this time upholding the display of a city-owned crèche in a public part in Pawtucket, Rhode Island, during the Christmas season.[28] Accommodationists' hopes were dashed, however, by several decisions handed down during the 1984 term. Among them were the Court's decision invalidating a Michigan program under which public employees were sent into religious schools to teach selected subjects and a decision striking down the Alabama moment-of-silence law.[29]

Taken together, these and other decisions in the 1984 term represented a reaffirmation of the separationist jurisprudence of the 1970s. The accommodationists were exasperated. Justice William H. Rehnquist, dissenting in *Wallace*, developed at length his view of the relevant history, concluding that Jefferson's "misleading metaphor" about a "wall of separation" should be "frankly and explicitly abandoned."[30]

Religion aside, by the summer of 1989 the Court appeared, in some areas at least, to have a conservative working majority. President Ronald Reagan's three appointees—Sandra Day O'Connor, Antonin Scalia, and Anthony M. Kennedy—have joined with two justices already on the Court—Rehnquist and Byron R. White—to create such a bloc. The new majority has begun to make itself felt in such areas as civil rights and abortion.[31] In religion cases, however, the conservatives find victory just beyond their fingertips.

In a case arising in Pittsburgh, a majority of the justices concluded that displaying a Christmas crèche on the grand staircase of the county courthouse violated the establishment clause.[32] The majority was made possible by Justice O'Connor. Usually to be found voting with other conservative justices, O'Connor, in the Pittsburgh case, thought that displaying the crèche conveyed a message to non-Christians that they were "not full members of the political community."[33]

For Justice Kennedy, who dissented, the majority's decision in the crèche case reflected "an unjustified hostility toward religion." Kennedy hotly protested the Court's imposing national norms in matters of church and state: "Obsessive, implacable resistance to all but the most carefully scripted and secularized forms of accommodation requires this Court to act as a censor, issuing national decrees as to what is orthodox and what is not." Kennedy's vote was for pluralism; both the establishment clause "and our Nation's historic traditions of diversity and pluralism allow communities to make reasonable judgments respecting the accommodation or acknowledgement of holidays with both cultural and religious aspects."[34]

As President George Bush took office, there were three octogenarians on the Supreme Court (Justices William J. Brennan, Jr., Harry A. Blackmun, and Thurgood Marshall). Bush will surely have one or more vacancies to fill, especially if he is elected for a second term as president. Recalling Bush's positions, both as candidate and as president, on such traditional values as the United States flag, it seems reasonable to suppose that a Bush nominee to the Court would be inclined to vote with Rehnquist and Kennedy and to be more indulgent of states' efforts to accommodate or acknowledge religion. If so, the Court will have begun to move away from its long-standing adherence to a national norm implied by the metaphor of the "wall of separation" of church and state.

Allowing more room for state standards in church-and-state cases would prove a mixed victory for the accommodationists. State constitutions often have quite detailed provisions limiting state aid to religion. It is not unusual to find a state constitutional provision that is more separationist than the First Amendment. A justice of the Texas Court of Appeals has noted, for example, that constitutional language and Texas's historical experience "clearly denote a stronger belief in the separation of church and state."[35] Likewise, a Missouri justice has commented that aid to students, such as transportation and the lending of textbooks, that would be permitted under the First Amendment is forbidden by Missouri's "more explicit constitutional provisions."[36]

G. Alan Tarr, in an exhaustive survey of state constitutional adjudication of church-state conflicts, has asked whether state constitutional guarantees might offer "surer and more consistent direction" than has the jurisprudence of the Supreme Court.[37] Tarr's thesis does not go unchallenged by commentators who prefer uniform national standards. Daniel O. Conkle argues that, given national mobility and communication, we must "provide *American* answers to our most fundamental issues of principle and policy," including issues of church and state.[38] Tarr's response is that the disarray in the Supreme Court's jurisprudence allows him to point to the state constitutional provisions as surer guides for action.[39]

Applying National Norms but Then Diluting Those Norms

In 1947 two justices of the Supreme Court, Hugo Black and Felix Frankfurter, dueled over the extent to which provisions of the Bill of Rights should be taken as applying to the states. In *Adamson v. California*, a majority of the Court held that the Fifth Amendment's privilege against self-incrimination did not apply to the states.[40] Justice Stanley F. Reed, who wrote the majority opinion, conceded that the Fourteenth Amendment's due process clause guaranteed a right to a "fair trial." Moreover, Reed assumed that a prosecutor's commenting on a defendant's failure to take the stand (as the prosecutor had done in *Adamson*) would, had the trial taken place in a federal court, violate the Fifth Amendment. Reed did not, however, see due process as requiring that the full scope of the Fifth Amendment apply in state trials.[41]

Hugo Black, who dissented, complained that the majority's constitutional theory endowed the Court with boundless power under "natural law" to expand and contract constitutional standards to conform to the Court's notion of "civilized decency" and "fundamental liberty and justice." Delving into the history of the Fourteenth Amendment, Black concluded that the amendment was meant to apply the guarantees of the Bill of Rights to the states.[42]

Justice Frankfurter, who concurred with the majority's reasoning, set out to rebut Black's "incorporation" theory. Rejecting the notion that the Fourteenth Amendment's due process clause is "a shorthand summary" of the first eight amendments, Frankfurter argued that Black's thesis would fasten "fetters of unreason upon the States." Frankfurter saw a relation between the federal system and a democratic and progressive society. Frankfurter expressed his concern that stripping due process of independent force by turning it into merely a summary of the Bill of Rights' specific provisions would "deprive the States of opportunity for reforms in legal process designed for extending the area of freedom." He predicted that, were Black to prevail, the Court would be obliged to warp provisions of the Bill of Rights "to bring within their scope conduct clearly condemned by due process but not easily fitting into the pigeon-holes" of those provisions.[43]

The debate over national standards under the Constitution flared with even greater force during the time of Chief Justice Earl Warren (1953–69). The Warren Court's majority was driven by an instinct for imposing national standards in order to achieve such values as equality and fairness. One recalls Justice Arthur Goldberg referring to the Supreme Court as the "nation's schoolmaster." Such an instinct helps explain such activist opinions as those laying down a requirement of mathematical exactness in the population of congressional districts and undertaking strict scrutiny of state measures alleged to discriminate on the basis of race.[44]

Nowhere was the Warren Court's appetite for national norms more evident than in cases concerning the Bill of Rights and criminal justice. In 1914 the Supreme Court had barred the use in federal courts of evidence seized in violation of the Fourth Amendment's ban on unreasonable searches and seizures.[45] In 1949, however, the Court had refused to apply this federal exclusionary rule to the states.[46] Revisiting the question, the Warren Court, in *Mapp v. Ohio* (1961), decided that the states, too, must abide by the exclusionary rule.[47] A wish for uniformity lies at the heart of *Mapp*. Justice Tom C. Clark reasoned that allowing tainted evidence to be admitted in state courts encourages disobedience to the Constitution. A double standard, he believed, would invite federal officers to give unconstitutionally seized evidence to state officers. Leaving open an "ignoble shortcut to conviction" would tend to undermine the whole system of constitutional restraints.[48]

The dissenters in *Mapp* saw the majority's approach as a "Procrustean bed." Justice John M. Harlan argued that, while a core principle of privacy restrained what the states may do, neither the Fourth Amendment as such, nor the federal precedents under that amendment, apply to the states. Problems of law enforcement, Harlan said, vary from state to state: "In my view this Court should continue to forbear from fettering the States with an adamant rule which may embarrass them in coping with their own peculiar problems in criminal law enforcement." It is clear that a concern for federalism itself moved Harlan to argue as he did. A state conviction, he noted, is "the complete product of a sovereign judicial system," and the Supreme Court should realize its remoteness from particular state problems.[49]

Hugo Black's argument for wholesale incorporation—applying the Bill of Rights in their entirety to the states—never succeeded in commanding the vote of a majority of the justices. Black did prevail, however, in retail fashion. In a series of cases, most of them decided during the mid-sixties, the Warren Court added provision after provision of the Bill of Rights to the constitutional norms that the states must observe. These included, among others, the Fifth Amendment's privilege against self-incrimination and the Sixth Amendment's rights to counsel, speedy trial, confrontation of opposing witnesses, and compulsory process for obtaining witnesses.[50]

As the Warren Court pursued the nationalization of criminal procedure, Justice Harlan continued to object. Dissenting in 1968 from the Court's holding that the Fourteenth Amendment guarantees jury trial in all cases which, were they tried in federal court, would come within the Sixth Amendment, he declared, "I have raised my voice many times before against the Court's continuing undiscriminating insistence upon fastening on the States federal notions of criminal justice, and I must do so again in this instance." Opposed to the Court's imposing "nationwide uniformity for its own sake," Harlan pointed to the states' "primary responsibility" for criminal justice and for "adapting it to their particular circumstances."[51]

The strain of what Harlan called "jot for jot" incorporation soon became evident. Applying a provision of the Bill of Rights to the states meant, in the Warren Court's approach, applying the full reach of federal standards, including the array of precedents glossing what the provision means as applied to federal proceedings. Critics of the Court's incorporation decisions had predicted that, in insisting on a single standard, the Court would be tempted to redefine a federal right in the context of a state proceeding. That temptation became reality in two cases decided in the early years of the Burger Court. Until those cases were decided, it was common to suppose that the Constitution's guarantee of a right to trial by jury in criminal cases meant that there must be twelve jurors and that a jury's verdict must be unanimous. In *Williams v. Florida* (1970), the Court held that the Sixth Amendment does not require twelve jurors; the justices upheld Florida's empaneling juries of six.[52] In *Apodaca v. Oregon* (1972), the Court ruled that the Sixth Amendment does not require that juries return unanimous verdicts.[53]

Concurring in *Williams*, Justice Harlan wrote an I-told-you-so opinion. He saw *Williams'* "true thrust" as recognizing that the incorporation doctrine must be tempered to allow the states more "elbow room" in ordering their own criminal justice systems. The Court, he said, "dilutes a federal guarantee" in order to reconcile the logic of incorporation with the "reality of federalism."[54] Likewise, Justice Lewis F. Powell, Jr., who concurred in *Apodaca*, saw the Court's "understandable unwillingness" to impose unnecessarily rigid requirements had led to its diluting federal rights that, until then, had never been seriously questioned.[55]

Both Harlan and Powell were carrying forward the federalism tradition articulated by Frankfurter in *Adamson*. All three justices looked to the Fourteenth Amendment as such to decide what restraints would be placed on state action. None saw the amendment as making federalism irrelevant. As Harlan put it, the amendment "did not unstitch the basic federalist pattern woven into our constitutional fabric."[56] Powell emphasized the importance of the states as laboratories in an age increasingly relying on empirical data. Diversity in criminal procedure, he thought, might lead to valuable innovations in determining, more expeditiously and fairly, defendants' guilt or innocence. Powell called, therefore, for recognizing the place for "imagination unimpeded by unwarranted demands for national uniformity"—a "legitimate basis for experimentation and deviation from the federal blueprint."[57]

During the decades since *Adamson*, while the justices have been debating the implications of incorporation, others have joined the fray. Soon after *Adamson*, Charles Fairman, in an exhaustive survey, concluded that the Fourteenth Amendment's legislative history provided a "mountain of evidence that the Amendment's Framers never intended to apply the bill of rights to states."[58] More recently, Lino Graglia has called incorporation "a proposition for which there is not a shred of historical evidence."[59] Much of the debate, in the academic literature, has shifted from the question whether the Bill of Rights should be incorporated, either wholesale or selectively, to arguments over interpretivism versus noninterpretivism.[60] Some argue for a return to "original intent"; former Attorney General Edwin Meese III believes that judges should "resurrect the original meaning of constitutional provisions" and confine their decisions accordingly.[61] Others believe in a "living Constitution"; Justice Brennan sees the job of the judges as adapting the Constitution to "cope with current problems and current needs."[62] Georgetown's Mark Tushnet, contending that the framers' intent is neither discernible nor dispositive, argued that "our interests, concerns, and preconceptions" must shape our construction of the framers' world.[63]

What does the future hold for this debate over national standards and the incorporation doctrine in criminal justice cases? There are conservative voices that would like to uproot the basic assumptions about incorporation. On the Court, three justices—Powell, Burger, and Rehnquist—joined together in 1978 in objecting to a majority opinion that assumed the "full incorporation" of the Sixth Amendment by the Fourteenth. Not "every feature of jury trial practice," these three justices argued, "must be the same in both federal and state courts."[64]

As the Rehnquist Court begins to mature, we begin to see unmistakable evidence of the emergence of a conservative working majority, at least in some areas of the Court's docket. For example, in the term that ended in the summer of 1989, the Court handed civil rights advocates a string of rebuffs in cases involving affirmative action and the interpretation of civil rights statutes.[65] Might this new majority on the Court decide to abandon the Warren Court's insistence on a national norm in criminal justice cases? One might suppose that just such a change is in the cards, but there are reasons to pause before predicting a shift of this kind.

Several factors counsel caution about predictions. One is that, of the three justices who objected in 1978 to "full incorporation," two (Burger and Powell) are no longer on the Court. The newest justices, the Reagan appointees, are, of course, conservative in their judicial philosophy, but as yet, we lack a clear reading as to their views on the incorporation debate. Voting patterns aside, it may fairly be said that incorporation—Ed Meese notwithstanding—is simply less of a real issue now. Some rights seem securely in place. This is especially true of those rights touching the fairness of the trial process itself. For example, it is hard to imagine the Court abandoning the rule, laid down in *Gideon v. Wainwright* (1963), that a criminal defendant unable to afford a lawyer must have one appointed for him.[66] As to the more controversial criminal justice rules, for example, it is in the area of decisions restricting police practices, such as interrogations and searches and seizures, that the conservative tide in the Supreme Court has been the strongest in the years since the Warren Court. The Fourth Amendment, in particular, has undergone major shrinkage. To the extent that the underlying constitutional right becomes more attenuated, there is less to which to attach the exclusionary rule. A majority that makes generous use of expectations to search-and-seizure limitations (such as the open-fields exception) or that takes a constrained view of when there is a reasonable expectation of privacy may find it unnecessary to worry about the incorporation doctrine as such.[67]

Applying National Norms but Permitting Local Standards

For over thirty years, the Supreme Court has struggled with the question of First Amendment limits on state efforts to ban or punish traffic in obscenity. In 1957, in *Roth v. United States*, Justice Brennan ruled that obscenity was not protected by the First Amendment but that state laws regarding obscenity must meet constitutional standards.[68] *Roth*'s test was whether, to the average person, applying contemporary community standards, the dominant theme of the material taken as a whole appeals to prurient interest.[69]

The years after *Roth* were for the justices years of groping for a stable approach to obscenity. *Roth* itself was a plurality opinion, and the cases following *Roth* saw no clear majority emerge. Per curiam opinions were common, a kind of unarticulated reminder of the justices' inability to agree on common ground. They differed, among other things, on what "community" was meant when *Roth* referred to "community standards." In *Jacobellis v. Ohio* (1964), Justice Brennan argued that national standards must apply; Chief Justice Warren believed that the standards could be those of a local community.[70]

By January 1972, all four of President Richard Nixon's appointees to the Supreme Court had taken their seats. A year later, in *Miller v. California*, Chief Justice Burger decided that the First Amendment did not necessarily require that the same results follow in obscenity cases everywhere in the country. He granted that, under a national constitution, "fundamental First Amendment limitations on the powers of the States do not vary from community to community. . . . " Nevertheless, it did not follow "that there are, or should or can be, fixed uniform national standards of precisely what appeals to the 'prurient interest' or is 'patently offensive.' " Burger opted for diversity:

These are essentially questions of fact, and our Nation is simply too big and too diverse for this Court to reasonably expect that such standards could be articulated for all 50 States in a single formulation, even assuming the prerequisite consensus exists. . . .

It is neither realistic nor constitutionally sound to read the First Amendment as requiring that the people of Maine or Mississippi accept public depiction of conduct found tolerable in Las Vegas, or New York City.[71]

In a companion case to *Miller*, *Paris Adult Theater I v. Slaton*, Chief Justice Burger made clearer the kinds of value judgments that localities could make in regulating traffic in obscenity. In *Paris* the Court rejected the argument that pornographic films acquire constitutional immunity because they are exhibited for viewing by "consenting adults" only.[72] Quoting Alexander Bickel, Burger said that allowing a man to gather, however discreetly, with others of like tastes "is to affect the world about the rest of us. . . . What is commonly read and seen and heard and done intrudes upon us all, want it or not." In short, Burger concluded, the public has an interest in "the quality of life and the total community environment," the right of a nation and state, in the words of Earl Warren, "to maintain a decent society."[73] (It is interesting, and a trifle ironic, that jurists as different in so many ways as Earl Warren and Warren Burger should have taken a like approach to the power of localities to shore up community standards regarding obscenity.)

The extent to which the Court in *Paris* was willing to allow states to make their own judgments about bans on obscenity is revealed by Burger's observation on legislatures' being free to make judgments about the relevant empirical data. The Court in *Paris* rejected the defendants' argument that there are no scientific data to demonstrate obscenity's having an adverse effect.[74] In rebutting their argument, Burger might well have been speaking of conventional state regulation of economic matters where no First Amendment value was involved: "From the beginning of civilized societies, legislators and judges have acted on various unprovable assumptions. Such assumptions underlie much lawful state regulation of commercial and business affairs."[75] In support of this proposition, Burger cited *Ferguson v. Skrupa* (1963) and *Lincoln Federal Labor Union v. Northwestern Iron & Metal Co.* (1949), cases that reflect the hands-off judicial approach to state economic regulations in the era since 1937.[76]

A year after *Paris*, the Court decided that diversity was permissible even in prosecutions in federal court. A federal statute prohibits the use of the mails for obscenity. In *Hamling v. United States* (1974), the Court held jurors in obscenity cases may draw on their knowledge of the local community or vicinage in deciding what community standards require.[77] It does not matter, said Justice Rehnquist, that distributors would thus be subject to varying community standards in various federal judicial districts. Distributors are, after all, subjected to varying state laws.[78]

Such diversity in juries' thinking poses obvious problems for those who produce and distribute material that may be seen by some as obscene. Dissenting in *Hamling*, Justice Brennan argued that distributors would "be forced to cope with the community standards of every hamlet into which their goods may wander." Fearing the expense and difficulty of defending prosecutions in remote communities, he concluded, distributors would be forced to undertake "debilitating self-censorship."[79]

In 1987 the Court put an important gloss on *Miller*. In *Pope v. Illinois*, Justice White, in his opinion for the Court, made it clear that only the first two prongs of *Miller*—appeal to prurient interest and patent offensiveness—are subject to the community standards test. The work's literary, artistic, political, or scientific value, however, does not depend upon the degree of local acceptance of the work. Under the First Amendment the proper enquiry is, not what an ordinary member of a given community might think, but whether a "reasonable person" would find value in the material, taken as a whole.[80]

Academic reaction, overall, to the Court's permitting varying community standards to be applied in obscenity cases has been negative. Some observers object that using community standards leads to inconsistency in the law; "instead of a discernible rule, the obscenity cases have been a source of confusion."[81] The most common criticism of a community standards approach is that it threatens First Amendment values.[82]

Publishers and distributors of material that might be considered on the borderline of obscenity, faced with ambiguous and conflicting standards throughout the nation, might simply curtail what they publish or distribute rather than risk prosecution. The critics might point to *Jenkins v. Georgia*.[83] There a small-town jury in Georgia convicted a local theater manager under an obscenity statute after he showed the film "Carnal Knowledge," a nationally distributed movie that had received both popular and critical acclaim. The Supreme Court reversed the conviction. *Jenkins* thus makes it clear that community standards will be subject to at least some judicial control, to avoid the chilling of expression. Juries are therefore not to go unfettered, but the facts of the case remind one of the extent to which local tastes may operate at variance with First Amendment standards. First Amendment concerns aside, some observers question whether a community standard approach is even workable. What is meant by "community"? Is a political subdivision, such as a county or a city, a community? How does one define community, at one extreme, in a thinly populated area or, at the other, in a vast metropolitan area? Are Chattahoochee County, Georgia, and greater Los Angeles both communities? Such questions offer obvious fodder for the social scientists.

STATE CONSTITUTIONAL LAW

Before the delegates met at Philadelphia in 1787 to frame the federal Constitution, individual states had already adopted constitutions of their own. State constitutions, both those of the founding period and those in force today, reflect a tradition distinct from that associated with the federal document. Whereas the

Constitution of 1787 put important restraints on popular government (for example, providing that senators were to be elected by state legislatures), the early state constitutions were based in a Whig tradition emphasizing direct and continuing popular control over the legislature and over government in general.[84] A glance at a typical modern state constitution reveals that the state documents continue, in important ways, not to be simply little editions of the nation's Constitution. The state constitutions typically are far longer and more detailed than their federal counterpart; they deal at length, for example, with education, a subject not mentioned in the federal Constitution.

In the two centuries since the adoption of the first state constitutions, the evolution of these documents has reflected the great movements and controversies of United States history. During the era of Jeffersonian and Jacksonian democracy, state constitutions were rewritten in ways that reflected the spirit of the time; for example, property qualifications for voting were progressively abolished, and representation in state legislatures was more nearly equalized.[85] As the nineteenth century gave way to the twentieth, state constitutions mirrored the age of populism and progressive reforms. Many state constitutions were revised to include forms of direct government—initiative, referendum, and recall.[86] Throughout United States history, state constitutions, because of their periodic revision and frequent amendment, have been barometers of social, economic, and political issues.

During the time of the Warren Court, state constitutions were overshadowed by the national Court's expansive reading of the United States Constitution. Attention focused on the Court's decisions imposing national norms on the states, making them conform to a national floor. State courts, with some exceptions, did not enjoy a strong reputation, and the states, in the sixties, were viewed by many as being part of the problem, not an avenue for solutions. The result was a desuetude of interest in state constitutional law.

The advent of the Burger Court brought a revival of interest in state constitutions and their interpretation. State jurists, such as Oregon's Hans Linde and California's Stanley Mosk, called for state courts to be more active in using state constitutions to create bodies of constitutional law going independently of federal constitutional law. States are obliged, of course, to live up to the standards imposed by the federal Constitution. A state can, however, choose to use state constitutions to create rights not recognized in federal constitutional law, so long as, in doing so, they do not infringe some other federal constitutional principle.

State courts have indeed been active in shaping areas of state constitutional law having an independent base.[87] They have thereby underscored another dimension of the question of allowing constitutional norms to vary within a national state. It is not the dimension explored earlier in this paper, the question of interpretation of the federal Constitution itself. It is the dimension created when states in a federal system undertake to create bodies of constitutional law flowing from their own constitutions, bodies of law that exist independently of the text of, or glosses on, the federal Constitution.

A few examples illustrate how important these bodies of state constitutional law have become.

1. In some areas, state courts have long been active in ways that are, in important respects, autonomous of the United States Supreme Court's jurisprudence. In the area of economic regulation, for example, the Supreme Court in the past half-century has abdicated its earlier posture of using the due process clause to second-guess state legislatures as to their regulation of business enterprise. Substantive due process persists, however, in many state courts. These courts are, of course, perfectly aware of the Supreme Court's posture, but they look to their state constitutions to police such measures as those allowing price-fixing or limiting access to trades or occupations.[88]

2. Some state court opinions are little more than reactions to Supreme Court opinions. As the Burger Court, beginning in the early seventies, began moving in a more conservative direction in criminal justice cases (notably those involving search-and-seizure issues), most state courts followed suit; these courts were not willing to read their state constitutions as granting rights broader than those grounded in the federal Constitution.[89] Other state courts have decided that a police practice that would be acceptable under federal rulings nevertheless violates the state constitution. Frequently, however, such state court opinions do not reflect a serious effort at exploring the state constitution as an independent source of rights and norms. It is not unusual to find a state court opinion that does little more than decide that the dissenters in a Supreme Court case have the stronger argument and adopt that as the better reading of the state constitution.[90]

3. Newer areas of constitutional adjudication offer striking examples of using a state constitution to create rights independent of federal constitutional law. Illustrations include the environment, gender discrimination, and education finance. Federal courts have refused to declare a federal constitutional right to a decent environment. Such federal environmental rights as may exist derive from statutes and regulations. Many state constitutions, by contrast, have provisions explicitly protecting the environment. Some of the provisions, such as expressions of a public trust doctrine, have ancient origins; more of the state provisions date from the 1970s, when the nascent environmental movement brought about amendments to some of the state constitutions.[91]

Proponents of the Equal Rights Amendment failed in their effort to amend the United States Constitution. Perhaps half of the states, however, have some form of equal rights provision in their state constitutions. The language of those state articles varies, as does judicial interpretation. But the state provisions furnish an explicit textual basis for state court action, in contrast to federal constitutional doctrine, which has been based on the general language of the Fourteenth Amendment's equal protection clause.[92]

Efforts to have the Supreme Court order the states to undertake a more equitable distribution of state school money were rebuffed in *San Antonio Independent School District v. Rodriguez* (1973).[93] Justice Powell made it clear that, however important education may be in a free society, it is not among the "fundamental" rights given special status under the Fourteenth Amendment.[94] Most state courts are as reluctant as is the Supreme Court to take on the delicate task of ordering legislatures to revise funding formulas. State constitutions do, however, give the proponents of reform opportunities not found in the federal Constitution. The federal document does not even mention education, but state constitutions have detailed articles laying down the basis for public education. Some states recognize education as a fundamental constitutional value; Virginia's constitution, as of 1971, includes education in the commonwealth's bill of rights.[95] Despite judicial reluctance in this area, a few state courts—New Jersey being the best-known example—have used the state constitution to require school money to be distributed in a more equitable fashion, the better to ensure a better chance at educational opportunity for school children throughout the state.[96]

The Supreme Court has accepted that state courts may use state constitutions to fashion an independent body of constitutional norms. The Burger Court was generally quick to reverse state court decisions going beyond Supreme Court precedents in expanding rights of criminal defendants based on the federal Constitution.[97] The adequate state ground doctrine, however, insulates decisions clearly based on state constitutions.[98] An example of the Supreme Court's acquiescing in state courts' using state constitutions to go beyond the Court's own opinions is *PruneYard Shopping Center v Robins* (1980).[99] The Supreme Court previously had held that there is no First Amendment right to expression on privately owned shopping centers.[100] In *PruneYard*, students wanted to solicit signatures for protest petitions at a shopping center, and the California Supreme Court interpreted the California Constitution as giving a right of access to the shopping center. Justice Rehnquist left no doubt about the premise of the Supreme Court's affirmation of the California ruling. The federal Constitution, he said, does not "limit the authority of the State to exercise its police power or its sovereign right to adopt in its own Constitution individual liberties more expansive than those conferred by the federal Constitution."[101]

UNIFORMITY AND DIVERSITY: AN APPRAISAL

In thinking about rights, what are the arguments for uniformity? For diversity? A nation, whether unitary or federal, may use considerations of convenience, cost, or other aspects of public policy in deciding whether, and to what extent, to decentralize aspects of public administration. Railroads or the postal service are commonly centralized; provision of municipal services, such as sewers and sidewalks, may well be left to local authorities. But what of rights? Should they be the same throughout a country? Or may they vary from one locale to another, specifically, from one state to another in a federal system?

Among the arguments that suggest uniformity of rights, one may suggest the following:

1. The very idea of "justice" suggests consistency in the law, the notion that all citizens enjoy the same rights. Ronald Dworkin, in his *Law's Empire*, states that the principle of consistency connotes "a single and comprehensive vision of justice." Dworkin's theory of "integrity" in the law "requires government to speak with one voice, to

act in a principled and coherent manner toward all its citizens, to extend to everyone the substantive standards of justice and fairness it uses for some.''[102] John Rawls, in his *A Theory of Justice*, citing the equal intrinsic value of individuals, concludes that the "citizens of a just society ought to have the same basic rights.''[103]

2. Common notions of rights may aid in building a sense of nationhood. It may fairly be argued that the idea of an American nation flowered with the debate over the ratification of the federal Constitution in the 1780s. Similarly, one may suppose that national standards of rights would foster a sense of common ties among people who may otherwise be divided by race, religion, or other barriers. The idea of a "political community" may be said to rest on an assumption by people who "accept that their fates are linked in the following strong way: they accept that they are governed by common principles.''[104]

3. Uniformity of norms may be more acceptable to lay perceptions of what rights are about. The layperson may be quite unsettled by the notion that rights could vary from one part of a country to another. In a nation like the United States, where people move about frequently from one state to another, the idea that one's protection against overreaching police conduct may be different in Georgia from what it is in California will be hard to explain to many who are not tutored in the law.

4. A common body of rights, a single set of judicial precedents, would make it easier for lawyers and judges to have a sure grasp of when constitutional rights are to be invoked. It is hard enough for United States lawyers and jurists to understand the nuances of federal constitutional law (just try and make sense of the six opinions in the *Bakke* case or to reconcile the Supreme Court's often wandering church-and-state opinions). It is that much harder to master two arenas of constitutional law, state and federal.

5. Uniformity makes it easier for government officials to keep their actions within constitutional guidelines. Focusing on a single set of guidelines, they may find they have a better understanding of the relevant constitutional rules and principles. This argument would have special force as regards police officers, for whom it cannot be easy to follow judicial opinions telling them what they may and may not do.

6. Rights are important for all citizens, but they are especially likely to be invoked on behalf of racial, religious, or other minorities needing the protection of national standards. In United States history, since the adoption of the Fourteenth Amendment, it is just such minorities who have put their greatest hopes in national norms to ward off discrimination made possible or even initiated by state and local governments. Thomas Jefferson's belief that, in the United States, the states are the "true barriers of liberty in this country" states an important facet of federalism as a buffer to overcentralization.[105] Jefferson's thesis, however, was sorely challenged by states' racist policies in the post-reconstruction era, when Jim Crow became state policy and, later, when states sought to deflect the civil rights movement's attacks on racially discriminatory laws.

Other arguments run in the direction of allowing diversity in the formulation and enforcement of constitutional rights. Among those arguments, one may advance the following:

1. Constitutions consist, not merely of bills of rights, but also of provisions for structure and institutions. In a federal system, certainly in the United States, federalism is an

essential component of the constitutional framework. In such a federal system, respecting diversity is a constitutional imperative, not a mere policy choice.

2. Allowing local choices as to rights strengthens the educational value of civic participation. It is deliberating together that makes for reflection on the meaning of a free society. Local governments are thus a school for citizenship.

3. The ambiguities of different sources and varying standards of rights may, paradoxically, be among diversity's appealing qualities. Federalism aims both at achieving unity and preserving diversity. The result is a dialogue, a dialectic, both between levels of government and among citizens who have allegiance to both. This produces a continuing referendum on first principles.

4. Diversity both reflects and encourages pluralism. An open society allows individual idiosyncracies to flourish. Federalism thus serves as a counter to uniformity and homogeneity, which undermine a healthy pluralism.

5. Allowing local definition and implementation of rights fosters a sense of community. The early state constitutions in the United States, drawing on the republican tradition, emphasize such community values as an aspiration for the common good. Reinforcing a sense, at the local level, of reciprocal rights and obligations helps define a community.

6. In shaping rights, as in other spheres, states in a federal system can be laboratories. Justice Louis D. Brandeis, in oft-quoted language, declared, "it is one of the happy incidents of the federal system that a single courageous State may, if its citizens choose, serve as a laboratory, and try novel social and economic experiments without risk to the rest of the country."[106] One should be more cautious about experimenting with rights than with economic arrangements, but the empirical opportunities, for example, in comparing state constitutional decisions, are obvious. Justice Powell has emphasized that "imagination unimpeded by unwarranted demands for national uniformity is of special importance at a time when serious doubt exists as to the adequacy of our criminal justice system." Powell's hope is that permitting diverse legislative innovations might lead to fairer and more expeditious determination of an accused's guilt or innocence.[107]

7. Making choices is the essence of political freedom. In the United States constitutional system, the right of individuals to participate in the process of making important choices is reinforced by such fundamental values as freedom of expression and the right to vote. State and local governments have often trampled those fundamental values. But the remedy for such abuses lies in the enforcement of constitutional guarantees at the national level. Within those national limits, local choices about rights are a part of the matrix of democracy and constitutionalism.

In evaluating these arguments—those cutting in favor of uniformity, and those suggesting diversity—it will be helpful to distinguish among rights according to the national and local interests involved. As to some rights, for example, the antidiscrimination principle (applied, in particular, to racial discrimination), the national interest in enforcing rights is especially great. In other areas, local interests are particularly strong, or local insights are especially useful. An example is land use and zoning, which lie at the heart of a community's effort to define itself. Another example may explain the survival of substantive due process under the state constitutions: State judges are better situated than their federal counterparts to be sensitive to the dynamics of state legislation that, whatever its surface appeal, in fact smacks of protection or favoritism.

Sorting out national and local interests can be a process somewhat like that suggested in the famous footnote four of the Supreme Court's *Carolene Products* case.[108] There Justice Harlan F. Stone suggested areas, including the protection of the political process or protection of racial and other unpopular minorities, that might be candidates for closer judicial scrutiny. A like canvass might argue for greater national uniformity of rights as to those subjects.

Whatever one's formula, the ultimate aim should be to give full rein to two values intrinsic to constitutionalism in a free society: individual liberty as safe-guarded by such constitutional provisions as the Bill of Rights and the Fourteenth Amendment; and individual liberty and rights of choice as fostered by international arrangements such as federalism.

NOTES

1. Robert Alan Rutland, *The Birth of the Bill of Rights 1776–1791* (1955), at 208–09.

2. Barron v. Baltimore, 32 U.S. 243 (1833).

3. Slaughter-House Cases, 83 U.S. 36 (1873).

4. Plessy v. Ferguson, 163 U.S. 537, 550, 552 (1896).

5. Ku Klux Klan Act, ch. 22, 17 Stat. 13 (1871) (certain provisions currently restated in 10 U.S.C. §333; 18 U.S.C. §§371, 372, 2384; 28 U.S.C. §§1343, 1344, 1861; 42 U.S.C. §§1983, 1985, 1986).

6. Civil Rights Act of 1964, Pub. L. No. 88–352, 78 Stat. 241 (1964) (codified as amended at 42 U.S.C. §§1971, 1975a et seq., 2000a et seq. [1982]).

7. Lochner v. New York, 198 U.S. 45 (1905).

8. Adkins v. Children's Hospital, 261 U.S. 525 (1923) (invalidating District of Columbia's minimum wage law).

9. Anson Phelps Stokes and Leo Pfeffer, *Church and State in the United States* (1964), at 77–78.

10. Permoli v. First Municipality, 44 U.S. 589 (1845).

11. Cantwell v. Connecticut, 310 U.S. 296 (1940).

12. Everson v. Board of Education, 330 U.S. 1 (1947).

13. 330 U.S. at 15–16.

14. Thomas Jefferson to Committee of the Danbury Baptist Association, January 2, 1802, *The Life and Selected Writings of Thomas Jefferson*, ed. Adrienne Koch and William Peden (1944), at 332–33.

15. 330 U.S. at 16.

16. For the text of Madison's Memorial and Remonstrance, see *Papers of James Madison*, ed. William T. Hutchinson, Robert A. Rutland, and William M. E. Rachal (1962–   ), VIII, 295–306. The Virginia Statute for Religious Freedom appears in 12 Hening's Statutes at Large 84.

17. 330 U.S. at 13.

18. Walz v. Tax Commission, 397 U.S. 664 (1970).

19. See *e.g.* Lemon v. Kurtzman, 403 U.S. 602 (1971); Committee for Public Ed-

ucation v. Nyquist, 413 U.S. 756 (1973); Wolman v. Walter, 433 U.S. 229 (1977); School District of the City of Grand Rapids v. Ball, 473 U.S. 373 (1985).

20. See, *e.g.*, the amicus brief of the Freedom Council, p. 21, and the amicus brief of the Legal Foundation of America, p. 3, filed in Wallace v. Jaffree, No. 83–812 (O.T. 1984).

21. Brief Amicus of the United States, pp. 19–20. In Lynch v. Donnelly, 465 U.S. 668, 678 (1984), Chief Justice Burger read the establishment clause in light of a constitutional tradition that encourages "diversity and pluralism."

22. Brief Amicus of the Center for Judicial Studies, p. 20.

23. Brief Amicus of the United States, pp. 23–24.

24. Estate of Thornton v. Caldor, Inc., No. 83–1158 (O.T. 1984), Brief Amicus of the United States, p. 24.

25. See A. E. Dick Howard, "The Burger Court," in Leonard W. Levy, Kenneth L. Karst, and Dennis J. Mahoney, eds., *Encyclopedia of the American Constitution* (1986), at 176.

26. See Stephen A. Saltzburg, "Foreword: The Flow and Ebb of Constitutional Criminal Procedure in the Warren and Burger Courts," 69 *Georgetown Law Journal* 151 (1980—1981).

27. Marsh v. Chambers, 463 U.S. 783, 786 (1983).

28. Lynch v. Donnelly, 465 U.S. 668 (1984).

29. School District of the City of Grand Rapids v. Ball, 473 U.S. 373 (1985); Wallace v. Jaffree, 472 U.S. 38 (1985). On these and other decisions of the 1984 term, see A. E. Dick Howard, "The Supreme Court and the Serpentine Wall," in Merrill D. Peterson and Robert C. Vaughan, eds., *The Virginia Statute for Religious Freedom* (1988), at 313.

30. 472 U.S. at 107 (Rehnquist, J., dissenting).

31. See, *e.g.*, City of Richmond v. J. A. Croson Co., 109 S.Ct. 706 (1989) (invalidating a city's affirmative action plan for construction contracts); Wards Cove Packing Co., Inc. v. Atonio, 109 S.Ct. 2115 (1989) (tightening the burden of proof for employment discrimination cases brought under Title VII of the Civil Rights Act of 1964); Patterson v. McLean Credit Union, 109 S.Ct. 2363 (1989) (holding that an 1866 statute forbidding discrimination in contracts does not apply to post-hiring discrimination); Webster v. Reproductive Health Services, 109 S.Ct. 3040 (1989) (upholding a Missouri statute restricting access to abortions).

32. County of Allegheny v. ACLU, 109 S.Ct. 3086 (1989).

33. 109 S.Ct. at 3118 (O'Connor, J., concurring).

34. 109 S.Ct. at 3134, 3146 (Kennedy, J., dissenting).

35. Bullock v. Texas Monthly, 731 S.W.2d 162, 166 n.1 (Tex. Ct. App. 1987) (Carroll, J., dissenting). Bullock reached the Supreme Court, which, relying on the establishment clause, struck down a Texas statute exempting from sales and use taxes periodicals published or distributed by a religious faith and consisting of writing sacred to a religious faith. 109 S.Ct. 890 (1989).

36. William Blackmar, "The Constitution and Religion," 32 *St. Louis University Law Journal* 599, 602 (1988), citing Paster v. Tussey, 512 S.W.2d 97 (Mo. 1974), which, in reliance upon Article IX, 8, of the Missouri Constitution, struck down the lending of textbooks to private-school students.

37. G. Alan Tarr, "Church and State in the States," 64 *Washington Law Review* 73, 75 (1989).

38. Daniel O. Conkle, "Toward a General Theory of the Establishment Clause," 82 *Northwestern University Law Review* 1113, 1188 (1988).

39. 64 *Washington Law Review* at 109–10.

40. Adamson v. California, 332 U.S. 46 (1947).

41. 332 U.S. at 53.

42. 332 U.S. at 69, 71 (Black, J., dissenting).

43. 332 U.S. at 62, 61, 67 (Frankfurter, J., concurring).

44. See Kirkpatrick v. Preisler, 394 U.S. 526 (1969) (congressional districts); Loving v. Virginia, 388 U.S. 1 (1967) (racial classifications).

45. Weeks v. United States, 232 U.S. 383 (1914).

46. Wolf v. Colorado, 338 U.S. 25 (1949).

47. Mapp v. Ohio, 367 U.S. 643 (1961).

48. 367 U.S. at 660.

49. 367 U.S. at 679, 681, 682.

50. Malloy v. Hogan, 378 U.S. 1 (1964) (self-incrimination); Gideon v. Wainwright, 372 U.S. 335 (1963) (counsel); Klopfer v. North Carolina, 386 U.S. 213 (1967) (speedy trial); Pointer v. Texas, 380 U.S. 400 (1967) (confrontation); Washington v. Texas, 388 U.S. 14 (1967) (compulsory process).

51. Duncan v. Louisiana, 391 U.S. 145, 171, 172, 173 (1968) (Harlan, J., dissenting).

52. Williams v. Florida, 399 U.S. 78 (1970).

53. Apodaca v. Oregon, 406 U.S. 404 (1972).

54. 399 U.S. 117, 118, 128, 129 (1970) (Harlan, J., concurring).

55. 406 U.S. 366, 375 (1972) (Powell, J., concurring).

56. 399 U.S. at 132.

57. 406 U.S. 366 at 376, 377.

58. Charles Fairman, "Does the Fourteenth Amendment Incorporate the Bill of Rights?" 2 *Stanford Law Review* 5 (1949).

59. Lino Graglia, "Constitutional Theory: The Attempted Justification for the Supreme Court's Liberal Political Program," 65 *Texas Law Review* 789, 797 (1987). See generally Raoul Berger, *Government by Judiciary: The Transformation of the Fourteenth Amendment* (1977).

60. On various views of the judicial function, see A. E. Dick Howard, "Five Men in a Bar: Judicial Review in a Democratic Society," in Roscoe Pound–American Trial Lawyers Foundation, *The Courts: Separation of Powers* (1983), at 5.

61. Edwin Meese, "The Supreme Court of the United States: Bulwark of a Limited Constitution," 27 *South Texas Law Review* 455, 465–66 (1986) (speech before the American Bar Association in Washington, D.C., on July 9, 1985).

62. William J. Brennan, "The Constitution of the United States: Contemporary Ratification," 27 *South Texas Law Review*, 433, 438 (1986) (speech delivered at Georgetown University on October 12, 1985).

63. Mark Tushnet, "Following the Rules Laid Down: A Critique of Interpretivism and Neutral Principles," 96 *Harvard Law Review* 781, 802 (1983).

64. Ballew v. Georgia, 435 U.S. 223, 245, 246 (1978) (Powell, J., concurring in the judgment).

65. See, e.g., cases cited in note 31 supra.

66. See Gideon v. Wainwright 372 U.S. 335 (1963). Indeed, the Burger Court, generally conservative in criminal justice matters, extended the *Gideon* principle from

felony cases (the subject of *Gideon*) to misdemeanor cases. See Argersinger v. Hamlin, 407 U.S. 25 (1972).

67. See, e.g., Florida v. Riley, 109 S.Ct. 693 (1989) (observation of greenhouse from helicopter circling 400 feet above did not constitute a "search" for which a warrant was required); United States v. Miller 425 U.S. 435 (1976) (no legitimate expectation of privacy in contents of bank records); United States v. Leon, 468 U.S. 879 (1984) (good faith exception to the exclusionary rule); New York v. Belton 453 U.S. 454 (1981) (police officers can search compartment of vehicle if search is incidental to arrest); Rakas v. Illinois, 439 U.S. 128 (1978) (no legitimate expectation of privacy when occupants of vehicle have no property interest in vehicle or its contents); Stone v. Powell, 428 U.S. 465 (1976) (no habeas corpus relief on grounds of violation of exclusionary rule). See generally Silas J. Wasserstrom and Louis Michael Seidman, "The Fourth Amendment as Constitutional Theory," 77 *Georgetown Law Journal*, 19 (1988); Silas J. Wasserstrom, "The Incredible Shrinking Fourth Amendment," 21 *American Criminal Law Review* 257 (1984).

68. Roth v. United States, 354 U.S. 476 (1957).

69. 354 U.S. at 489.

70. Compare Jacobellis v. Ohio, 378 U.S. 184, 192–95 (1964) (Brennan, J.), with id. at 200–01 (Warren, C.J., dissenting).

71. Miller v. California, 413 U.S. 15, 30, 32 (1973).

72. Paris Adult Theatre I v. Slaton, 413 U.S. 49, 57 (1973).

73. 413 U.S. at 58–60. Burger was quoting from an article by Bickel in *The Public Interest*, XXII, 25–26 (Winter 1971), and from Warren's opinion in Jacobellis v. Ohio, 378 U.S. 184, 199 (1964) (Warren, C.J., dissenting).

74. 413 U.S. at 60.

75. 413 U.S. at 61.

76. Ferguson v. Skrupa, 372 U.S. 726 (1963); Lincoln Federal Labor Union v. Northwestern Iron & Metal Co., 335 U.S. 525 (1949).

77. Hamling v. United States, 418 U.S. 87 (1974).

78. 418 U.S. at 106.

79. 418 U.S. at 144 (Brennan, J., dissenting).

80. 481 U.S. 497 (1987).

81. Richard Shugrue and Patricia Zieg, "An Atlas for Obscenity: Exploring Community Standards," 7 *Creighton Law Review* 157, 159 (1974).

82. See Note, "Community Standards, Class Actions, and Obscenity under *Miller v. California*," 88 *Harvard Law Review* 1838 (1975); Note, "*Miller v. California*: A Cold Shower for the First Amendment," 48 *St. John's Law Review* 568 (1974).

83. 418 U.S. 153 (1974).

84. See Willi Paul Adams, *The First State Constitutions: Republican Ideology and the Making of the State Constitutions in the Republican Era* (1980), at 129–275.

85. See Merrill Peterson, *Democracy, Liberty, and Property: The State Constitutional Conventions of the 1820's* (1966); Fletcher Green, *Constitutional Development in the South Atlantic States, 1776–1820* (1930).

86. M. Barbara McCarthy, *The Widening Scope of American Constitutions* (1928), at 74.

87. See generally Howard, "The Renaissance of State Constitutional Law," 1 *Emerging Issues in State Constitutional Law* 1 (1988); Howard, "State Courts and Constitutional Rights in the Day of the Burger Court," 62 *Virginia Law Review* 873 (1976).

88. See, e.g., Lincoln Dairy Co. v. Finigan, 170 Neb. 777, 788, 104 N.W.2d 227, 234 (1960), in which the court declared its responsibility to guard against "pressure groups which seek and frequently secure the enactment of statutes advantageous to a particular industry. . . . '' See generally James C. Kirby, "Expansive Judicial Review of Economic Regulation under State Constitutions: The Case for Realism," 48 *Tennessee Law Review* 241 (1981).

89. See, e.g., Hughes v. State, 522 P.2d 1331, 1333–34 (Okla. Crim. App. 1974), following United States v. Robinson, 414 U.S. 218 (1973). (Once a custodial arrest is based on probable cause, a search incident to that arrest requires no additional justification.)

90. See, e.g., State v. Santiago, 53 Hawaii 254, 263–65, 492 P.2d 657, 663–64 (1971), in which the court merely quoted at length from Justice Brennan's dissent in Harris v. New York, 401 U.S. 222, 229–32 (1971) (Brennan, J., dissenting), and adopted that as the law in Hawaii. The majority in *Harris* permitted the use, for impeachment purposes, of a statement that, because obtained in violation of the Miranda rules, would have been inadmissible as part of the prosecution's case in chief.

91. See generally Howard, "State Constitutions and the Environment," 58 *Virginia Law Review* 193 (1972).

92. See generally G. Alan Tarr and Mary Cornelia Porter, "Gender Equality and Judicial Federalism: The Role of State Appellate Courts," 9 *Hastings Constitutional Law Quarterly* 919 (1982); Comment, "Equal Rights Provisions: The Experience under State Constitution," 65 *California Law Review* 1086 (1977).

93. 411 U.S. 1 (1973).

94. 411 U.S. at 37.

95. Article I, Section 15.

96. See Robinson v. Cahill, 62 N.J. 473, 303 A.2d 273, (1973), *cert. denied sub nom.* Robinson v. Dickey, 414 U.S. 976 (1974); for a discussion of public school finance cases, see generally Note, "To Render Them Safe: Analysis of State Constitutional Provisions in Public School Finance Reform Litigation," 75 *Virginia Law Review* 1639 (1989).

97. See, e.g., Oregon v. Hass, 420 U.S. 714 (1975).

98. Justice Robert H. Jackson explored the basis for the adequate and independent state ground doctrine in Herb v. Pitcairn, 324 U.S. 117 (1945). For a more recent discussion, see Michigan v. Long, 463 U.S. 1032 (1983).

99. 447 U.S. 74 (1980).

100. See Lloyd Corp. v. Tanner, 407 U.S. 551 (1972); Hudgens v. NLRB, 424 U.S. 507 (1976).

101. 447 U.S. at 81.

102. Ronald Dworkin, *Law's Empire* (1986), at 134, 165.

103. John Rawls, *A Theory of Justice* (1971), at 211, 61. See also H. L. A. Hart, *The Concept of Law* (1961), at 156–60, 190–92.

104. Dworkin, *Law's Empire*, at 211.

105. See Jefferson Powell, "The Compleat Jeffersonian: Justice Rehnquist and Federalism," 91 *Yale Law Journal* 1317, 1365 (1982).

106. See New State Ice Co. v. Liebmann, 285 U.S. 262, 311 (1932) (Brandeis, J., dissenting).

107. Johnson v. Louisiana, 406 U.S. 356, 376 (1972) (Powell, J., concurring).

108. United States v. Carolene Products Co., 304 U.S. 144, 152–53 n.4 (1938).

6

Conclusion

MARK TUSHNET

One is tempted to respond to the juxtaposition of studies of federalism in the United States and in the European Community by calling the former a mature federalism and the latter an incipient one. I intend to succumb to that temptation, at least for purposes of framing these concluding observations. The preceding chapters suggest, however, that although the distinction between incipient and mature federalism may offer some useful insights into constitutional federalism, it is ultimately misleading to characterize the United States and European systems in that way. Taken together, the chapters suggest two issues: the relationships among integration in politics, economics, constitutional forms, culture, and other social domains and the tensions that persist in federal systems as a result of the normative attractiveness of certain social forms that integration places under pressure.

THE TENSIONS OF INTEGRATION

The intuition that lies behind the terms *mature* and *incipient* is that somehow political, social, cultural, economic, and constitutional integration "go together"—not at the same rates, of course, but in some dynamic relation such that increases in the one form of integration lead to increases in the other forms. Perhaps the weakest formulation of this intuition, suggested for example through the structure of Varat's argument, would be that increases in one form of integration facilitate the emergence of increased integration elsewhere. Thus, the intuition goes, increasing economic integration leads to increased political integration, and vice versa. This intuition seems to make sense of the United States experience, in which constitutional integration facilitated political integration, for example, through the formation of national political parties, and economic integration. It also appears to be the basis for the fears expressed by the present government in Great Britain that the completion of the European Common Market in 1992 (economic integration) will lead to the demise of the distinctive British political and perhaps even cultural system.[1]

Despite the appeal of this intuition, there are reasons to be skeptical. First, it seems to be a version of the political scientists' modernization thesis, which, developed in connection with Third World nations, appeared to assert precisely that modernizing nations would come to resemble advanced Western societies in the degree of coordination of integration in various social domains. Prescriptively, the modernization thesis urged developing nations to adopt Western forms of political and constitutional integration in order at least to facilitate and perhaps to cause economic development. As it turned out, the modernization thesis failed both descriptively and prescriptively.[2] To the extent that the "mature/incipient" distinction applies the ideas of the modernization thesis to advanced Western societies, then, it may lack support in the very territory from which it emerged.

Second, the mature/incipient distinction rather plainly requires some specification of the rates of integration in the different social domains. One might contend, in a weak version of the argument, that all we need is that the signs of the first derivatives of the functions describing integration in each domain be the same. That is, a weak version of the argument is that as integration increases in one domain, integration increases in other domains as well. This version makes no claims about how much integration you get in the economic domain when there is a great deal of integration in the political domain, and no claims about how fast integration in economics will occur in relation to how fast political integration proceeds. We might weaken the argument further by positing that there are threshold effects, so that we might not observe changes in the amount of integration in any given domain unless the amount of change in some other domain exceeded some specified level.

Even so weak a version of the mature/incipient distinction is unlikely to be persuasive. It can be attacked from at least two directions. First, as the contributions by Rakove and Mackenzie-Stuart to this volume suggest, even if we take the United States as a paradigm of mature federalism, the length of time it took to reach even a modest level of political and economic integration is quite striking, particularly given the rather high degree of cultural integration, the existence of slavery in the South notwithstanding, that existed from the outset. Where the levels of cultural and constitutional integration are lower at the start, it seems likely that the causal connections among integration in constitutional, political, cultural, and economic structures will be confounded by many other aspects of social life.

If the preceding skepticism is that we will be unable to identify causal connections among integration in the various domains, another skepticism is that there is already so much integration in at least some domains that it would be either silly to expect that integration to produce integration elsewhere that has not yet emerged (that is, the threshold must be extremely high) or uninteresting to notice some modest increases in integration given that there is so much already. I refer here to two facts. There is an identifiable West European culture that encompasses the United States, Western Europe, and some other nations as well. That is, the level of cultural integration is already quite high in this complex of nations. If, in the weak version of the distinction, integration in one domain—here, the cultural—leads to integration in others, for example, the political, the high level of cultural integration and the low level of political integration strongly suggest either that the threshold before we observe effects is quite high or that the rate of influence across domains is so low as to be uninteresting. The second fact is that, similarly, and 1992 notwithstanding, the economies of Japan, Western Europe, and the United States are already rather highly integrated, and the same observations hold.

Finally, to the extent that this volume has focused on constitutional aspects of federalism, it is particularly implausible to think that we would discover many interesting connections between constitutional federalism and economic or cultural integration. Here, the intuition may well be that, if there are such connections, they run from culture or economics to constitutional forms. That is, to use the image of threshold effects again, perhaps at some point the cultural and economic arrangements of a group of people are so close that they choose "naturally" to affiliate themselves in some overarching constitutional system.[3]

In one sense, the narrow focus of this volume ought to make the intuition about coordinated integration implausible in the context presented here. It would seem unlikely in the extreme that mere constitutional arrangements could have much effect on another form of integration. Although I will argue that the proposition is basically correct, there are some suggestive points to be made against it.

How might constitutional arrangements affect integration? The domain nearest the constitutional one, of course, is the political domain, and it might seem almost obvious that constitutional arrangements of a certain sort, at least, could facilitate political integration. To avoid making the proposal tautological, though, we have to consider constitutional arrangements that fall short of complete centralization. That makes concern with constitutional federalism important. Yet once the constituent elements, the states or nations of a federal system, have some significant role in structuring the institutions of the federated system (national, confederated, or whatever), it is no longer so clear that constitutional integration leads to or facilitates political integration.

The relatively rapid emergence of a national two-party system in the United States does suggest that there might be a connection between constitutional and political integration. That system emerged for a number of clearly contingent reasons, such as the situation the United States found itself in with respect to European powers. The primary reason for the emergence of that system, considered in constitutional terms, though, is that the states almost uniformly adopted systems of representation in which delegates to the national Congress were selected on the basis of winning a plurality in geographically defined constituencies. The contemporary experience of the Greens in Western Europe, where some nations have proportional representation while other have plurality and constituency-based representation, shows that the mere existence of some centralized representative body, of the sort created by constitutional arrangements alone, need not facilitate the emergence of political parties with programs coordinated across the federation's constituent elements. Rather, where such parties emerge, their outgrowth may result from prior commitments, shared across boundaries, to such things as proportional or plurality representation. Conversely, the history of so-called "proletarian internationalism," which along with the Socialist International is one of the precursors of the Greens, suggests that the mere sharing of ideological commitments is insufficient to guarantee that a political program coordinated across boundaries will emerge.

An instructive example of the lack of close connection between constitutional integration and the coordination of economic regulation (a form of economic integration) is provided by an episode in the history of regulation in the United States.[4] In 1868 the United States Supreme Court held that the national government did not have power, under the Constitution, to regulate insurance.[5] As the interstate dimensions of the insurance business increased, and as consumers in the various states began to procure local regulation of the insurance business, state insurance commissioners found it helpful to attempt to develop a coordinated system of regulation. In 1871 they formed what is now the National Association of Insurance Commissioners, which developed model laws and other forms of coordinated regulation, such as the exchange of information. Even in the absence of constitutional integration, then, when political and economic conditions were favorable, it proved possible to develop an integrated system of economic regulation nonetheless.

Taken together, these observations suggest, in a modest version, that constitutional and other types of integration are jointly necessary for the completion of a program of integration across many domains; or, in a less modest version, that the various types of integration do indeed go together, but are so strongly connected that unless everything happens at once, nothing very much will happen at all.

A second constitutional arrangement that might be thought to have implications for political and, especially, economic integration is the creation of some sort of supervisory judiciary, one of whose tasks is to determine, at the initiative of some agency other than the government of a constituent of the federated system, whether legislation enacted by one of the constituent elements is inconsistent with the norms of the wider system.[6]

Here too it is important to avoid something close to a tautology. If one assumes that the wider system, or federation, is created to achieve greater economic integration, for example by allowing the federation's legislature to enact rules designed to eliminate trade barriers and these rules are effective within each constituent element of the federation, the creation of a judicial enforcement mechanism adds almost nothing to the creation of the federation itself. In the absence of a judiciary, noncompliance with federation legislation would be subject to political negotiation and sanction. But even the presence of a judiciary does not make the national norms directly enforceable. The experience of the United States prior to the Civil War shows that decisions by the federation judiciary must be accepted by the constituent states or nations if they are to be enforceable, and that such acceptance is, once again, a contingent historical fact that does not automatically flow from the creation of the federation.

Even apart from the problem of compliance, there is a problem of defining the federation norms that the judiciary is to enforce. As Varat's chapter shows, the United States Supreme Court has developed a number of "tests" to apply to subnational legislation that is challenged as interfering with the economic integration that is part of the constitutional design. The Court is most suspicious of legislation that is expressly protectionist, applying different rules to commerce that originates outside the state from those applied to identical activities within the state, and it applies a generous balancing test to determine whether neutral rules, which may or may not disproportionately affect commerce originating outside the state, interfere with national free trade norms.

Two points should be noted about the United States experience. First, even with respect to clearly protectionist legislation, the Court has developed a test that allows compelling state interests to override the national free trade norm, and it recently invoked that test to uphold protectionist legislation that aided environmental interests.[7] Thus, even at the core of the free trade concept, the United States Supreme Court, and its doctrine, can allow protectionist legislation. It therefore does not follow from the mere creation of a judiciary to enforce the free trade norm that free trade actually will be promoted; rather, what matters is the stance the judiciary takes toward the competing values of free trade and locally asserted interests.

Second, once one moves beyond clearly protectionist legislation and considers the area of social legislation, the United States Supreme Court has applied its balancing test in a way that almost routinely upholds state legislation whose nominal purpose is the promotion of some social agenda, even if that legislation imposes substantially greater costs on commerce originating out of state than on that originating within the state.[8] The generosity of the United States Supreme Court may result, of course, from the almost complete absence in the United States of a socialist movement that would support substantial local regulation, in the name of socialist ideals, of the relations among capitalists, workers, and consumers, and were the Court to be presented with social legislation that acted closer to the core of managerial prerogatives, it might adopt a different stance. Because of the presence of a substantial socialist movement in most of the member states of the European Community, it has developed stronger rules dealing with government subsidies than are present in United States law. And, clearly, in a system with substantial socialist influences it would be quite impossible to have anything like the "market participant" doctrine that Varat discusses, which operates to insulate government action in the market from challenges based on the claim that the government is interfering with the operation of a free market. Again, one should note that the mere existence of a judiciary does not necessarily lead to aggressive supervision of local legislation.

Further, the problem of compliance would be substantially enhanced were a federation's judiciary to supervise aggressively strong social legislation that was the result of locally powerful socialist groups. At the very least, and in many ways consistent with the themes stated by Rakove and Mackenzie-Stuart, one can expect that developing the political preconditions for effective supervision of that sort is likely to take a rather long time.

Despite the rather negative conclusions of this analysis, there is one way in which the creation of a judicial institution with power to supervise legislation adopted by the constituent elements of a federation system is necessarily connected to greater economic integration. Although there are no guarantees, the judiciary can be rather aggressive in overseeing local legislation, either through its interpretation of legislative norms adopted by the federation or through its interpretation of the organic constitution of the federation. This possibility arises simply from the existence of the judiciary, and would not exist if the only institution available to supervise local legislation were the federation's legislature. In that sense creating a judiciary leads to a greater possibility of economic integration.

The preceding observations suggest that neither the most expansive hopes of "Eurocrats" nor the greatest fears of Mrs. Thatcher are well founded; 1992 need not be the beginning, or, as Mackenzie-Stuart points out, another step in the direction, of a complete integration of Europe in many domains, as the former hope and the latter fears. Yet it is worth noting as well that 1992 need not be such a step in itself, but it may have significance for further integration anyway. The impulses that led to 1992, after all, may influence the development of other forms of political and cultural integration; 1992, that is, may be less a step in the direction of more complete integration than a symptom of deeper forces already driving in that direction. If that is so, the only real function of 1992 can be as a source of propaganda for or against further integration; the completion of the European Common Market will not itself bring about more integration.

CULTURAL INTEGRATION AND THE POWER OF THE FEDERATION

The contributions of Minow and Majone to this volume define the enduring problems of what can be called, for convenience only in light of the argument just concluded, a mature federalism. Minow describes certain general problems of the connection between cultural diversity and constitutional, political, and economic integration; while Majone suggests, provocatively, that the dynamics of integration addressed above in fact do not terminate with full-scale integration in all domains but in fact may have another stage, in which devolution of various functions to new subnational units may occur, thereby rearranging the geographic basis for the federal system.

The basic problem that Minow identifies is that the national regimes that encompass culturally diverse populations recognize, and indeed in some sense are constituted by their recognition of, the value of specific human rights, that is, rights that inhere in every person without regard to his or her membership in any particular group, be it a nation or a sub- or transnational culture. At the same time, however, cultural diversity implies, and indeed in some sense may be constituted by, the possibility that specific cultures will reject the values of human rights, or some of them. Federations are designed to protect some degree of cultural diversity, if only that diversity specifically linked to the geographical territories that are the usual basis of federations. Yet if the federation has the power to enforce human rights against deviant cultures, it may use that power to enforce broader concepts, beyond the minimal requirements of human rights. The difficulty, then, is to determine whether it is possible to confine the exercise of the federation's power only to those situations compellingly demanded by the concept of human rights. The experience of the United States illustrates the proposition, suggested as well by the broader experience of Western society, that that task may be impossible.

Here it may be useful to revert to the intuition discussed in the first section of this chapter, that there are dynamic connections between the various domains of integration. Although there are no necessary connections among those domains, the intuition gains its credibility from the historical experience of Western society, in which integration of the various domains has indeed taken place. That is, one might broadly describe the history of Western society as the story of the construction of the historical individual, whose identity is constituted only by his or her human rights and the exercise thereof. The construction of the individual proceeded by eliminating such alternative sources of identity as the guild, the church, the neighborhood, and the like. Put in a way more compatible with the themes in this volume, the construction of the individual occurred as a result of the integration of various domains. As the economy was integrated, guild and other localistic economic interests were stripped away; as the political realm was integrated into the nation-state, neighborhood and regional interests were stripped away; and so on through the many domains of human endeavor.

In this story, the persistence of cultural diversity is essentially a remnant of the past or perhaps exemplifies the incomplete integration of social life, which is, however, in the course of being eliminated. And, in Minow's account, there is a certain nostalgia attached to the communities whose cultural diversity ought to be preserved. They are the communities of the indigenous peoples of the Americas or the communities of marginal religious denominations. Strikingly, Minow does not discuss other types of culturally diverse communities, such as the communities located in what used to be called Bohemia but that have been

eliminated by the processes of urbanization and, in the United States, gentrifi-
cation, as well as the general reduction in the level of intellectual discourse that
has characterized "high" culture in the United States.[9]

As Minow's analysis suggests, it is precisely because the communities she
discusses are residual that they may not respect the human rights that are one
aspect of the definition of the modern nation-state. If one considers other possible
communities, including Bohemia as well as various quasi-utopian intentional
communities, the picture becomes more complex. Here Howard's chapter is
suggestive, for one way to characterize Bohemia and other such communities is
that they are the location for the definition of emerging or potential human rights.
Again, the metaphor may be misleading to the extent that it suggests a line of
progressive development. The basic point, however, is that there is no particular
need to take the definitions of human rights that modern nation-states have arrived
at as the end of the historical process of the definition of rights. Howard shows
that local governments in the United States have not only provided different
specifications of widely agreed-upon human rights than have the national courts
but have also defined a substantially more expansive set of rights, human or
otherwise, that many people have come to respect.

Once we have the contrasting communities of Bohemia and the residual communities that concern Minow in mind, though, the problem she discusses becomes even more pressing. For on what basis are we to say that the values
asserted by the former are emerging and those asserted by the latter are residual?
The difficulty is that both types of community claim that the values they assert
are, in the most basic sense, truly human. For Bohemia, society has not yet
recognized, but will, its values; for the residual communities, society has mis-
takenly put aside their values, but given the example of the residual communities,
may take them up again. Minow argues, surely correctly, that some substantive
concept of human rights is essential to resolve this dispute. Yet, one might note,
the claim that there is such a discoverable concept is precisely the result of the
historical processes of cultural integration, which we know as the Enlightenment,
that both Bohemia and the residual communities stand against. Minow's claim
about the existence of a substantive concept of human rights, that is, does not
have the kind of ontological authority that it must have if it is to command
rational respect. This is not to say, of course, that her claim *will be* rejected;
indeed, the chances are that she will be vindicated by the increasing integration
of Western society. It is only to say that the reason she is likely to be vindicated
is that the notion of human rights to which she appeals is likely to settle in even
more firmly as time goes on. The reason, I suggest, is just that the historical
processes of integration have gone so far as to be nearly irresistible. Yet, of
course, if that is true, it is unclear that the values of the residual communities
can possibly be respected or preserved in the long run, except perhaps to serve
as examples for citizens of the integrated West of what they have left behind;
in short, the communities would be rather like human zoos.

This is not a prospect many people are likely to relish; preserving certain communities as human zoos, after all, does not sound much like respecting cultural diversity or even the humanity of the members of those communities, although their human rights, as defined by the wider community, may be respected. Majone's chapter suggests a more hopeful direction of development.

Majone points out that throughout Europe one can observe the emergence of regional groupings that cross national borders and that seem likely to be increasingly important as locations for economic and perhaps political (semi) integration based upon their preexisting cultural integration. Before exploring the significance of this observation for questions of federalism and cultural diversity, it is important to note two possibly misleading, or at least less interesting, interpretations of the phenomenon Majone describes. First, regionalism might be chosen by the federation's government as the most effective instrument by which to carry out national programs. The instrumental use of regional groupings by that government merely reproduces in a different, geographically more extended form, the basic dilemma that Minow discusses, for it makes regionalism entirely dependent upon the toleration of the federation. In this interpretation, then, regionalism presents no novel options. Second, Majone's specific examples rather strongly suggest that one should see regionalism as a corrective to errors made in the course of constructing the nation-states of Europe. For particular historical reasons, that is, geographical areas that in some sense belonged together were artificially separated, leaving us today with nation-states that have "misdrawn" boundaries. Regionalism, in this interpretation, is simply a correction of these historical errors, made easier as the significance of the existing boundaries of nation-states diminishes. Again, however, this interpretation leaves no novel insights into federalism, for if the corrective process were carried through to its conclusion, we would be left with a reconstituted system of nation-states with more consistent geographical boundaries.

Yet, if one explores the meaning of "more consistent" in that formulation, one may come up with some useful insights. In Majone's account, it seems as if the regional groupings he discusses would not have to face the problem of preserving cultural diversity, because they would be internally homogeneous, or at least sufficiently homogeneous to make the problem of internal cultural diversity quite marginal. And, whatever Majone's intent, I want to examine the possibility of a federation of internally homogeneous constituent elements.

The most important point to note is that in such a federation the problem of preserving cultural diversity becomes the problem of sustaining the federation as an entity. That is, if each constituent element is internally homogeneous, diversity exists in the very heart of the federation, and nowhere else. If the problem is seen in this way, Minow's difficulties disappear, or are transformed in interesting ways. For Minow, the fundamental problem of preserving cultural diversity is to figure out how to deploy the power of the federation against cultural minorities, or conversely, how to restrain the deployment of that power.

If the federation is *constituted by* its diversity, though, there is no federation power available to deploy against the constituent elements. When some of the aggregated elements of the federation attempt to deploy the federation's power against another constituent element, the potential victim can simply withdraw from the federation. At that point, ordinary problems of international relations and coercion or war arise, but nothing distinctively federal is at issue.

Of course, that overstates the matter. As I have described federal systems, they necessarily adhere to the theory of states' rights that animated the slave-holding states of the United States prior to the war of 1861–65. Yet the northern states believed that the federal system of the United States did not allow, as a legal matter, withdrawal of states when they disagreed with national policies. The example of the United States, however, may actually support the stringent definition of federal systems that I have offered. After all, it did indeed take a war to eradicate the theory of federalism that I have sketched. Further, I refrained from giving a label to the war of 1861–65 precisely in order to be able to point out that the competing labels given to that war—the Civil War, that is, a war within a single system, in the North, and the War for Southern Independence, that is, a war between two systems, by some in the South—derive from the very competition of theories of federalism that were the predicate, in constitutional theory, of the war itself.

Even so, the theory is overstated because it assumes that the options available to a constituent element of a federation that objects to proposed exercises of federation power are confined to submission or withdrawal. The governing theory of federalism in the United States is to the contrary, in the sense that there is another option. The Tenth Amendment to the United States Constitution provides that the powers not delegated to Congress are reserved to the states. As is commonly observed, as a linguistic formulation this is a tautology, yet the Tenth Amendment does express a principle of federalism that the Supreme Court continues to treat as important. In *Garcia v. San Antonio Metropolitan Transport Authority*, the Supreme Court held that the courts would not enforce principles of federalism, but it did not deny that federalism was important.[10] Rather, it held that the values of local autonomy were to be promoted by processes of political negotiation and bargaining in Congress.

Garcia may be vulnerable as a precedent,[11] but it expresses an important insight into the possibilities of federalism. For, in addition to submission or withdrawal, constituents of federations may use the ordinary processes of political bargaining to protect their interests, which, on the assumption being made at this point, are culturally homogeneous internally but culturally diverse in the federation as a whole. They may point out that if the federation imposes a program they dislike, they are in a position to withdraw and thereby eliminate at least some of the benefits of the federation. By a process of political negotiation and compromise, then, if the preservation of the federation is seen by its participants as an important value, the cultural diversity embedded in the federation may be preserved. There is a sense in which this replicates Minow's dilemma, for the federation might have the raw power to impose its will, particularly if the benefits of remaining in the federation are so great as to overwhelm the benefits of one or more of its constituent elements' cultural diversity. Yet one wonders whether exercising that raw power ought to count as preserving the federation rather than, for example, transforming it into a system with a central government and a semicolonized subnational unit.

There is another way in which the preceding analysis rests on an overly strong premise of internal homogeneity. Clearly, the regions that Majone describes are not in fact completely homogeneous, simply more homogeneous than the nation-states of which they are parts. What is the analytical significance of the incomplete homogeneity of these regions? The first point to note is that, once a certain degree of integration of the larger system exists, one can say that the residents of each region have accepted the amount of diversity and the like that the region has. That is, once the larger system protects the mobility of residents and other factors of economic production, people can be expected to relocate themselves until they find the place that provides them with the mix of economic forms, political arrangements, and cultural tolerance or intolerance with which they are most comfortable. Varat's suggestion that the personal liberty dimensions of protecting interregional mobility have been more important in United States law than the political and economic dimensions may thus be defended on the structural ground that protecting the personal liberty dimensions is more important than protecting the others. Once the process of reshuffling is carried through to its conclusion, most of Minow's normative concerns might disappear.

Of course, in contemporary societies the fact that mobility is protected does not guarantee that people reside where they find the most acceptable mix of economics, politics, and culture. People are constrained in the exercise of their right to relocate by, most obviously, differential economic opportunity. Given the economic disparities among the regions of Europe, for example, there is no reason at all to think that "guest workers" freely choose to relocate and abandon their cultural ties to their regions or nations of origin. Again, however, it is important to see that one may simply be observing a process of incomplete integration in the sense that, once all factors of production are freely mobile, economic disparities ought, in theory, to be eliminated. Were that to occur, one would then be in a position to treat residents' choices as free.

Here too, however, one of Minow's concerns would recur. In the possible scenarios that might result from these postulated processes, there is little reason to rule out the possibility that some community will oppress some of its residents, who will, in some sense, choose to accept their subordination. The possibility is limited by the fact that, by hypothesis, mobility both out of and into such communities is protected, which means that those who object to what they describe as oppression can either leave the community or, if they are outside it, flood it and use its political processes to change its system. Nonetheless, there is still some possibility that people will not object to what others, using for example the criteria for oppression described in Minow's chapter, will see as oppression. I am not entirely convinced that we can develop a normatively acceptable account of false consciousness that would justify the imposition of outside norms on such communities.[12] It may be, though, that the possibility of mobility would provide enough constraint on the development of these problematic communities that we would not find ourselves troubled by the few that might sustain themselves.

CONCLUSION

It should be obvious that I have been discussing a rather utopian vision of the way in which constitutional federalism might address the normative problems raised by Minow in light of the suggestion, developed from Majone's analysis, that integration is only an intermediate stage in long-term historical processes. Perhaps the utopianism may be justified by the suggestion made in the first section of this chapter, that the intuition about "mature" federalism is in an important sense just as utopian, yet it provided the reason for addressing comparative constitutional federalism in the first place. I believe that we have shown that the enterprise of comparative constitutional federalism, though it may be motivated by certain utopian intuitions or yearnings, leads to the open confrontation of enduring questions of institutional design and normative evaluation.

NOTES

1. It may be suggestive in this connection that apparently the first real consequence of the rather modest degree of political integration of the member states of the European Community has been the emergence of a transnational "Green" not-quite-party. (The relationships among the various national Socialist parties of course predate the Community.)

2. In the legal literature the best discussion of the prescriptive failure is David Trubek and Marc Galanter, "Scholars in Self-Estrangement," 1974 *Wisconsin Law Review* 1062.

3. Perhaps, too, just before the threshold is reached, political leadership can utilize constitution-framing as a mechanism for pushing the group across the threshold.

4. The importance of the example was suggested to me by Thierry Bourgoignie and David Trubek, *Consumer Law, Common Markets and Federalism in Europe and the United States* (1987), which is Volume 3 of *Integration Through Law: Europe and the American Federal Experience*.

5. Paul v. Virginia, 75 U.S. 168 (1868).

6. The judiciary must be able to act at the insistance of some agency other than a government, for example, at the initiative of a private party, lest it degenerate into another forum for simple political negotiations between sovereign nations.

7. Maine v. Taylor, 477 U.S. 131 (1986).

8. The most dramatic recent example is Exxon Corp. v. Governor of Maryland, 437 U.S. 117 (1978), where the Court upheld a rule that barred almost all out-of-state gasoline companies from operating gasoline stations but that had almost no effect on in-state companies.

9. For a confused but nonetheless suggestive discussion of these communities, see Russell Jacoby, *The Last Intellectuals* (1987).

10. 469 U.S. 528 (1985).

11. Four justices dissented, stating that they would like to use the earliest opportunity to overrule *Garcia*.

12. In the legal literature in the United States, the most elaborate recent discussion of this and associated problems is Cass Sunstein, ''Legal Interference with Private Preferences,'' 53 *University of Chicago Law Review* 1129 (1986).

Bibliographical Essay

There are many general works on comparative federalism, describing the legal arrangements, political dynamics, and cultural characteristics of individual federal systems. There are fewer analytic works, especially those that attempt to link systematically the constitutional forms of federalism with the economic, political, and cultural aspects of the systems from which they emerge and which they simultaneously structure. It may be that the most important analytic insights are all available in two of the earliest works: *The Federalist* and Alexis De Tocqueville, *Democracy in America*, both available in various editions. In addition, general works on United States constitutional law, such as Laurence Tribe, *American Constitutional Law* (Mineola, N.Y., 2d. ed., 1988), and Leonard W. Levy, Kenneth L. Karst, and Dennis J. Mahoney, eds., *Encyclopedia of the American Constitution* (New York, 1986), contain important analytic discussions. Perhaps the most important recent contribution is Albert Hirschman, *Exit, Voice, and Loyalty: Responses to Decline in Firms, Organizations, and States* (Cambridge, Mass., 1970).

More explicitly comparative works that contain important analytic contributions include Thierry Bourgoignie and David Trubek, *Consumer Law, Common Markets and Federalism in Europe and the United States* (Berlin and New York, 1987); Peter Hay and Ronald Rotunda, *The United States Federal System: Legal Integration in the American Experience* (Dobbs Ferry, N.Y., 1982); *Courts and Free Markets* (Terrence Sandalow and Eric Stein, eds, Oxford, 1982); *Regulation, Federalism, and Interstate Commerce* (A. Dan Tarlock, ed., Boston, 1981); and *Integration Through Law: Europe and the American Federal Experience* (Mauro Cappelletti, Monica Seccombe, and Joseph Weiler, eds., Hawthorne, N.Y., 1986), all of which focus on the European Community and the United States. See also Commission of the European Communities, *Thirty Years of Community Law* (Brussels, 1981), and Commission of the European Communities, *Completing the Internal Market: White Paper from the Commission to the European Council*

(Brussels, 1985). In addition, general studies of legal pluralism are useful; see John Griffiths, "What is Legal Pluralism?" 24 *Journal of Legal Pluralism* 1 (1986), and Marc Galanter, "Justice in Many Rooms: Courts, Private Ordering and Indigenous Law," 19 *Journal of Legal Pluralism* 1 (1981).

Historical studies of the development of federalism in the United States, especially in the early years, are particularly rich. A sampling would include Gordon S. Wood, *The Creation of the American Republic, 1776–1787* (North Carolina, 1969); Jack N. Rakove, *The Beginnings of National Politics: An Interpretive History of the Continental Congress* (Baltimore, 1979); Jack P. Green, *Peripheries and Center: Constitutional Development in the Extended Polities of the British Empire and the United States, 1607–1788* (Athens, Ga, 1986); Michael G. Kammen, *Deputyes and Libertyes; The Origins of Representative Government in Colonial America* (Philadelphia, 1969); Peter S. Onuf, *The Origins of the Federal Republic: Jurisdictional Controversies in the United States, 1775–1787* (Philadelphia, 1983); Peter S. Onuf, *Statehood and Union: A History of the Northwest Ordinance* (Bloomington, Ind., 1987); James H. Kettner, *The Development of American Citizenship, 1608–1870* (Chapel Hill, N.C., 1978); and Edmund S. Morgan, *Inventing the People: The Rise of Popular Sovereignty in England and America* (New York, 1988).

Overviews of the ideological context of the development of federalism in the United States are provided by Louis Hartz, *The Liberal Tradition in America* (New York, 1965); Bernard Bailyn, *The Ideological Origins of the American Revolution* (Cambridge, Mass., 1967); Frank Michelman, "Law's Republic," 97 *Yale Law Journal* 1493 (1988); and Suzanna Sherry, "Civic Virtue and the Feminine Voice in Constitutional Adjudication," 72 *Virginia Law Review* 543 (1986). Examining the development of constitutional law in the states are Willi Paul Adams, *The First American Constitutions: Republican Ideology and the Making of the State Constitutions in the Republican Era* (North Carolina, 1980); Merrill Peterson, *Democracy, Liberty, and Property: The State Constitutional Conventions of the 1820's* (Indianapolis, 1966); Fletcher Green, *Constitutional Development in the South Atlantic States, 1776–1820* (New York: 1930); and M. Barbara McCarthy, *The Widening Scope of American Constitutions* (Washington, D.C., 1928).

Works focusing on the political dimensions of federalism include *The Formation of National States in Western Europe* (Charles Tilly, ed., Princeton, N.J., 1975); *The State in Europe* (Arthur Cyr, ed., Chicago, 1975); Ernest Gellner, *Nationalism and the Two Forms of Cohesion in Complex Societies* (New Hampshire, 1983); Rudolf Schlesinger, *Federalism in Central and Eastern Europe* (Westport, Conn., 1970, reprint of 1945 edition); and Albert O. Hirschman, "Three Uses of Political Economy in Analyzing European Integration," in *Essays in Trespassing* (New York, 1981).

The classic statements of the relation between constitutional federalism and national integration in the United States are Herbert Wechsler, "The Political Safeguards of Federalism: The Role of the States in Composition and Selection of the National Government," 54 *Columbia Law Review* 543 (1954), and Jesse Choper, "The Scope of National Power Vis-à-Vis the States: The Dispensability of Judicial Review," 86 *Yale Law Journal* (1977), which are criticized in Richard Stewart, "Pyramids of Sacrifice? Problems of Federalism in Mandating State Implementation of National Environmental Policy," 86 *Yale Law Journal* 1196 (1977); Andrzej Rapaczynski, "From Sovereignty to Process: The Jurisprudence of Federalism after *Garcia*," 1985 *Supreme Court Review* 341 (1985); Lewis Kaden, "Politics, Money, and State Sovereignty: The Judicial Role," 79 *Columbia Law Review* 847 (1979); Michael McConnell, "Federalism: Evaluating the Founders' Design," 54 *University of Chicago Law Review* 1484 (1987). These analyses are quite suggestive in their treatment of the possibility that it will prove difficult to sustain the diversity that makes federalism attractive in a system with a substantial degree of political centralization.

In the constitutional literature of the United States, the richest explorations of the relation between political and economic integration are contained in the extensive literature on the constitutionality of local regulations of national commerce. Much of that literature examines the argument that some form of national control over local regulation is essential to compensate for the fact that out-of-state interests are not adequately represented in local legislatures. A representative sampling of the major articles includes Julian Eule, "Laying the Dormant Commerce Clause to Rest," 91 *Yale Law Journal* 425 (1982); Robert Sedler, "The Negative Commerce Clause as a Restriction on State Regulation and Taxation: An Analysis in Terms of Constitutional Structure," 31 *Wayne Law Review* 885 (1985); Gary Simson, "Discrimination Against Nonresidents and the Privileges and Immunities Clause of Article IV," 128 *University of Pennsylvania Law Review* 379 (1979); Mark Tushnet, "Rethinking the Dormant Commerce Clause," 1979 *Wisconsin Law Review* 125 (1979); David Pomper, "Recycling *Philadelphia v. New Jersey*: The Dormant Commerce Clause, Postindustrial 'Natural' Resources, and the Solid Waste Crisis," 137 *University of Pennsylvania Law Review* 1309 (1989); Mark Gergen, "The Selfish State and the Market," 66 *Texas Law Review* 1097 (1988); Michael Smith, "State Discriminations Against Interstate Commerce," 74 *California Law Review* 1203 (1986); Martin Redish and Shane Nugent, "The Dormant Commerce Clause and the Constitutional Balance of Federalism," 1987 *Duke Law Journal* 569; Thomas Anson and P. M. Schenkkan, "Federalism, The Dormant Commerce Clause, and State-Owned Resources," 59 *Texas Law Review* 71 (1980); Saul Levmore, "Interstate Exploitation and Judicial Intervention," 69 *Virginia Law Review* 563 (1983); Richard Collins, "Economic Union as a Constitutional Value," 63 *New York University Law Review* 43 (1988); Donald Regan, "The Supreme Court and State Protectionism: Making Sense of the Dormant Commerce Clause," 84 *Michigan Law Review* 1091 (1986); and Daniel Farber, "State Regulation and the Dormant Commerce Clause," 3 *Constitutional Commentary* 395 (1986).

In the same vein are treatments of the constitutional requirement barring states from discriminating with respect to "privileges and immunities" of state citizenship, discussed in Jonathan Varat, "State 'Citizenship' and Interstate Equality," 48 *University of Chicago Law Review* 487 (1981), and George Carpinello, "State Protective Legislation and Nonresident Corporations: The Privileges and Immunities Clause as a Treaty of Nondiscrimination," 73 *Iowa Law Review* 351 (1988). A related constitutional provision limiting the degree of state experimentation with governmental forms is the guaranty clause of Article IV; for discussion, see Arthur Bonfield, "The Guaranty Clause of Article IV, §4: A Study of Congressional Desuetude," 46 *Minnesota Law Review* 513 (1962), and Deborah Jones Merritt, "The Guarantee Clause and State Autonomy: Federalism for a Third Century," 88 *Columbia Law Review* 1 (1988).

A rich, rather technical literature in the United States deals with the problem of coordinating legal jurisdiction between states and nation; the more interesting examinations of the problem address the implications of the existence of a dual jurisdictional system for political and cultural integration. The basic source is of course Paul Bator, Daniel Meltzer, Paul Mishkin, and David Shapiro, *Hart & Weschler's The Federal Courts and the Federal System* (3d ed., Westbury, N.Y., 1988); probably the most interesting short analysis is Robert Cover, "The Uses of Jurisdictional Redundancy: Interest, Ideology, and Innovation," 22 *William & Mary Law Review* 639 (1986). More recent is

Richard Fallon, "The Ideologies of Federal Courts Law," 74 *Virginia Law Review* 1141 (1988). For a complete examination of the technical problems that arise in the course of constructing a dual jurisdictional system, see American Law Institute, *Study of the Division of Jurisdiction Between State and Federal Courts* (Philadelphia, 1968).

The preceding studies tend to focus on the ways in which the national courts can accommodate state diversity. From the other direction the problem involves ensuring that state courts respond appropriately to national legal norms. Representative studies of the issue include G. Alan Tarr, "Church and State in the States," 64 *Washington Law Review* 73 (1989); Richard Shugrue and Patricia Zieg, "An Atlas for Obscenity: Exploring Community Standards," 7 *Creighton Law Review* 157 (1974); Note, "Community Standards, Class Actions, and Obscenity under *Miller v. California*," 88 *Harvard Law Review* 1838 (1975); Note, "*Miller v. California*: A Cold Shower for the First Amendment," 48 *St. John's Law Review* 568 (1974); A. E. Dick Howard, "The Renaissance of State Constitutional Law," *Emerging Issues in State Constitutional Law* 1 (Washington, D.C., 1988); A. E. Dick Howard, "State Courts and Constitutional Rights in the Day of the Burger Court," 62 *Virginia Law Review* 873 (1976); A. E. Dick Howard, "State Constitutions and the Environment," 58 *Virginia Law Review* 193 (1972); G. Alan Tarr and Mary Cornelia Porter, "Gender Equality and Judicial Federalism: The Role of State Appellate Courts," 9 *Hastings Constitutional Law Quarterly* 919 (1982); Comment, "Equal Rights Provisions: The Experience under State Constitutions," 65 *California Law Review* 1086 (1977); Note, "To Render Them Safe: Analysis of State Constitutional Provisions in Public School Finance Reform Litigation," 75 *Virginia Law Review* 1639 (1989); and James C. Kirby, "Expansive Judicial Review of Economic Regulation under State Constitutions: The Case for Realism," 48 *Tennessee Law Review* 241 (1981).

The equal protection clause of the United States Constitution provides some degree of protection for religious, cultural, and other forms of diversity, while at the same time, because it is a national norm enforced by the national courts, it limits the way in which federalism can promote diversity. For a general study informed by comparative perspectives, see D. G. T. Williams, "Aspects of Equal Protection in the United Kingdom," 59 *Tulane Law Review* 959 (1985). Focusing on the United States, see Jill Norgren and Serena Nanda, *American Cultural Pluralism and Law* (New York, 1988); Robert Cover, "The Supreme Court, 1982 Term—Foreword: Nomos and Narrative," 97 *Harvard Law Review* 47 (1983); Martha Minow, "The Supreme Court, 1986 Term—Foreword: Justice Engendered," 101 *Harvard Law Review* 10 (1987).

Ethnic diversity is one characteristic of federal systems. For a general political study, see Donald Horowitz, *Ethnic Groups in Conflict* (Berkeley, 1985). In the United States, recent controversies over bilingual education have provoked scholarship examining the tension between local and national norms. See *Bilingual Education* (K. A. Baker, ed., Lexington, Mass., 1982); Rachel Moran, "Bilingual Education as a Status Conflict," 75 *California Law Review* 321 (1987); Rachel Moran, "The Politics of Discretion: Federal Intervention in Bilingual Education," 76 *California Law Review* 1249 (1988); Note, " 'Official English'—Federal Limits on Efforts to Curtail Bilingual Services in the States," 100 *Harvard Law Review* 1345 (1987). See also Sarah Deutsch, "Women and Intercultural Relations: The Case of Hispanic New Mexico and Colorado," 12 *Signs* 719 (Summer 1987).

Another source of pluralism is religion. Religious minorities sometimes are concentrated in particular geographic locations, and their programs may then come into conflict with the programs of a national religious majority. For general studies, see R. Laurence Moore,

Religious Outsiders and the Making of Americans (New York, 1986), and Robert Bellah, *Habits of the Heart: Individualism and Commitment in America* (New York, 1986). Broader still is Marshall Berman, *All That is Solid Melts Into Air: The Experience of Modernity* (New York, 1983). Examinations of the constitutional dimensions of religious pluralism in the United States are Michael McConnell, "Accommodation of Religion," 1985 *Supreme Court Review* 1 (1985); Mark Tushnet, "The Emerging Principle of Accommodation of Religion (Dubitante)," 76 *Georgetown Law Journal* 1961 (1988); and Tanina Rostain, "Note: Permissible Accommodations of Religion: Reconsidering the New York Get Statute," 96 *Yale Law Journal* 1147 (1987). A general study is Anson Phelps Stokes and Leo Pfeffer, *Church and State in the United States* (Westport, Conn., 1964).

Carol Weisbrod, "Family, Church and State: An Essay on Constitutionalism and Religious Authority," 26 *Journal of Family Law* 241 (1987–1988), examines related problems at the intersection of religious and family diversity. For related studies, see Gillian Douglas, "The Family and the State Under the European Convention on Human Rights," 2 *International Journal of Law and the Family* 76 (1988), and Chai Feldblum, Nancy Fredman Krent, and Virginia Watkins, "Legal Challenges to All-Female Organizations," 21 *Harvard Civil Rights–Civil Liberties Law Review* 171 (1986). Finally, Deborah Rhode, "Association and Assimilation," 81 *Northwestern University Law Review* 106 (1986), provides a comprehensive overview of the tensions between diversity and uniformity within a single national legal framework. Kenneth Karst, *Belonging to America: Equal Citizenship and the Constitution* (New Haven, Conn., 1989), is a recent and insightful study of the overall issue of cultural diversity in a unified nation.

Because of its geographic proximity and the influence of United States culture and economy, Canada provides an interesting case study in the effects that varying types of federalism, culture, and economy have on each other. See Jane Jacobs, *The Question of Separatism: Quebec and the Struggle Over Sovereignty* (New York, 1980); Robert Harney, " 'So Great a Heritage as Ours': Immigration and the Survival of the Canadian Polity," 117 *Daedalus* 51 (Fall 1988); Lloyd Axworthy, "The Federal System—An Uncertain Path," 117 *Daedalus* 129 (Fall 1988); Eleanor Cook, " 'A Seeing and Unseeing in the Eye': Canadian Literature and the Sense of Place," 117 *Daedalus* 215 (Fall 1988); Ronald Watts, "The American Constitution in Comparative Perspective: A Comparison of Federalism in the United States and Canada," in *The Constitution and American Life* 109 (David Thelen, ed., Ithaca, N.Y., 1988).

References

GENERAL WORKS

Griffin, Susan. "The Way of All Ideology." 7 *Signs* 641 (Spring 1982).
Lugones, Maria, and Elizabeth Spelman. "Have We Got a Theory for You! Feminist Theory, Cultural Imperialism and the Demand for the 'Woman's Voice.' " 6 *Women's Studies International Forum* (1983) (no.6).
McWilliams, Wilson Carey. "American Pluralism: The Old Order Passeth." In *The Americans* 293 (Irving Kristol and Paul Weaver eds. 1976).
Sunstein, Cass. "Legal Interference with Private Preferences." 53 *University of Chicago Law Review* 1129 (1986).
Wolff, Robert Paul, Barrington Moore, Jr., and Herbert Marcuse. *A Critique of Pure Tolerance* (1965).
Young, Iris. "Five Faces of Oppression." 19 *Philosophical Forum* 270 (Summer 1988).
Order, Freedom, and the Polity: Critical Essays on the Open Society (G. Carey ed. 1986).

FEDERALISM IN THE UNITED STATES

Anderson, Alison Grey. "The Meaning of Federalism: Interpreting the Securities Exchange Act of 1934." 70 *Virginia Law Review* 813 (1984).
Balkin, J. M. "Federalism and Conservative Ideology." 19 *Urban Lawyer* 459 (Summer 1987).
Cappalli, Richard. "Restoring Federalism Values in the Federal Grant System." 19 *Urban Lawyer* 510 (Fall 1987).
Chapin, Russell. "Reinvigorating Federalism." 19 *Urban Lawyer* 523 (Fall 1987).

Kozyris, John. "Corporate Takeovers at the Jurisdictional Crossroads: Preserving State Authority Over Internal Affairs While Protecting the Transferability of Interstate Stock Through Federal Law." 36 *U.C.L.A. Law Review* 1109 (1989).

Powell, Jefferson. "The Compleat Jeffersonian: Justice Rehnquist and Federalism." 91 *Yale Law Journal* 1317 (1982).

HISTORICAL STUDIES

Banning, Lance. "Republican Ideology and the Triumph of the Constitution, 1789 to 1793." *William and Mary Quarterly*, 3d ser., 31 (1978), pp. 167–188.

Hobson, Charles F. "The Negative on State Laws: James Madison, the Constitution, and the Crisis of Republican Government." *William and Mary Quarterly*, 3d ser., 36 (1979), pp. 215–235.

Marston, Jerrilyn Greene. *King and Congress: The Transfer of Political Legitimacy, 1774–1776* (1987).

McCoy, Drew. "James Madison and Visions of American Nationality in the Confederation Period: A Regional Perspective." In *Beyond Confederation: Origins of the Constitution and American National Identity* (Richard Beeman, Stephen Botein, and Edward C. Carter II eds. 1987), pp. 226–258.

McCoy, Drew. *The Last of the Fathers: James Madison and the Republican Legacy* (1989).

Morgan, Robert J. "Madison's Theory of Representation in the Tenth Federalist." *Journal of Politics*, 36 (1974), pp. 852–885.

Onuf, Peter S. *Statehood and Union: A History of the Northwest Ordinance* (1987).

Rakove, Jack N. "The Madisonian Moment." *University of Chicago Law Review*, 55 (1988), pp. 473–505.

Rakove, Jack N. "The Great Compromise: Ideas, Interests, and the Politics of Constitution Making." *William and Mary Quarterly*, 3d ser., 44 (1987), pp. 424–457.

Rakove, Jack N. "The Legacy of the Articles of Confederation." *Publius*, 12 (1982–83), pp. 62–63.

Rutland, Robert Alan. *The Birth of the Bill of Rights 1776–1791* (1955).

Scheiber, Harry N. "Federalism and the American Economic Order, 1789–1910." *Law and Society Review*, 10 (1975–76).

Stagg, J. C. A. *Mr. Madison's War: Politics, Diplomacy and Warfare in the Early American Republic, 1783–1830* (1983).

Three British Revolutions: 1641, 1688, 1776 (J. G. A. Pocock ed. 1980).

SPECIFIC CONSTITUTIONAL ISSUES IN THE UNITED STATES

Criminal Procedure

Fairman, Charles. "Does the Fourteenth Amendment Incorporate the Bill of Rights?" 2 *Stanford Law Review* 5 (1949).

Saltzburg, Stephen A. "Foreword: The Flow and Ebb of Constitutional Criminal Procedure in the Warren and Burger Courts." 69 *Georgetown Law Journal* 151 (1980–1981).

Wasserstrom, Silas J. "The Incredible Shrinking Fourth Amendment." 21 *American Criminal Law Review* 257–401 (1984).

Religion

Blackmar, William. "The Constitution and Religion." 32 *St. Louis University Law Journal* 599, 602 (1988).

Conkle, Daniel O. "Toward a General Theory of the Establishment Clause." 82 *Northwestern University Law Review* 1113, 1188 (1988).

Howard, A. E. Dick. "The Supreme Court and the Serpentine Wall." In Merrill D. Peterson and Robert C. Vaughan, eds., *The Virginia Statute for Religious Freedom* (1988), p. 313.

Federal Jurisdiction

Fletcher, William. "The General Common Law and Section 34 of the Judiciary Act of 1789: The Example of Marine Insurance." 97 *Harvard Law Review* 1513 (1984).

Friendly, Henry. "In Praise of Erie—And of the New Federal Common Law." 39 *New York University Law Review* 383 (1964).

Commercial Regulation

Chase, Jonathon. "Does Professional Licensing Conditional Upon Mutual Reciprocity Violate the Commerce Clause?" 10 *Vermont Law Review* 233 (1985).

Cohen, William. "Federalism in Equality Clothing: A Comment on *Metropolitan Life Ins. Co. v. Ward*." 38 *Stanford Law Review* 1 (1985).

Day, James. "The National Conference of Commissioners on Uniform State Laws." In *The Life of the Law* 324 (John Honnold ed. 1964).

Hafter, Jerome. "Toward the Multistate Practice of Law Through Admission by Reciprocity." 53 *Mississippi Law Journal* 1 (1983).

Index

About the Editor and Contributors

MARK TUSHNET, Professor of Law, Georgetown University Law Center, served as a law clerk to Justice Thurgood Marshall and previously taught at the University of Wisconsin. Among his many books are *The American Law of Slavery, 1818–1860*, *Central America and the Law*, and *Constitutional Law*, and he is the author of numerous articles on constitutional law and history.

LORD MACKENZIE-STUART, former President, Court of Justice of the European Communities.

JACK N. RAKOVE, Associate Professor of History, Stanford University.

JONATHAN D. VARAT, Professor of Law, University of California at Los Angeles.

GIANDOMENICO MAJONE, Professor of Public Policy Analysis, European University Institute.

MARTHA MINOW, Professor of Law, Harvard University.

A. E. DICK HOWARD, White Burkett Miller Professor of Law and Public Affairs, University of Virginia.